AGAINST ALL ODDS

DEMOCRACY IN AFRICA SERIES VOL 2

AGAINST ALL ODDS

OPPOSITION POLITICAL PARTIES IN SOUTHERN AFRICA

BOTSWANA LESOTHO MAURITIUS MOZAMBIQUE NAMIBIA SOUTH AFRICA SWAZILAND ZAMBIA ZIMBABWE

EDITED BY HUSSEIN SOLOMON

KMM REVIEW PUBLISHING COMPANY
Johannesburg

SOUTH AFRICAN INSTITUTE OF INTERNATIONAL AFFAIRS

All rights reserved.
No part of this publication may be reproduced,
stored in a retrieval system or transmitted, in any form or by any means,
electronic, mechanical, photocopying, recording or otherwise,
without written permission from the publisher and copyright holder.

© KMM Review Publishing 2011

Published by KMM Review Publishing Company (Pty) Ltd
PO Box 78214, Sandton, 2146

ISBN 978-O-620-47600-3

Democracy in Africa series
Volume 1
The Struggle for the Eastern cape
1800 - 1854
Subjugation and the roots of South African democracy.
Volume 2
Against All Odds
Opposition political parties in southern Africa

Cover, design, typesetting and reproduction: Brandon van Heerden, Johannesburg
Printing and binding : Colors, Johannesburg.

Contents

Acknowledgements		vi
Contributors		vii
Chapter 1:	Conceptual overview of opposition political parties in southern Africa. **Hussein Solomon**	1
Chapter 2:	Botswana: Opposition political parties within a fraying dominant party system. **Balefi Tsie**	14
Chapter 3:	Lesotho: Political parties in a fraying polity. **Francis Makoa**	46
Chapter 4:	Mauritius: Beyond elite compacts and incestuous politics. **Sheila Bunwaree**	68
Chapter 5:	Mozambique: From civil war to loyal opposition. **Fivejoa Pereira, Sandra Manuel, Carlos Shenga**	90
Chapter 6:	Nambia: Opposition parties stuck in the sand. **Andre du Pisani, Bill Lindeke**	119
Chapter 7:	South Africa: Opposition politics post apartheid. **Dirk Kotze**	152
Chapter 8:	Swaziland: Opposition politics within a feudal system. **Petros Magagula, Zwelibanzi Masilela**	177
Chapter 9:	Zambia: Between the politics of opposition and incumbency. **Jotham Momba**	203
Chapter 10:	Zimbabwe: Opposing an authoritarian system - The case of the MDC. **John Makumbe**	223
Bibliography		245

Acknowledgements

Most of the chapters in this edited volume were originally commissioned as part of a programme developed by the South African Institute of International Affairs (SAIIA) on Parliaments of the Southern African Development Community (SADC). The programme's central aim was to better understand the relationship between parliaments and civil society within SADC and to suggest practical methods to strengthen these relationships.

This book is the result of the work and dedication of many. In particular, SAIIA wishes to recognise the intellectual contribution of SAIIA Research Fellow, Mr Tim Hughes, who headed the SADC Parliaments programme. Mr Hughes conceptualised and developed the original terms of reference for a series of papers on opposition parties in southern Africa, on which the chapters in this volume are based. His work in this area drew on his research over more than seven years into democracy and the role of parliaments, political parties and other organs of civil society in southern Africa.

In addition, SAIIA would like to gratefully acknowledge the Danish International Development Agency (DANIDA) for its financial support of the SADC Parliaments programme; Ipuseng Kotsokoane of KMMR; and last but not least, Professor Hussein Solomon, a SAIIA research associate and professor at the University of the Free State, who edited this volume....

Elizabeth Sidiropoulos
National Director
South African Institute of International Affairs

Contributors

Editor Hussein Solomon
Professor Hussein Solomon lectures in the Department of Political Sciences at the University of the Free State. He is currently a visiting Professor at the Global Collaboration Centre at Osaka University, Japan and a visiting Fellow at the Mackinder Programme for the Study of Long-Wave Events at the London School of Economics and Political Science.

Botswana Chapter:
Balefi Tsie is Associate Professor of Political Science at the University of Botswana (UB). He served as Dean of the Faculty of Social Sciences at UB from 2003 to 2009. He was Head of the Department of Political and Administrative Studies from 1993 to 1998. Prof. Tsie has a Ph.D. from the University of Leeds in England. His research interests are: Globalization and Regional Integration in Southern Africa; The State and Development in SADC; Civil Society and Developmental Democracy in Southern Africa; International Political Economy and Democratic Governance in Southern Africa.

Lesotho Chapter:
Professor Francis Makoa, former Dean of the Faculty of Social Sciences of the National University of Lesotho, served in the Department of Political and Administrative Studies of this university up to 2010. He has published extensively in wide-ranging topics such as Democracy and Governance, Elections, Political Development, Political Parties, Public policy, conflict resolution, national security, labor relations, regional integration, gender Politics. He is a member of the Association for African Public Administration and Management (AAPAM), South African Association for Public Administration and Management (SAAPAM), the Organization for Social Science Research in Eastern and Southern Africa (OSSREA)
and South Africa Institute of Africa (SAIA).

Mauritius Chapter:
Sheila Bunwaree is Professor of Gender and Development Studies at the University of Mauritius. She has also served as the Director of the Research Department at the Council for the Development of Social Science Research in Africa (CODESRIA), based in Dakar, (Senegal). More recently she was senior researcher at the Centre for Conflict Resolution, in Cape Town. Her research interests include governance, gender and globalisation. Sheila Bunwaree has numerous publications to her record.

Mozambique Chapter:
João C. G. Pereira is Auxiliary Professor at the Faculty of Social Science Department of Political and Public Administration (Eduardo Mondlane University, Mozambique) and Director of Civil Society Support Mechanism (CSSM). He is also associated with

the Institute for Economic and Social Studies (IESE), Afrobarometer, and Comparative National Electoral Project in Mozambique. His research interests include: Voting behavior; Public opinion, Party Politics, Urban Politics, Political representations, Political Communication, Civil Society, Government Accountability and Responsiveness.

Sandra Manuel is a PhD Candidate in Anthropology and Sociology, School of Oriental and African Studies, University of London, and Lecturer at the Department of Archeology and Anthropology, Eduardo Mondlane University in Mozambique. Her area of interest includes Gender and Politics Studies, Sexual Behaviour, Lesbian & Gay studies, AIDS & HIV, Medical Anthropology, Youth Behaviour, and Medical Sociology.

Carlos Shenga PhD Candidate in Political Science, Research Assistant in Democracy in Africa Research Unit of the Centre for Social Science Research, both at the University of Cape Town, and Principal Investigator of the Afrobarometer Network in Mozambique.
He has been involved in CNEP (Comparative National Election Project) and CSES (Comparative Studies of Electoral Systems) networks. His area of interest includes Comparative Politics, Democracy, Elections and Parliament.

Namibia Chapter:

André du Pisani is Professor of Political Studies and former Dean of Faculty at the University of Namibia (UNAM) and former Director in Namibia of the Southern African Defence and Security Management Network (SADEM). He serves as National Coordinator for the Volkswagen Foundation funded Angola-Namibia Project of the Arnold Bergstraesser Institut. He is the author, editor or co-editor of several books and numerous articles on Namibian politics and security issues in the SADC region.

William A. Lindeke now serves as the Senior Research Associate for Democracy and Governance at the Institute for Public Policy Research (IPPR) in Windhoek, Namibia. He was Professor of Political Studies at the University of Massachusetts Lowell (retired). He has authored or co-authored several book chapters and articles on Namibian politics and on SADC issues. He is Co-national Investigator for Round Four of the Afrobarometer in Namibia and a Senior Researcher on the Angola-Namibia Project.

South Africa Chapter:

Professor Dirk Kotzé is the Head of the Department in the Political Sciences at the University of South Africa (UNISA). He is a member of the International Political Science Association and as National Secretary/treasurer of the South African Association of Political Studies. Moreover, he is also involved in the official training programme in South Africa for the Government of Southern Sudan. He was a member of the ministerial panel on ownership of land by foreigners in South Africa. Academic publications and media contributions include topics like the Negotiation Process in South Africa and The Transition, Political Cartoons, Elections, Democratic Consolidation,

The ANC and SACP, The quality of democracy, and conflict resolution.

Swaziland Chapter:

Petros Magagula is Political Science Senior Lecturer with the Department of Political and Administrative Studies (PAS) in the Faculty of Social Science at the University of Swaziland. He has also served as a member of the Governing Body for the Conciliation, Mediation and Arbitration Commission (CMAC) of Swaziland, served as the Chairperson of the Social Science Sub- Committee of the National Research Council, based in Swaziland. His research interests include Foreign Investments in Swaziland and its Politico-Socio-Economic effects, Post- independence Political Development in Swaziland.

Zwelibanzi Masilela is a former Political Science Lecturer with the Department of Political and Administrative Studies, Faculty of Social Science in the University of Swaziland. He is currently working at the Department of Trade and Industry in the International Trade and Economic Development (ITED) under the Southern African Customs Union (SACU) Directorate. He has published for various institutions including the Electoral Institute for Southern Africa – EISA (2008), Transparency International - TI Zimbabwe (2007), Open Society for Southern Africa – OSISA (2006), and worked for the National Democratic Institute for International Affairs (NDI) and the Council of Swaziland Churches.

Zambia Chapter:

Jotham Momba is an Associate Professor of Political Science at the University of Zambia. He has written a number of articles on issues of governance and liberal democracy in Zambia. He is former head of the Department of Political and Administrative Studies. He also taught at the Drew University in the USA as a Fulbright Fellow and at the University of Swaziland. He was president of the Organisation for Social Science and Research in Eastern and Southern Africa (OSSREA) from 2007 to 2011. He obtained his BA from the University of Zambia and his MA and PhD from the University of Toronto, Canada.

Zimbabwe Chapter:

John Makumbe is an Associate Professor of Political Science at the University of Zimbabwe. Author of Behind the Smokescreen: The Politics of Zimbabwe's 1995 General Elections, (with Daniel Compagnon), and several other books. Actively involved in civic action and, until recently, founder Chairman of the Zimbabwe Chapter of Transparency International (TI). He also sat on the international Board of Directors of TI. He is the founder Chairman of the Zimbabwe Albino Association (ZIMAS), and sits on the Board of the African Development Educators' Network (ADEN). He is also a board member of the Mass Public Opinion Institute (MPOI).

CHAPTER ONE
CONCEPTUAL OVERVIEW OF OPPOSITION POLITICAL PARTIES IN SOUTHERN AFRICA
HUSSEIN SOLOMON

In February 2010, Tendai Biti, an official of the Movement for Democratic Change (MDC) and Zimbabwe's Minister of Finance, bluntly stated, 'ZANU-PF cannot continue to urinate on us'.[1] What Biti was complaining about was the penchant of the dominant Zimbabwe African National Union–Patriotic Front of President Robert Mugabe to ignore the opposition MDC in the governance of Zimbabwe, even though both parties were part of a supposedly inclusive unity government in Harare.

Indeed the frustration that caused Biti to utter these words is felt by much of the political opposition in southern Africa. These feelings are either arrogantly dismissed or condescending tolerated by incumbent parties across the region. In other cases, opposition political parties have no one else but themselves to blame as a result of internal divisions, poor party organisation and a concomitant lack of party discipline.

The generally ineffective and moribund nature of much of the political opposition points to a grave democratic deficit in southern Africa. The reason for this is not hard to fathom. Like it or not, the political party is the major organising principle of modern politics. Andrew Heywood[2] notes that political parties are, '...the vital link between the state and civil society; between the institutions of government and the group and interests that operate within society'.

Yolanda Sadie[3] goes even further and states that no democracy can function without political parties. She argues that democracies are based on the principle of representation of the people. It is political parties that represent and articulate the interests of the people through their duly elected representatives.

Both ruling and opposition parties play a crucial role here, with the party securing the most votes forming the government and executing the policies of its constituency whilst the political opposition serves to hold the ruling party accountable and provides inputs into the legislative process. In this way, too, both ruling and opposition political parties give the entire political process legitimacy. Dominant interests in society, through the various checks and balances in place, are not so dominant that they can ride roughshod over other segments of society. The opposition, meanwhile, despite their party not having won the election, can still play important roles in demanding accountability from the ruling party whilst at the same time playing an important role in the legislative process. Thus there is a buy-in from all sectors of society into the political system. In this process, as Balefi Tsie argues in this volume, political parties contribute to political stability.

Political parties, operating within the context of electoral competition and within a liberal polity where a democratic political culture prevails through all segments of society, are therefore guardians of democracy. On the other hand, Heywood warns against regime parties that monopolise political power, giving rise to the so-called dominant party system where ruling political parties are often seen as 'instruments of manipulation and political control'[4]. In similar vein, Sadie argues that without rotation in office, dominant parties fail to distinguish between party and state interests, centralise power, and grow increasingly arrogant as they ignore criticism from other political parties and broader civil society.[5]

In southern Africa, this arrogance of power of the incumbent political parties, with its resultant democratic deficit, holds dire consequences for the region's people from poor policy formulation resulting in poor living standards to human rights abuses – most notably in the Democratic Republic of the Congo and Zimbabwe.[6] Without a vibrant political opposition such poor policy formulation and human rights abuses will remain unchecked to the detriment of the region's people. More importantly, the authoritarian tendencies of ruling parties will be merely reinforced in the absence of such effective political opposition. Thus, a vibrant political opposition in each of the polities of southern Africa needs to be entrenched if the region's people are to enjoy a future of economic prosperity and political stability.

This is seen most graphically perhaps in feudal Swaziland, one of the most politically repressive states in the region and one of the most economically backward. We see this in the torture and unjustified use of lethal force by so-called law enforcement agencies as well as in the nearly 70 per cent of the population who live in poverty.[7] Indeed, as we shall see in this volume, Petros Magagula and Zwelibanzi Masilela point to the fact that part of the poor policy-making undertaken in Swaziland relates directly to the fact that opposition parties had not played a legislative role in the country since independence. To put it differently, the parliaments of the kingdom never had the benefit of learning from, or of being buttressed by, the contributions of the opposition parties.

This, of course, raises important questions. Why is the political opposition so weak and fragmented in the region? Are the challenges that they confront largely those of internal weaknesses or state repression? How does the political opposition relate to their constituencies as well as wider civil society? What is the legal framework in which they operate? How do the state and its constituent organs in their interaction with the political opposition interpret that legal framework? How does funding to political parties operate in each of the countries? How do political parties engage with the media to articulate the interests of their constituencies?

In seeking to answer these questions, this volume assembled a number of prominent scholars from the region to respond from the experiences of their own country. This volume is unique in that it is the first time that a comprehensive survey of opposition political parties in southern Africa has been attempted. As Dirk Kotze notes in this volume, scholarly work on the subject is severely limited. Moreover, the diversity of countries included – from tiny island-state Mauritius to regional behemoth South Africa, from democratic Botswana to feudal Swaziland – allows one to draw comparative lessons and indeed generalisations about the region.

In the first chapter, Balefi Tsie examines opposition political parties in Botswana from the country's independence in 1965 up to the 2009 elections. He explores both the character of the political opposition and its contribution to democracy. Importantly, Tsie examines opposition political parties within the broader context of the political economy of the country. He concludes by looking into the future – examining pathways to a stronger political opposition and thereby a more vibrant democratic polity.

Jotham Momba, meanwhile, focuses his attention on Zambia from 1990 when Article 4 of the Zambian Constitution was amended to allow for the formation of political parties other than the ruling United National Independence Party (UNIP). Whilst this opened political space for both the political opposition and civil society, Momba makes clear that the situation is far from a level playing field, with incumbents having the benefit of patronage networks and interpreting legislation to their benefit. At the same time, internal weaknesses also prevent the political opposition from playing as effective a role as they need to play in order to ensure accountability from the ruling party.

In their analysis of Namibia since 1990, Andre du Pisani and Bill Lindeke examine the genesis, nature and performance of the political opposition. In the process, they provide penetrating insights into the constitutional provisions for opposition politics, electoral systems, party performance, support bases and party funding. Despite the fact that Namibia has experienced 15 elections at three different levels of government since independence, the reality remains that the country experiences major challenges surrounding the dominant one-party system of the South West African Peoples' Organisation (SWAPO).

Francis Makoa's examination of Lesotho's opposition politics is also done through a historical lens and investigates the changing nature of the political opposition within a wider political and economic context. In a wide-ranging analysis he explores civil-military relations, the role of the king and trade unions, the development of political parties within Lesotho since the 1950s and the institutional framework in which these operate. Makoa's analysis also points to the role of dominant personalities within Lesotho's fragile polity since independence. In this way African politics differs very much from its counterparts elsewhere, because institutions have been historically weaker; personalities matter more at state and party level.

The issue of the personalisation of politics is displayed more evidently in opposition politics in Mozambique. In their chapter, Joao Pereira, Sandra Manuel and Carlos Shenga examine opposition politics in Mozambique since November 1990 when a new Constitution provided for a multiparty political system. In a comprehensive analysis, the authors critically discuss the electoral system in Mozambique, the ethnic basis of party support, issues of internal cohesion and the organisation of parties, party funding and intra-party democracy. As in Namibia, Angola, Botswana and increasingly South Africa, one-party dominance characterises politics in the country.

In his chapter on South Africa, Dirk Kotze examines opposition political parties since 1994, focusing on those opposition political parties with a national footprint. As he points out, 80 per cent of the official political parties registered with the Independent Electoral Commission focus only on municipal elections. By narrowing his attention to those political parties which stand a chance of unseating the dominant African National Congress (ANC), he adds a greater level of depth to his analysis. Very importantly, Kotze also examines how the opposition view themselves and how the ruling party views the political opposition.

At face value, Mauritius gives one the impression of a vibrant and democratic multiparty system with regular elections, the peaceful transfer of power and voter turnout in elections at a remarkable 80 per cent. Yet, in her incisive chapter, Sheila Bunwaree notes that the democratic deficit is also evident in Mauritian politics, largely on account of the dynastic nature of political parties. Moreover, she points to the need to de-ethnicise and de-racialise the party system as well as to ensure greater participation of women in the political process.

Opposition political parties in Swaziland, meanwhile, confront unique challenges. In their chapter, Petros Magagula and Zwelibanzi Masilela point out that Swaziland is the only southern African country to be ruled by a monarch wielding real political power and traditional authority and institutions to bolster his rule. Whilst opposition political parties cannot legally operate and there is a ban on political campaigning, these do exist and do operate. Magagula and Masilela provide fascinating insights into the nature of the Swazi system as well as a thorough examination of the various political formations in the country and their interaction with Swazi civil society from 1968 to 2009.

In the final case study, that of Zimbabwe, John Makumbe provides an erudite study of opposition political parties in the country since 1980, with an emphasis on developments since the establishment of the MDC in 1999. Like Swaziland, the political opposition in Zimbabwe operates under repressive conditions. Unlike Swaziland, however, the two MDC factions together with ZANU-PF are all part of a government of national unity. What has this meant for the MDC and its constituency? What has it meant for democracy in Zimbabwe? How have internal divisions hurt the political opposition? How has the international community engaged in promoting democracy in Zimbabwe? These are some of the questions

Makumbe attempts to answer in this important chapter.

Whilst the challenges confronting the political opposition are ultimately unique in each country, there are broad similarities too. These provide us with an understanding of not only the broad challenges but opportunities confronting the political opposition in southern Africa.

Sheila Bunwaree begins her illuminating chapter quoting two pre-eminent thinkers – Robert Dahl and Van de Walle. Both thinkers note how the quality of political competition and the power of the political opposition are closely related to how democratic a country is. For Dahl, no political opposition translates into no democracy. After all, as Dahl notes, without political opposition, there is no choice, and without choice, citizens cannot exercise their rule.

In similar vein Francis Makoa argues that a key hallmark of multiparty democracy is effective representation underpinned by strong political institutions founded on and guided by the principle of freedom and the right to choose. Pereira, Manuel and Shenga passionately argue that opposition political parties have a critical role to play in the governance process and are a key element in monitoring government performance and mobilising citizens to participate in public life.

Balefi Tsie also examines political parties' wider contribution to society by pointing out how they achieve societal cohesiveness. Indeed, this is the common thread running through all the chapters in the volume. Magagula and Masilela accept this position but take it a step further and point out how the lack of participation of the political opposition has resulted in mismanagement of finances, lack of accountability and poor policies. Dirk Kotze goes further still, and quotes Adam Przeworksi who made the observation that a democracy is not yet consolidated until the government has lost an election and handed power to the opposition who now forms the government.

Despite the importance of political opposition and resultant competition, the reality in the southern African region is a major democratic deficit resulting from the lack of a vibrant political opposition. The reasons for this are varied emanating from both the external environment and internal factors.

First among the external factors is the institutional framework in which political parties are compelled to operate. The institutional framework varies from the relatively benign as in Botswana, Mozambique, Namibia, South Africa and Zambia to the highly repressive as in Swaziland.

In their penetrating chapter on Namibia, André du Pisani and Bill Lindeke point out how Namibia's 1990 Constitution is regarded as one of the most liberal in Africa, making provision for individual liberties, media freedom and a multiparty political framework. One would expect that under these conditions, multiparty democracy would be flourishing in Namibia. The reality though is that it is not, with opposition parties having been held to less than 30 per cent of the vote in elections since 1989. Amongst the reasons is the discrepancy between what is said in the Constitution and the reality on the ground. Thus when the opposition Rally for Democracy and Progress was formed and broke away from the ruling SWAPO, its leaders were targeted with stinging verbal abuse and vengeful dismissals. The most serious violence post-independence then broke out.

In Botswana, whilst the political opposition welcomed the changes to the Constitution in 1997, allowing the formation of an Independent Electoral Commission, they were appalled to find that the supervisor of elections still reported to the Office of the President. Similarly in Mozambique, whilst the November 1990 Constitution allows for a multiparty political system with a minimum of five per cent electoral threshold in the national vote to gain representation in parliament, the reality is that FRELIMO benefits from the politics of incumbency so that it is far from a level playing field. The same could be said of South Africa.

In Zambia, whilst the amendment of Article 4 of the Constitution allows for the provision of political parties other than the then-ruling UNIP, other laws like the Public Order Act and its application by the police have worked against multiparty democracy.

Perhaps the difference between constitutional provisions and reality is seen most graphically in Zimbabwe where despite constitutional provisions for a multiparty democracy, MDC members have had to bear the brunt of state-sanctioned violence and repression. In Swaziland, the February 2006 Constitution does not define the principle of democracy and is unclear on whether political parties are allowed to operate in the kingdom. This ambiguity then allows the state to make use of such legislation as the Suppression of Terrorism Act of 2008 to infringe on the rights of people to freely form political parties and engage in political activities.

Another aspect of the institutional framework that impacts on political parties is the nature of the electoral system. In Mauritius, the first-past-the-post system runs the risk of a parliament without an opposition. This system has also resulted in parties forming coalitions or alliances to prevent annihilation at the polls. However the downside of these coalitions is that it robs citizens of choice and results in a tiny political elite being recycled from election to election. In addition, there is an absence of a culture of opposition politics – of wanting to ensure that government performance is monitored and accountability is enforced. Instead those parties not in power seek ways to get into the coalition in power.

The case of Lesotho demonstrates that jettisoning the first-past-the post-system and its replacement by the mixed member proportional electoral model has made little difference to the prospects of the political opposition to unseat the ruling party. The lesson learned may be that whilst the change of the electoral model towards one of inclusion is to be welcomed, other changes need also to be effected if the political opposition is to have any chance of replacing the ruling party. These range from rectifying intra-party problems to issues of neutralising the benefits of incumbency. Neither is the politics of incumbency a uniquely Lesotho affair.

We have seen how in Zambia, the ruling party uses loopholes in the Electoral Code of Conduct to gain an unfair advantage over the political opposition.

Closely related to the institutional framework is the issue of party funding. As Pereira, Manuel and Shenga remind us, the issue of party funding in Africa takes on increased urgency because of the poverty of party members, many of whom are unable to pay party membership fees. Without party funding, no political party can campaign effectively, mobilise its constituency and thereby stand a chance of unseating incumbents. This is a fact that ruling parties in the region understand well and they go out of their way to starve opposition parties of funding whilst at the same time building patronage networks for their own party, using state resources. In Zimbabwe, ZANU-PF uses state resources for itself whilst the political opposition has no access to the same resources. At the same time the Mugabe regime has been critical of any foreign donor agencies providing support to both civil society and the political opposition. However in Mozambique, where RENAMO has been the recipient of public funds as well as foreign donations, gifts and grants, such foreign support has made no difference to the party's political prospects.

In South Africa, too, opposition parties are relatively free to raise funds privately in addition to the public funds they receive. Despite this, there is little hope that these funds could translate into unseating the incumbent. The lesson here is also clear: additional funds do not serve to bolster the opposition's political prospects at the polls unless they are used effectively and the parties' internal problems are fixed.

In Lesotho, the Independent Electoral Commission provides R20 000 towards campaigning for all political parties having 500 members on registration. This token amount hardly covers the cost of the campaign. Thus opposition parties need to find funds to supplement the minuscule amount received from public funds. This, however, is extremely difficult in a context where society is poverty-stricken. Here, too, the politics of incumbency provides the ruling party with an unfair advantage.

In Mauritius public funding of political parties does not exist. Politicians however do receive so-called 'donations' from 'well-wishers'. The problem with this scenario is that such donations are unofficial and unacknowledged. Such a situation can only promote corruption since one has no idea what favours the 'well-wisher' may want in return for the 'donation'. Greater transparency is essential if this scenario is to be avoided.

The relationship between the private sector and party funding is also seen in Namibia, where businesses which seek to access government contracts and licences contribute to SWAPO coffers. Balefi Tsie's point on Botswana is however relevant to all dominant party systems in the region when he eloquently argues that private companies invariably support the ruling party in such systems, since this is where they get their tenders. Once more this is the politics of incumbency. In Zambia, perhaps more malevolently, the Zambian Revenue Authority is allegedly utilised to harass those businesses seen to be making donations to opposition political parties.

Another key factor is the role of the media. When government has a monopoly over the media, greater advantages accrue to the ruling party, whilst the political opposition languishes in political obscurity – with the ruling party enjoying the limelight provided by public broadcasting authorities. This monopoly is seen most graphically in the tight control exercised by the Swazi Ministry of Public Service and Information over both the Swaziland Broadcasting and Information Service and the Swaziland Television Broadcasting Corporation. In Mozambique, meanwhile, publicly funded media organisations are deployed against the political opposition during elections. In Namibia, SWAPO's political dominance is reinforced by its dominance of the government-owned media where content bias as well as intensity of coverage reinforces the political status quo. Even in politically tolerant Mauritius, the incumbent government often abuses its power to access much more time on state-owned media than its rivals.

One way to break the ruling party's media dominance is the establishment of the private media outlets that we see in South Africa, which so successfully acts as a check on the ruling African National Congress (ANC). There are, however, three problems here:

First, there is the resource question. Given the distressed economic circumstances in tiny Lesotho or Swaziland, it is rather unlikely that they would be able to follow the South African example of creating a vibrant alternative media outlet.

Second, there is the problem of state repression. In Zambia, for instance, we have the example of a private radio station in the Copperbelt, which was deemed to be anti-government; the station was attacked by Movement for Multi-Party Democracy (MMD) cadres during the 2001 elections whilst police looked on. It is, however, Zimbabwe where state repression against any media critical of ZANU-PF is taken to its logical extreme – where journalists are beaten up, editors are arrested and printing presses are blown up.

Third, current media legislation on the table in South Africa suggests that the ruling party is flexing its muscle and raises questions for how long even private media can serve as an effective check on the ruling ANC.

The fourth external factor is the relationship between the political opposition and broader civil society. Given the dominance of the ruling party in many countries of the region and the politics of incumbency, a good relationship between the political opposition and broader civil society may serve as a force-multiplier effect, assisting in levelling the playing field somewhat. In Zimbabwe, for instance, the opposition MDC grew out of the Zimbabwe Congress of Trade Unions (ZCTU) and made use of ZCTU's organisational infrastructure to expand its reach as the political opposition.

In Swaziland, too, it is the labour movement that is assisting in the creation of a multiparty democracy, by challenging the authoritarian basis of the state. This is further cemented by the historically close ties between PUDEMO (People's United Democratic Movement) the Swaziland Federation of Trade Unions. However the tensions emanating from PUDEMO's call for a blockade of the Swaziland-South Africa border in April 2006 has resulted in this relationship souring. If a democratic polity is to be achieved in Swaziland, it is imperative that the political opposition works together with other broader structures of civil society. Here, the formation of the Swaziland Coalition of Concerned Civic Organisations and the National Constitutional Assembly are good indicators that this might well be taking place.

In Mauritius, the current economic difficulties may well have a positive impact on the cause of political pluralism by opening up party processes and hopefully breaking the dynastic politics that has so come to characterise the political landscape. The economic uncertainties plaguing the island state are resulting in trade unions organising better, mobilising their members better and seeking to more effectively represent the interests of their constituency by lobbying political parties. For opposition political parties, taking on board organised labour's concerns might well provide them with a return ticket to power. This creates a win-win scenario for both labour and the political opposition. More importantly, though, it might well create the conditions where some of the labour leaders are incorporated into the leadership of political parties – thus breaking the hold of dynastic politics.

In Namibia, the positive role civil society could play in fostering genuine political competition and moving away from one-party dominant politics is undermined by the fact that most large civil society organisations are either affiliated to SWAPO or dominated by it. To a limited extent the same could be said of the Congress of South African Trade Unions (COSATU) in its tripartite relationship with the ANC in South Africa. However the diversity of civil society structures and the recent tensions between COSATU and the ANC might well prove positive towards the country's political health in the long-term. The overall point made by Francis Makoa in the chapter on Lesotho is an important one: that the political opposition needs to deepen their involvement with civil society if they intend to play a meaningful role in the political landscape.

Fifth, opposition political parties have an added difficulty going up against governments that emanate from liberation movements. Mugabe and ZANU-PF constantly remind the electorate that they rescued them from the evils of Ian Smith's minority rule. SWAPO in Namibia, FRELIMO in Mozambique and the ANC in South Africa all make similar claims. This allows incumbents to dress themselves in the garb of revolutionary righteousness whilst the opposition is cast as 'reactionaries'. Dirk Kotze demonstrates how this impacts on the attitudes of an ANC that refuses to call itself a political party and insists that it remains a national liberation movement – whilst members of the opposition are relegated to being viewed as spokespersons of minority and sector interests.

However, this is changing across the region. With the passing of years, this talk of liberation politics has less resonance to a new generation of citizens who never experienced the ravages of the Portuguese in Mozambique or the brutality in Rhodesia or the excesses in South West Africa. Moreover, the development of opposition political parties that emerged from the liberation movements – SWAPO and the ANC – also serve to undermine the incumbent monopoly of this liberation legacy.

The sixth and final external factor is the role played by the international community. As was pointed out earlier, foreign donor support for an opposition political party like RENAMO in Mozambique will have no effect if there are no structural and personnel changes inside the party to make use of such foreign largesse effectively. But the role of the international community in furthering the cause of multiparty democracy may also be both positive and negative. Pressure from the international community might well have the positive impact of compelling a repressive state to change. This we have seen to a certain extent in Swaziland, where pressure from the International Labour Organisation, Amnesty International, the Southern African Development Community and the United States impelled King Mswati III to enact some reforms. Whilst the reforms certainly did not go far enough, the fact that the kingdom did bend under pressure is an important precedent that should be exploited further.

The case of Zimbabwe shows the limitations of what international pressure can accomplish. Robert Mugabe has made use of international support for the political opposition and civil society to accuse them of being agents of foreign 'imperialists'. On the other hand, the fact that the international community is so divided, especially on the axis between SADC and Western countries, has resulted in dispersed and contradictory international efforts. In 2009, under pressure from SADC, ZANU-PF was compelled to share power in a unity government with the two factions of the MDC. However, more than a year later, after the unity government came into effect, Robert Rotberg notes that there has been little unity, and even less partnership between the MDC and ZANU-PF.[8] ZANU-PF has thus effectively dismissed the MDC as junior partners to be co-opted despite the fact that the MDC won the March 2008 parliamentary elections outright.

In a blistering critique of such unity models of government John Githongo asserts, 'The unity model is an inclusive one, and has been championed in some academic and political circles as the new model for African democracy. It is no such thing. The coalitions are the result of democratic failures, not successes. Throughout Africa, uniting belligerents under one roof has resulted in policymaking paralysis and resentful voters, angry that the governments they have are not the ones any of them elected'.[9] It is, however, precisely this failed unity model that SADC has foisted on the hapless citizens of Zimbabwe.

It is not only external factors, but also internal factors – factors within the control of the political opposition – that prevent them from realising their potential. Jotham Momba brilliantly demonstrates how internal dynamics have served to undermine the Zambian political opposition – the jostling for leadership positions along with the concomitant 'big-man' syndrome in African politics have served to undermine intra-party democracy. This is also visible in Botswana politics where one witnesses the factionalisation of both opposition and ruling party. We see this phenomenon in Mozambique where the personalisation of politics is all too evident with the leader, Afonso Dhlakama, himself, is seen as embodying RENAMO. In Mauritius this is seen in the transfer of party leadership within the family. In Namibia, the tiring circulation of old elites as opposed to a renewal of leadership has seen the electorate growing increasingly disenchanted with the political opposition. All this suggests that if multipartyism is to be strengthened in the region, what is needed is not merely the strengthening of opposition political parties but also the instilling of a democratic political culture across all sectors of society. If this is not done, we might well see what happened in Zambia, with the opposition MMD toppling UNIP but then also behaving in an authoritarian style.

Ongoing quarrels and divisions within the opposition threaten to marginalise them ever further. In Zimbabwe, the October 2005 split inside the MDC has served not only to weaken the opposition but also to play into the hands of ZANU-PF. In Swaziland, the debate on whether or not to participate in the existing political system fractured the Ngwane National Liberatory Congress. In Namibia, meanwhile, an internal leadership battle in 2007 threatened to destroy the Congress of Democrats. In Botswana, the main opposition Botswana National Front split in April 1998 – sowing a new opposition party, the Botswana Congress Party – in the process diluting the opposition's weight and influence over the ruling Botswana Democratic Party. In South Africa, we have witnessed how the Congress of the People, launched with so much hope, has essentially failed to be a credible challenger to the ruling ANC on account of its internal divisions. The overall point is that such divisions reinforce the dominant political status quo.

Still another aspect of concern that negatively impacts on the performance of opposition political parties is ethnic politics. In Mozambique, for instance, RENAMO draws its support largely from the Ndaw, Sena and Makwa ethnic groups. In Namibia, too, much of the political opposition is ethnically based, such as the Kavango-based All Peoples' Party. The problem with such ethnic politics is that few opposition parties have a national footprint and are therefore in a position to realistically challenge the incumbent. Even the so-called 'rainbow nation', post-apartheid South Africa, has witnessed this phenomenon, which makes it unlikely that the opposition Democratic Alliance (DA) will be able to capture another province beyond the Western Cape – precisely because no other province has the same demographic make-up as that province. In Mauritius we witness ethnicity, religion and caste coalesce in an unholy trinity. The two largely Indian and Hindu-based parties – the Mouvement Militant Socialiste Mauricien and the Labour Party – have always had a Hindu of the Vaish caste as their leaders. This once more reinforces the elitist nature of Mauritian politics.

Finally, the political opposition is also confronted with a set of organisational challenges. A vast array of opposition political parties exists in Lesotho. Of these only the Basotho National Party has a significant presence in the countryside.

It might well be that it is more difficult to organise in the countryside than in the urban areas, but unless they start mobilising in the rural areas, there is no possibility of the opposition toppling the ruling Lesotho Congress for Democracy from power.

In Mozambique, the same problem persists but from the opposite side – RENAMO works in the rural areas but has no significant urban presence. Until the opposition party's political machinery is in place throughout the country, there is no chance of displacing the incumbent party.

One realises that the depth and penetration of party machinery is intimately related to issues like party finance as well as skill sets. On the latter point, it must be acknowledged that whilst the MDC in Zimbabwe as well as the DA in South Africa have been very successful in attracting talented professionals to assist in the running of the party, most opposition parties remain moribund because of an inability to attract such talent. Indeed, the elitist politics these parties pursue and the undemocratic nature of internal party processes result in a reluctance of intellectuals to be part of these parties.

Against all odds, though, it must be acknowledged that the political opposition continues to exist and, in some cases, even thrive in southern Africa. But at the same time it also needs to be acknowledged that the political opposition is not performing as well as it should be. In the process, democracy is undermined, as is the will of the region's people. Each country case study in this volume is rich with lessons for policymakers, politicians, scholars and members of civil society on how to entrench a vibrant multiparty democratic system in which the strengthening of opposition political parties is seen as a vital aspect of democratic consolidation. It is time to implement these lessons if we are to have a peaceful and prosperous region.

ENDNOTES

1 Quoted in Rotberg Robert 2010., 'Mugabe Uber Alles: The Tyranny of Unity in Zimbabwe'. Foreign Affairs, 89(4), July/August, p10.

2 Heywood Andrew 2002. Politics, 2nd edition. London: Palgrave Macmillan, p247.

3 Sadie Yolanda 2001. 'Political Parties and Interest Groups', in Venter Albert (ed) Government and Politics in the new South Africa. Pretoria: Van Schaik Publishers, p277.
4 Heywood, op.cit., p251.
5 Sadie, op.cit., p294.
6 Amnesty International 2010. Amnesty International 2010: The State of the World's Human Rights. www.thereport.amnesty.org/en/download. [accessed: 31 May 2010]
7 Ibid
8 IRotberg, op.cit., p10.
9 Githongo John 2010. 'Fear and Loathing in Nairobi'. Foreign Affairs, 89(4), July/ August, p3.

CHAPTER TWO
BOTSWANA: OPPOSITION POLITICS WITHIN A FRAYING DOMINANT PARTY SYSTEM
BALEFI TSIE

Introduction

Political parties – whether in power or opposition – are key actors in the development and sustainability of multiparty democracy. Modern representative democracy is inconceivable without the active involvement of different political parties competing for political office or state power. To our knowledge no country has democratised without the involvement of political parties.

Political parties are organised associations of people with common interests and objectives, seeking to capture or retain political power – to remain in government or become one. As Schumpeter correctly observed, 'the first and foremost aim of each political party is to prevail over others in order to get into power or stay in it'.[1] State power is the ultimate objective of every political party, no matter how small its inception. This is what distinguishes political parties from interest groups, which merely seek to influence government policy in certain directions. Political parties, together with legislative bodies, are part of what is called political society. Unlike civil society, which is outside the state, political society permeates the state and parts of it are organs of the state. A good example is the legislature.

Political parties perform several important functions in modern representative democracy. The first is to contribute to nation-building, especially in multiethnic and multiracial societies; to strive to unify the nation and achieve societal cohesiveness by bringing various diverse interests and competing aspirations together; and above all, to promote political stability. Political parties are not expected to divide the nation or to destabilise it.

The second function is interest articulation. Political parties articulate the interests of their followers into coherent programmes of action called party manifestos. They collect, sift and prioritise a myriad of specific demands and aspirations into manageable packages which in due course can become party policies on a variety of issue areas. Thus, 'parties play a crucial role in bringing together diverse interests, and providing alternative policy proposals from which voters can make an informed choice at the time of elections'.[2]

Thirdly, political parties actively influence and shape political attitudes and values in society. They recruit and socialise people into politics in ways that favour their interests. Parties usually articulate their own particular vision for the society they exist in. Seen in this light, all political parties have normative stances or philosophical bases no matter how blurred or inchoate. They have an ideological position or world-view even if they do not explicitly state it.

Fourthly, parties in power have the enormous responsibility of steering the ship of state; that is, managing and directing the affairs of state for a specified period of time with the overarching objective of being returned to power if they have delivered on their election promises as spelt out in their manifestos.

Fifthly, opposition political parties perform the critical function of serving as a watchdog for the electorate; indeed, for society as a whole, by keeping ruling parties in check, thereby helping to make the government of the day open to public scrutiny and truly accountable. This is an important responsibility because accountability, openness, transparency and responsiveness are key mediating values in a functioning representative democracy. In short, the opposition too is expected to contribute to a vibrant multiparty democracy by rigorously keeping the ruling party in check.

The sixth function of political parties is representation. Parties are expected to represent and articulate the interests of the people who elected them to legislative bodies – be they parliaments, provincial legislatures, regional assemblies or district and town councils. Finally, political parties serve as recruiting agents and training grounds for future political leaders. This is an equally important function of political parties because in every society leaders come and go and yet political offices – from the highest in the land to the lowest – must be filled.

It should be clear by now that political parties are vital links or mediating agents between state and society, connecting citizens to the government and feeding the government with information about the needs and aspirations of citizens. They are pivotal and integral to modern politics. Modern political parties are all catch-all parties; broad churches with their own left-wing and right-wing tendencies. They 'seek electoral support from wherever they can find it'.[3]

This study focuses specifically on opposition political parties in Botswana. Opposition parties in Botswana have failed to unseat the ruling Botswana Democratic Party (BDP) for the last 45 years. Their contribution to the quality of representative democracy in Botswana is questionable because only one party has been in power since independence in 1966. Botswana would not qualify as a consolidated democracy if the transfer of power test is used as the only criterion. This criterion says: 'A democracy is consolidated when a government that has itself been elected in free and fair elections is defeated at a subsequent election and accepts the results'.[4]

Fortunately, the alternation of parties in power is not the only test of democratic consolidation.[5] But it cannot be dismissed lightly, especially in view of the dismal performance of the opposition in the 2009 general elections. This study will, among others, seek to explain why Botswana has had a dominant party system since the pre-independence general elections of March 1965. By focusing on opposition political parties, we should be able to unravel another side of politics in Botswana which can provide important insights into the nature of politics in peripheral capitalist societies. The central argument is that underdevelopment and dependence structure politics in ways that have not been carefully studied.

The study is laid out in three sections. Section One is an historical overview of opposition politics in Botswana since 1965. It provides a context against which we assess the nature and character of opposition parties in Section Two. The thrust of the argument in section two is that the opposition is fragmented, disorganised and weak. Why this is the case is explored at length in this same section. We also briefly look at the role and contribution of the opposition to Botswana's multi-party democracy. The argument offered is that weakness does not automatically translate into uselessness. Section Three looks at future possibilities for opposition political parties. It seeks to identify credible pathways to a strong opposition in Botswana. Without a strong opposition Botswana's representative democracy would remain weak and vulnerable to reversals. The final section is the Conclusion. It sums up key issues raised in the body of the chapter.

Opposition Politics in Botswana in historical perspective: 1965-2010

A strategic entry point for a better understanding and appreciation of opposition politics in Botswana (and politics in general) is the country's political economy and how it has evolved since 1966. Of course, other relevant variables to take into consideration are the traditions, customs and culture of the inhabitants of Botswana.

When Botswana attained independence in September 1966 it was one of the poorest countries in the world, with a per capita income of approximately US$80. It had no known minerals or significant agricultural potential except in cattle rearing. Even then, periodic droughts made cattle rearing a risky venture. Hence many commentators dismissed Botswana as a barren desert. Botswana appeared destined to become a bantustan or a pan-African outpost surviving on international charity.[6]

To compound matters, independence coincided with the most devastating drought in living memory; i.e. the 1960-65 drought. The drought had decimated more than half of the cattle population and roughly 60 per cent of the population were living on food aid donated by international donor agencies such as United States Agency for International Development (USAID), the World Food Programme (WFP) and Oxfam. 'Literacy levels were among the lowest in Africa (the country had a mere 22 university graduates) and there were only eight kilometres of tarred road in the entire country'.[7] Attaining statehood under these difficult conditions appeared to be a lost cause or only for those who were either 'very brave or very foolish'.[8]

The story of Botswana's transformation from a basket case to 'an African miracle' is now a standard diet in the literature on Botswana's political economy.[9] There is no need to rehearse it here. But some brief remarks are in order, if only to refresh our minds and further clarify the context for this discussion.

The discovery of minerals, especially diamonds, in 1967 dramatically changed the fortunes of this small African nation. The Botswana government entered into a lucrative partnership with the De Beers company of South Africa to exploit diamonds in Orapa, Letlhakane and later Jwaneng under the auspices of Debswana. These diamond pipes proved to be very large and profitable. 'By 2003, Botswana was the largest producer of diamonds by value in the world'.[10] Another deal was struck with the Roan Selection Trust to exploit copper-nickel deposits in Selibe-Phikwe under the auspices of Bangwato Copper Limited (BCL). The latter venture has not been profitable until recently, when copper prices skyrocketed.

Revenue from diamond exports has been the driving force behind Botswana's phenomenal economic growth, and with it, a very impressive record of development performance which places Botswana in the medium category of the Human Development Index (HDI), ahead of many sub-Saharan African states, except Namibia, Mauritius and South Africa. As one study notes, 'Botswana is generally regarded as a developmental state with impressive capabilities because it has been able to deliver public goods and services. There [have] been ... deliberate efforts to reduce poverty, and maintenance of social harmony and political stability'.[11] Indeed, there have been significant improvements in the lives of ordinary citizens. Until the outbreak of the HIV/AIDS pandemic in the early 1980s, life expectancy in Botswana was 67 years in 1997 from a low point of 42 years in 1966.[12] The fundamental point being made here is that the opposition in Botswana is up against a ruling party which has performed relatively well, both in terms of infrastructure development and of human development. To emphasise the point, it is very hard to dismiss the BDP when it says it is 'the only party in town' with a proven track record. This is the context within which we should analyse opposition politics in Botswana in the post-colonial period.

The period 1960 to 1970

As indicated earlier, the immediate post-independence period did not confer any special advantages on the BDP. It is therefore important to revisit the period between 1960 and 1970 in order to find out why the BDP has emerged as the dominant force in party politics in Botswana. The British colonial administration took a deliberate decision in the mid-1950s to grant the Bechuanaland Protectorate (now Botswana) independence and this prompted sections of the indigenous political elite to form political parties. The history of political parties in Botswana has been ably discussed by, among others, Nengwekhulu, Parson, Ramsay and Parsons, Lekorwe, Somolekae and Selolwane.[13] All these scholars acknowledge the influence of South African politics on the development of political parties in Botswana, noting in particular that one of the oldest parties in the country – the Bechuanaland Peoples Party (BPP) – was founded by Batswana who had been activists in the African National Congress and the Pan Africanist Congress of South Africa.

They further note that the radical pan-Africanist stance of the BPP alienated dominant interests in Botswana; that is, chiefs, sub-chiefs, headmen, European settlers and the 'new men' of commoner background who by the early sixties were firmly part of the dominant class in Botswana. The BPP publicly stated that it would abolish chieftainship, introduce a planned socialist economy, nationalise land owned by European settlers or absentee landlords and redistribute cattle.[14] The campaign slogan of the BPP was Lefatshe! (meaning Land!). There was just no way in which dominant interests in Botswana – then and now – could support such a party. And dominant interests in Botswana were then, just as now, cattle interests; the cattle bourgeoisie had long been supported by the colonial state through breeding and borehole drilling programmes from the early 1920 onwards.

As is widely known, the BDP was founded in 1962 by Seretse Khama, Quett Masire and others. Unlike the BPP and the Botswana Independence Party (BIP) – a splinter group from the BPP – the BDP immediately adopted a moderate and pragmatic position, assuring chiefs that it would not abolish chieftainship if voted into power, that it would respect private property and encourage free enterprise and that it would strive for a multiracial liberal democratic order. Above all, Khama, its leader, was a paramount chief by birth. He was unique in many ways. 'He alone could muster support from the commercial cattle ranching interests, the educated Tswana elite, the traditionalists and the colonial public service'.[15] In particular, the BDP went out of its way to offer white settlers, most of whom were wealthy cattle owners and businessmen, an olive branch, recruiting them into its own ranks.

Admittedly, the one advantage that the BDP had was that it was favoured by the British colonial administration. Khama and the team he led had been groomed for leadership by the departing colonial administration. Khama, Masire and Chief Bathoen II, who later joined one of the opposition parties, served together in the Legislative Council from 1960 to 1965. In fact, out of the 12 seats in the Legislative Council, ten were occupied by BDP members. So in effect, the BDP was 'the incumbent party in the 1965 elections'.[16] But there was no other advantage beyond that. The key question is: how come the BDP won the pre-independence elections so decisively?

First of all, it has to be acknowledged that the BDP enjoyed support from wealthy European settlers. Emergent businessmen supported the BDP because it promised to remove all discriminatory commercial laws and to provide credit and extension services to the private sector. Chiefs also supported it covertly because of its moderate position on chieftainship. Taken together, this was earned or well deserved support. It has also been argued that the BDP was better organised than its rivals.

Indeed, these are important factors behind the rise of BDP to pre-eminence. But they still do not adequately explain why the BDP has enjoyed so much support. It is a fact that the BDP has enjoyed overwhelming support from the peasantry, the most numerous class in the country. Why? The key to a better understanding of the dominance of the BDP lies in unravelling the dominant relations of production in the countryside. Besides their reverence for tradition, their strong attachment to chieftainship and their noted conservatism worldwide, peasants in Botswana are caught up in patron-client relations built by cattle accumulators since pre-colonial times.

There are two pertinent aspects in these social relations. 'The first and most important of these social relations is the age-old system of farming out cattle to poorer kinsmen as *mafisa* (loaned cattle). The system has continued into the post colonial period albeit with significant modifications. The second is the control of grazing land by the cattle-based bourgeoisie through borehole ownership. For ordinary peasants to access that grazing land, permission to water their cattle has to be secured from the owners of boreholes in the first place.'[17] These are the principal means by which dominant cattle interests in Botswana have sustained their legitimacy and support amongst the peasantry. Robert Fatton's observation about patron-client relations is particularly apposite in this regard: He says:

'Patron-client relationships contribute to routinisation and legitimation of coercive dependence by projecting a form of benevolent paternalism: they facilitate the establishment of moral authority of obedience and stifle a sense of injustice. They tend to freeze the emergence of class conflict and enshrine as natural the existing hierarchy of domination and subordination.'[18]

Chiefly authority and influence simply reinforced these social relations in favour of the BDP in the 1965 general elections and subsequent ones; more so because its leader was royal. The BDP became even more popular in the post-colonial period when it introduced various agricultural schemes to help farmers and peasants. The core argument here is that the BDP was able to bring together a grand coalition of dominant interests with a strong rural support base way before any other political party could do so. In addition, it propounded an inclusive, hegemonic development agenda and systematically implemented it. In that way, there has been considerable mutuality of interests between dominant interests and sub-altern classes in Botswana, especially the peasantry.

Opposition political parties in Botswana found it very difficult to break or penetrate the 'benevolent paternalism' of the BDP in the countryside, especially in the Central and Kweneng districts where there are more constituencies. The BDP also proved to be a formidable force in urban areas such as Lobatse. However, it should be remembered that the working class was very small at that time. In the 1965 general elections the BDP won 28 out of 31 parliamentary seats. The BPP won only three and the BIP failed to win a seat. Formally speaking, opposition politics began in Botswana when the first session of the first parliament was convened. The leader of the BPP, Philip Matante, became the leader of the opposition in parliament. Before then, there were no opposition political parties because each of the parties contesting the 1965 elections could in theory win those elections. So opposition politics in Botswana began in 1965.

The number of opposition parties increased to three in 1966 when the Botswana National Front (BNF) was formed. The political programme of the BNF has been succinctly summarised by Lekorwe.[19] The BNF describes itself as 'a progressive popular democratic movement ... unified by its social democratic programme'.[20] It was conceived as a broad church to unite all patriotic elements in the country against the 'neocolonial' BDP. Its overriding objective was to conscientise and mobilise dominated classes and their middle-class allies for the purpose of launching a national democratic revolution. The leadership of this 'revolution' was designated to be radical socialist BNF members. In essence the BNF has since its inception been a Marxist socialist-oriented party seeking to mobilise the working class and other low orders in society against the 'neocolonial' BDP government. Its founder and leader for a long time – Dr K Koma – was a hardcore Marxist. The BPP and BIP were pan-Africanist in their orientation.

The fortunes of the opposition improved somewhat in the 1969 general elections. In June 1969 Chief Bathoen II of Bangwaketse resigned from the chieftainship and joined the BNF. Bathoen was unhappy about the centralisation of power by the BDP government because that process stripped chiefs of their traditional powers. He did not join the BNF because he was a socialist, let alone a democrat. He was aggrieved by the manner in which chiefs were rapidly losing their traditional powers.

Three pieces of legislation are particularly relevant here. The first is the District Councils Act of 165. This Act transferred all facets of local government from the tribal administration to district councils. The second is the Chieftainship Act of 1967. This Act 'vested the powers of recognition, appointment, deposition and suspension of chiefs in the president'.[21] It virtually made chiefs paid civil servants of the central government. The third is the Matimela Act of 1968. This transferred the power to dispose of unclaimed stray cattle to councils. Before then, chiefs were entitled to possess all unclaimed stray cattle.

This is the background against which the BNF became a force to reckon with in the Ngwaketse areas of the Southern District. It won three seats in the 1969 elections. Bathoen stood in those elections and defeated the BDP candidate – Masire, who was by then vice-president – with an overwhelming majority. The two other BNF candidates also won comfortably. The BNF became the main opposition party from 1969 onwards. And let it be said: the BNF won in these constituencies because of the chiefly authority and influence of Bathoen and not because voters believed in its socialist ideology. It should also be pointed out that a significant section of Bangwaketse remained in the BDP camp. So Kanye and Ngwaketse West constituencies were never safe constituencies for the BNF in the same way

Serowe has been for the BDP since 1965. Nevertheless, the BNF has since 1969 given the BDP a tough time in these constituencies, including Ngwaketse South.

Elsewhere in the country the BIP won a seat in the Okavango Constituency. Its leader became an MP. Meanwhile the BPP retained its three seats of Francistown, North East and Mochudi. The BDP won overwhelmingly in the remaining 24 seats. By any count, the dominance of the BDP remained intact.

Opposition politics at this time revolved around the following issues: poverty and unemployment (BNF), elitist education that did not impart survival skills (BNF), the 'failure' of the BDP to 'expropriate' land in the north-east owned by absentee landlords, especially land owned by the Tati Company (BPP); the 'subservience' of the BDP government to foreign interests (BNF, BPP); the 'failure' of the BDP government to address the plight of the poor, especially the working class (BNF); the 'failure' of the BDP government to address the issue of chieftainship in an innovative manner (BNF) ; and the 'refusal' of the BDP government to give full recognition to minority ethnic groups (BIP).

This assessment may not be an accurate summation of opposition politics between 1965 and 1970. What is certain, however, is that the opposition was able to hold on to the seats it had won in 1965 and 1969 in the subsequent elections of 1974 and 1979.

The 1970s and 1980s

The land question in the north-east was a rallying point around which the BPP mobilised support. The issue of the rights of minorities raised most consistently by the BIP enabled it to retain this seat in 1974 but lost it for good in 1979 because newly naturalised Angolan refugees voted in large numbers for the BDP. The rights of ethnic minorities remained a burning issue in opposition politics and rightly so. We will return to this issue later on. One might ask though: Where was Bathoen's chiefly authority and influence when the BDP snatched back Ngwaketse West from the BNF in the 1974 general elections? The answer is that not all residents of Ngwaketse West are Bangwaketse, Bathoen's subjects. There are Bakgalagadi as well in this constituency and some of them have 'historical grievances' against Bangwaketse, whom they accuse of having abused them in the past by treating them like serfs.

The fortunes of the opposition did not improve in any significant fashion between 1974 and 1984. In fact, the opposition suffered setbacks in 1974 when the BDP snatched Ngwaketse West from the BNF and Mochudi Constituency from the BPP. In early 1973 the BDP government promulgated the Accelerated Rural Development Programme (ARDP) through which it sought to demonstrate its commitment to develop the rural areas.

According to Picard[22] the objective of the government was that by the time of elections in 1974, there must be visible developments on the ground. And indeed they were there, across the country in September 1974 in the form of tangible infrastructural projects such as schools, stand-water pipes, tarred or gravel roads, clinics etc. These projects improved the lives of the poor in many parts of the country.

One can only surmise that this is why the BDP improved its performance in the 1974 general elections. This conclusion is reinforced by the fact that the BDP did not lose any rural constituency to the opposition during this period. 'The persistence of traditional patron-client relations, the government's provision of social services across the country, the insignificant tax burden on the rural population and the absence of strong and stable opposition parties to articulate the agenda of social justice' enabled the BDP to consolidate its dominance in the decade of the 1970s.[23] Actually, the BDP snatched Francistown Constituency from the BPP in the 1979 general elections.

Starting from the early 1980s onwards several small opposition parties emerged in Botswana. The Botswana Progressive Union (BPU) was formed by Daniel Kwele in 1982. Before then, he was a member of the BNF. He left the BNF in 1979 to join BDP as a specially elected MP and was appointed assistant minister of local government and lands almost upon arrival. He was apparently very much annoyed by the government when it rebuked him for misuse of a government vehicle in late 1981. He unceremoniously left the BDP and formed his own party the following year. The BPU never really made any impact nor did it raise any pertinent issues except the question of the rights of minorities, specifically the language rights of the Bakalaka ethnic group where its leader came from. It was a one-man show from the beginning until it disappeared. In 1983 another small party called the Botswana Labour Party (BLP) was formed by Lenyeletse Koma, who nevertheless remained a staunch member of the BNF.

What we wish to highlight here is that in Botswana the legal framework is supportive of and friendly to the formation of political parties. All that is required to register a party with the Register of Societies is a party constitution which should be credible enough by legal standards and a small fee and the party will be registered within a week.

Because of the friendly legal environment there have been many small parties in Botswana which have no seats in parliament and in councils. These are: BIP, BPU, The Botswana Freedom Party, which split from the BNF in 1989, the United Democratic Front, United Action Party (UAP) also known as Bosele, the Social Democratic Party, BLP, Marx-Engels Leninist and Stalinist Movement (MELS), the Peoples United Socialist Organisation, National Democratic Front (NDF), also a splinter group from the, Botswana Liberal Party and Lesedi la Batswana (which split from the BDP in 1993). These last two have been deregistered because of their inactivity. Actually, 'there are no restrictions on the formation, numbers or functioning of political parties. The opposition parties are allowed to organise meetings, rallies and campaigns without undue restrictions'.[24] Currently, there are 13 opposition political parties in Botswana. Most of them are splinter groups from the BNF. For a country with a population of approximately two million people, 13 political parties are more than too many.

Although the opposition was almost depleted after the 1979 general elections, it is significant that for the first time in its history the BNF won two council wards in high-density parts of Gaborone, far away from the chiefly influence of Bathoen II. This signalled that the message of the BNF to the working class was beginning to pay dividends. The party intensified its campaign in the 1980s, concentrating mainly on urban areas. Its mobilisation strategy was anchored mainly on poverty and unemployment, low wages for the working class and the shortage of accommodation for the urban poor. Its leader, Dr Kenneth Koma, had moved from Mahalapye to contest the Gaborone South constituency in the 1984 general elections because the party felt that it stood a good chance of winning in Gaborone and thus enabling its leader to become leader of the opposition in parliament.

Initially when the results were announced, the BNF had only won in Gaborone North. Koma had lost to Vice-President Peter Mmusi of the BDP in Gaborone South. A week later an unopened ballot box was found in Tshiamo Primary School, a polling district in Gaborone South constituency. This meant that not all ballot papers had been counted. The BNF petitioned the High Court for a by-election and this was granted. Koma subsequently won the by-election comfortably. It can be surmised that the BNF was able to win the two parliamentary seats of Gaborone North and South in the 1984 general elections because of its sharply focused mobilisation strategy. Koma became leader of the opposition in parliament.

Botswana's fifth general elections were held on 7 October 1989. Six parties contested these elections. Earlier on, there had been efforts to hold 'unity talks' between different opposition parties. But nothing came out of these 'talks'. As in 1984, the main opposition party – the BNF – 'demonstrated an increasing ability to recruit and field candidates'.[25] Demographic factors seemed to be in favour of the opposition. Nearly 25 per cent of Botswana's population was urban in 1989 and the BDP appeared to be losing support in urban areas. The BNF continued to improve its support base by capturing 27 per cent of the popular vote although this translated into only three seats in parliament. Under proportional representation, the BNF would have secured at least nine seats. The BDP remained as strong as ever, especially in the rural areas. It won 31 seats out of the 34 that were contested for. The balance of power continued to be overwhelmingly in favour of the BDP. However, 'in 1989...the BNF won control over several more town councils, including Selibe-Phikwe'.[26]

The 1990s

This was a harbinger of important shifts in Botswana politics in the 1990s. The 1990s witnessed a steady rise in the support base of the political opposition as a whole in Botswana. Paradoxically, the BDP's dominance in the 1990s was being steadily undermined by its successful management of Botswana's economy. From the late 1970s onwards the BDP government embarked upon an ambitious road-building programme that literally 'democratised' travel.[27] It made it easier for the opposition to reach faraway rural constituencies which it could never have accessed in the 1970s. There were also massive improvements in education, health and sanitation services throughout the 1980s and early 1990s. Private newspapers such as the *Guardian* and *Mmegi* sprang up in the early 1980s, giving voters alternative viewpoints and analysis of the political situation in the country. Previously, the only source of information had been the state-controlled media; namely Radio Botswana and *Botswana Daily News*. In fact, *Mmegi* and the *Guardian* were highly critical of the BDP government and continue to be to a significant degree. Thus, the Motswana voter of the 1990s (and onwards) was by far better informed than their counterpart of the 1960s and 70s.

The performance of the opposition in the 1994 general elections must be understood within this context. The first serious threat to BDP dominance occurred in the 1994 general elections. For the first time in Botswana's electoral history, the BNF was able to win 13 parliamentary seats and many more local government seats. It literally pushed out the BDP from the main urban centres, especially the city of Gaborone. Besides, there were several scandals in the early 1990s which tarnished the image of the BDP. One was about the illicit allocation of land in the peri-urban area of Mogoditshane which implicated Vice-President Mmusi and Daniel Kwelagobe, who was the BDP secretary general and a cabinet minister. Both were forced to resign their cabinet positions by the findings of the Presidential Commission that had been appointed to investigate the allegations (i.e. the Kgabo Report; so named after the chairman of that commission, E Kgabo). The differences that emerged within the BDP following the release of the Kgabo Report actually constitute the origins of BDP factions which have since then been festering and threatening to divide the party.

Many political pundits were convinced that the opposition stood a good chance of ousting the BDP from power in the next general elections which were to be held in 1999 or at least giving it good run for its money. But this was not to be. The BDP undertook extensive self-introspection which culminated in the appointment of a consultant to assess the situation and make appropriate recommendations.

One of the recommendations of the consultant – Prof Lawrence Schlemmer – was that the old guard should give way to a new leadership untainted by factionalism. President Masire was at this point unable to deal decisively with factionalism in the party. It was thought the party would be better off if he stepped down. And indeed he announced in early 1998 that he would be retiring from politics on 31 March. Between February and March 1998 Masire went around the country bidding the nation farewell. He had been in power for 18 years. It was pleasantly surprising to see how popular and highly respected he was.

Masire's vice-president, Festus Mogae, took over as president of the republic in April 1998. He immediately nominated Lt General Ian Khama, eldest son of the founding president, paramount chief of Bangwato and former commander of the Botswana Defence Force, as his vice-president and minister of presidential affairs and public administration. Parliament endorsed Mogae's nomination as required by law.

Before Masire's retirement, important political changes had taken place in the country. First, the Constitution had been amended in 1997 to facilitate the automatic succession of a retiring president by a sitting vice-president. In the same amendment a president's tenure in office was limited to two terms of five years each. Although automatic succession has turned out to be very controversial, the term limit has been widely endorsed. Many see it as a vindication of the principle that no one is indispensable in a democracy.

Second, a few crucial electoral reforms were introduced. Before that, a referendum was held in October 1997 as required by the Constitution. Some of the proposed changes touched on entrenched clauses in the Constitution. These electoral reforms:
- established an Independent Electoral Commission (IEC);
- lowered the voting age from 21 years to 18 years of age; and
- allowed Batswana resident outside the country to vote.

The IEC was finally established in July 1998.

The opposition had long demanded these changes and. In fact, the BNF had threatened to boycott the 1994 general elections if these changes were not introduced. Hitherto general elections in Botswana were administered by a political appointee of the sitting president; in fact, by the permanent secretary to the president until after the 1984 elections. A slight modification was introduced in 1988 when an Office of Supervisor of Elections was introduced. The opposition insisted that this was still not enough because 'the supervisor of elections still reported to the Office of the President'.[28] What was required was an independent election management body made up of impartial persons of the utmost integrity commanding the respect and confidence of all political parties. By all accounts, Botswana now has such a professional, impartial IEC, although its independence has been questioned, mainly by the opposition.

The opposition welcomed these electoral reforms. It fancied its chances of winning the 1999 elections because it believed it had strong support amongst the youth and thousands of mine workers in South Africa. There was some basis for this, at least superficially. The BDP's share of the popular vote has been declining over the years: 55 per cent in 1994, 54 per cent in 1999, 51 per cent in 2004 and 52 per cent in 2009. It was indeed conceivable that the opposition could unseat the BDP if they cooperated. But alas! The main opposition party – the BNF – split at its annual conference held in Palapye over the Easter weekend in April 1998. The split resulted in the formation of the Botswana Congress Party (BCP).

Eleven BNF MPs left the party to form the BCP. Instantly, the BCP became the main opposition in parliament, enjoying all the perks that accompany that status. The causes and ramifications of the split have been extensively discussed by, among others, Molomo.[29]

Many people were disappointed by the split. It appears that the cause of the split was the growing influence and strength of social democrats in the party. The traditional socialists in the BNF were not prepared to allow the social democrats to take over the leadership of the party. But there is no doubt that the main cause was poor leadership. Inability to constructively manage conflict between competing factions within a party seems to be an incurable disease afflicting all political parties in Botswana. The opposition therefore contested the 1999 elections very much fragmented. Surprisingly, the BNF won 12 parliamentary seats whilst the newly formed BCP won only one. The remaining 27 seats were won by the BDP. These were the first elections to be administered by the IEC.

The decade of the 1990s was the high point of opposition politics in Botswana. There was such a high degree of optimism amongst intellectuals and civil society activists that Botswana would at long last have a strong opposition. This proved to be unwarranted 'optimism of the intellect' and no more. As we have seen, the opposition fragmented towards the end of that decade.

Into the Twenty-First Century

Destructive factionalism continued unabated within the BNF even after the departure of 'reactionary social democrats' to the BCP. A new Central Committee of the BNF led by Otsweletse Moupo was elected in the Kanye Congress in 2001. Koma, the former leader of the party, who had voluntarily stepped down, disputed the election results, citing some 'irregularities'. His preferred candidate for the presidency of the party had been defeated by Moupo. Eventually, Koma left the BNF to form the NDF in 2003, just a year before general elections.

So as in 1999, the opposition (especially the BNF) went to the 2004 general elections very much disorganised. Prior to the elections there was a series of negotiations among the BCP, BNF, NDF and the Botswana Alliance Movement (BAM) to form a united front that would face the BDP. It has since been established that there were serious disagreements regarding the model of cooperation to be used for the 2004 elections. The BNF strongly favoured an alliance model in which all opposition parties would be affiliated to it and campaign under its umbrella. Others favoured an electoral pact in which each party would retain its identity and field candidates only in those constituencies/wards in which it stood a chance of winning, based on the results of the 1999 elections and other considerations. They feared, and rightly so, that they would eventually be swallowed by the BNF if they embraced the alliance model.

Riding high on its electoral performance in the 1999 general elections and thinking that it could single-handedly take on the BDP, the BNF pulled out of the negotiations towards the elections. Hence the collapse of 'unity talks' was blamed on the 'big brother mentality' of the BNF. The BCP, BAM and BPP entered into an electoral pact for the 2004 elections, but the pact failed to dislodge the BDP because these three parties were just too small.

The 'Each Man for Himself – God for Us All' approach proved suicidal for the opposition. The BNF lost some of the constituencies it had won in 1999, but won, notably, Gaborone North. It managed to retain a significant presence in parliament mostly because constituencies had been increased from 40 to 57 after the population census of 2001. A few additional constituencies such as Gaborone West South, Kanye South and South East North were actually in BNF strongholds. The party also benefited from ethnic discontent against 'Tswana domination' in the Kweneng District where it managed to win two seats by very narrow margins.

The BCP won only one seat in Gaborone Central. However, its share of the popular vote had increased significantly, making it the fastest growing party in the country.[30] The BDP won 44 seats in the 2004 elections, emphasising once again its dominance in Botswana politics.

What is striking, however, is the constant share (and even slight increase) of the popular vote that went to the combined opposition in the 2004 elections. The BDP share of the popular vote declined slightly to 51 per cent whereas that of the opposition increased marginally. The verdict of the 2004 elections in terms of the popular vote is somewhat surprising, given the fact that the BDP government had performed relatively well in terms of infrastructure and human development. Furthermore, 'data generated by Afrobarometer between 1999 and 2008 show that 75 per cent of citizens said they were satisfied/very satisfied with democracy in Botswana in 1999, 58 per cent in 2003, 59 per cent in 2005 and 83 per cent in 2008'.[31] The only conclusion one can reach from these trends is that support for the BDP has reached a plateau. The main reason for this is increasing dissatisfaction by the youth, who are the hardest hit by unemployment and poverty. It has been shown that had the opposition parties cooperated during the 2004 elections they would have won ten additional seats.[32]

The performance of the opposition was very disappointing in the 2009 elections, especially that of the main opposition party, the BNF. The BNF went to the polls deeply divided. Some members had been expelled from the party for 'il discipline'. Others had been barred from contesting the elections until just a month before the poll even though they had won the party's primary elections. An example was A Magama, former MP for Gaborone South. One former BNF MP contested the elections as an independent candidate and won. Simply told, the BNF leadership dismally failed to manage factionalism in the party. The leadership was inept and so incompetent that the party did not even have a manifesto for the 2009 elections. The campaign also started late in many constituencies. On the other hand, the BCP and BAM entered into an electoral pact, and the BCP was the only party in the country that was not bleeding from destructive factionalism.

The BDP also went to the 2009 elections very much divided along factional lines. Two factions have been at each other's throat in the BDP: namely the Barata-Party faction led by D Kwelagobe and the A-Team, allegedly led by the vice-president, Lt Gen Mompati Merafe. Factionalism within the BDP has been ably discussed by Molomo.[33] Suffice it to say that the origins of these factions can be traced to the Kgabo Report on Land Allocation in Mogoditshane and small outlying settlements. Following the findings of the Kgabo Commission, some senior BDP members condemned Mmusi and Kwelagobe for corruption when actually they were not guilty at all. Kwelagobe's name was, in fact, cleared by the High Court later on. Since then, factionalism in the BDP has manifested itself every time the party holds a congress to elect new office bearers for the Central Committee. The 2009 BDP Congress held in Kanye was no different. In fact, this one was worse because Khama, the party leader, took sides by openly de-campaigning Kwelagobe whom he described as 'old and in poor health'.[34] Still the Barata-Party factioned trounced the A-Team, winning all the Central Committee positions that were in competition.

Unlike the political opposition, the BDP fielded candidates in all 57 constituencies and all council seats. The BCP-BAM pact fielded 46, BNF 44, BPP six and MELS fielded four. What is clear is that the political opposition does not have enough manpower to match the BDP. They do not have functioning party structures in all constituencies and regions.

The party that suffered the most in the 2009 elections is the BNF. It lost its three constituencies in Gaborone as well as the Kanye North constituency, Letlhakeng East and West in Kweneng District to the BDP. It also lost the Lobatse constituency to its former MP – N Modubule – who contested the elections as an independent candidate. It narrowly escaped defeat in South East North constituency where its sitting MP and vice-president – O Gaborone – won by a slender margin of 17 votes. The BNF won a paltry six seats in the 2009 elections. The BCP-BAM pact won five seats.

The combined opposition won 12 parliamentary seats in 2009. The remaining 45 seats were taken by the BDP, confirming it as the dominant party in Botswana. The annihilation of the BNF in Gaborone is amply demonstrated by the fact that it won one council seat in the Gaborone South constituency, its traditional stronghold, by a margin of one vote. The results of the 2009 elections underlined the fact that, collectively, the political opposition is by far weaker than the BDP.

However, there have been new developments in opposition politics in Botswana since then. A new party called the Botswana Movement for Democracy (BMD) has been formed. A series of conflicts within the BDP precipitated the formation of the BMD. Just before the 2009 elections one of the founding members of the BMD – S Pilane – wrote a scathing open letter to the president, accusing him of, among others, putting his personal interest above public interest. Pilane went on to say 'his style of governance, verging on authoritarianism as it does, has reduced what before were able and credible ministers into his mouthpieces'.[35] In effect, Pilane was accusing the president of ruling the country with an iron fist.

Matters did not stop at that. G Motswaledi, who had been elected secretary general of the BDP at the Kanye Congress, was recalled by Khama as the BDP candidate for Gaborone Central and suspended from the party until 2014; in effect banished from the party. Motswaledi had openly condemned a law firm which had made its legal opinion public allegedly before such an opinion was availed to the party central committee. Apparently, the law firm in question had been given authority to make its opinion public by Khama. The law firm made it known that Khama had meticulously followed the party constitution when he appointed 77 party members into various party committees. Some members of the central committee, including Motswaledi, were unhappy at this 'unilateral decision'. But the BDP constitution actually gives the party leader such authority.

Motswaledi took the leader of the BDP to the High Court, asking the court to reinstate him as a BDP candidate for Gaborone Central and to lift his suspension from the party. He lost the case because a sitting president in Botswana enjoys absolute immunity. Motswaledi appealed to the Court of Appeal, the highest in the land, and lost, and the BDP found an alternative candidate for Gaborone Central from within its ranks, Mrs K Mogami.

The Motswaledi episode deepened divisions within the BDP so much that even mediation efforts by the two former presidents failed to heal the rift. But what the Motswaledi case has brought to the attention of the public is the sweeping powers of the presidency in the Constitution of Botswana. One opposition MP from the BMD tabled a motion in parliament calling for a comprehensive review of the Constitution. Indeed, by today's democratic standards, the Constitution of Botswana is way behind. Besides giving a sitting president total immunity, Section 47(i) stipulates that executive power is vested in the president who is not obliged to take advice from any person or authority when taking decisions. The president has indicated that he is open to suggestions on this important matter.

After the 2009 elections some BDP MPs, notably B Ntuane and W Molotsi, were charged by the party Central Committee for indiscipline and undermining party unity by conniving with opposition MPs to block the appointment of some of the four elected MPs. Both MPs were known members of the Barata-Party faction. Apparently, the two MPs wanted Pilane to be amongst the four specially elected MPs. Before the case was heard, the two MPs together with MPs for Kgatleng West, Maun West, Kweneng South and Tati East, G Mangole, T Moremi, M Raletobana and G Moyo, and hundreds of members of the Barata-Party faction thronged the Big 5 Lodge where they voiced their unhappiness at the way the BDP was being run. The BDP had issued a stern warning to its members against attending such a meeting. The disgruntled group ignored this warning. This group made a series of demands amongst which was the lifting of Motswaledi's suspension. The group said it would return to the fold only if their demands were met unconditionally. The party described these demands as 'outrageous'. It was at this meeting that the idea of forming a new party was mooted.

After about a month, seven BDP members defected to the BMD with their seats. The initial four MPs were B Ntuane (former executive secretary of the BDP), G Moyo, G Mangole and W Molotsi. They were later joined by MPs for Mogoditshane, Shoshong and South East South, namely P Masimolole, P Makgalemela and O Motlhale respectively. The independent MP for Lobatse, N Modubule, also joined the BMD. Thus, the BMD had more MPs than the BNF. Its deputy chairperson, B Ntuane, became the leader of the opposition in parliament. The BMD has since its formation held rallies in Gaborone, Francistown and Maun, all of which have been described as highly successful. Motswaledi, its interim chairperson, left his job at the University of Botswana to 'grow the party'. Thus, the BDP gave birth to a new party mainly because the leadership failed to manage factionalism in a constructive fashion.

The preceding pages have shown that the opposition in Botswana is too weak to unseat the BDP, let alone pose a threat to its dominance. It is too early to tell what the impact of the newly formed BMD will be. But there is no doubt that the formation of the BMD has seriously dented the BDP. As can be expected, the BDP is insisting that its support base is intact. Interestingly, former president Masire was quoted in one newspaper as having said that 'anyone who cannot see that the party had lost brilliant young men in Motswaledi and Ntuane should buy themselves a pair of spectacles' (The Telegraph).[36] Masire later declined to join a group of party elders invited by Khama to help stem the tide of defections to the new party, saying he prefers to remain 'independent'.

The vexing question of how the opposition can become a credible force in Botswana is discussed later on. For now we focus attention on the nature and character of the opposition in Botswana in the next section.

The Nature and Character of the Political Opposition in Botswana

The political opposition in Botswana is responsible, loyal and patriotic. The opposition has never at any time attempted to destabilise the country or undermine the government. Even when Koma, as leader of the opposition, frequently complained that his party had been 'cheated' in elections, he did not incite his followers to engage in violent acts. Neither did he refuse to accept the results.

Furthermore, the opposition has not attempted to use ethnicity as a mobilisation tool even when it called for the restoration of the rights of minority ethnic groups. Admittedly, some elements of the political opposition are confined to particular regions of the country. For example, the BIP has been confined to the north-west since its inception while the BPP has largely been a party of the north-east since its establishment. These are the regions where BIP and BPP initially cultivated their political support. They claim that they are not sufficiently resourced to expand to other parts of the country.

The political opposition is also patriotic. The national anthem of Botswana was actually composed by K Motsete of the BPP. In his honour, the government decided that his picture should be permanently on the national currency, on the P20 note, to be specific. One of the most impressive and enduring features of politics in Botswana is the peaceful co-existence between the ruling party and the opposition. Both camps have reached an understanding that Botswana is 'ours together', a conviction so strongly expressed in the national anthem. A visitor may be pleasantly surprised to see a prominent member of the opposition having a friendly chat with a BDP cabinet minister. This tradition that binds the opposition together for the furtherance of the national interests of Botswana derives from pre-colonial consensual democracy, and not liberal democracy as some may think.

The political opposition in Botswana is also loyal. A loyal opposition is one that opposes the government of the day, and not the entire political system. It also respects the Constitution and the institutions it has given birth to, that adheres to democratic norms and practices in its campaigns and one that unconditionally accepts the legitimacy of the government once the people have spoken through the ballot box. The opposition in Botswana meets these requirements of loyalty. Its loyalty is also amply demonstrated by the fact that it has not attempted to frame its own development plans for councils under its control. For more than a decade the BNF was in control of the Gaborone City Council. The BNF adhered to the development plan of the city as framed by the government.

The opposition in Botswana has long been habituated to representative democracy. Together with the ruling party, it is characterised by 'bounded uncertainty'. This phrase simply means willingness to accept defeat with the firm conviction that another opportunity to contest elections will come as provided for in the Constitution and that the party in power will not use its incumbency to prevent its opponents from competing for office in future. This is what 'consolidationists' call the 'principle of contingent consent'. The opposition in Botswana has embraced the 'principle of contingent consent'. It exhibits a democratic outlook that says no other method of gaining power is legitimate except regular, free and fair elections in which all political parties and independent candidates are given equal opportunity to compete. It can therefore be said that Botswana's democracy has been consolidated.

Political opposition in Botswana.

The first point to note is that very few opposition parties in Botswana have a national appeal. So far only the BCP and the BNF have significant national appeal. For instance, the BNF has won parliamentary seats in Gaborone, Francistown, Lobatse, Letlhakeng East and West, Kgalagadi North and South and Kgatleng East and many more council seats across the country. It also performed relatively well in Gantsi East and West. The BCP too performed relatively well in the 2009 elections. The rest of the political opposition is made up of small parties with a narrow support base confined to certain parts of the country. A good example is the BPP which is confined to the north-east only. There are just too many small political parties in Botswana. In short, the opposition in Botswana is fragmented. Collectively, the opposition in Botswana is just too weak to unseat the BDP. A compounding factor is the electoral system which skews the translation of the popular vote into parliamentary seats in favour of the BDP. In other words, the first-past-the-post (FPTP) electoral system over-represents the BDP in parliament and under-represents the opposition. But things may change in the future if the BCP, BMD and BNF cooperate

The second point is that the political opposition in Botswana has collectively failed to provide voters with a consistent and clear-cut alternative socio-economic programme to that of the BDP. Part of the problem is, of course, due to neo-liberal global hegemony. The narrowing of ideological differences in the post-Cold War era has made it very difficult, but not impossible for political parties to clearly distinguish themselves from their opponents in their manifestos. Policy space has shrunk considerably so much so that some scholars are complaining about the birth of 'choiceless democracies' and 'the disempowerment of democratisation' in Africa.[37] Even in advanced democracies such as Britain it has become increasingly difficult to discern a clear distinction between the Conservative Party and the Labour Party in terms of their policies and practices when in office. Clearly, the BNF articulates a social democratic programme. Still, it is difficult in practice to find how different it is from that of the BDP.

Many of the programmes that the BNF has historically advocated have gradually been implemented by the ruling party. Examples are the old-age pension scheme and the Integrated Support Program for Arable Agricultural Development (ISPAAD).

Even the burning question of the rights of ethnic minorities has been partially addressed by the BDP government. Similarly, it is very hard to discern what actually differentiates the BCP from the BNF. In fact, one gets a sense that what the opposition is saying is that Botswana should be far better than it currently is given its resources. And that is a valid criticism considering that from 1998 to 2008 Botswana's diamond exports fetched historically unprecedented high prices. Of course, the BDP government can argue that the money was spent on the campaign to combat HIV/Aids and on anti-retrovirals for distribution to those already infected.

Besides the above-mentioned internal factors, there are other external factors which account for the weakness of the political opposition in Botswana. These are the lack of funding of political parties by the state and unequal access to state media. The private media – both print and electronic – adequately covers the opposition. A code of conduct for equitable coverage of all political parties was also developed by the IEC and agreed to by broadcasting media in the run-up to the 2009 elections and it worked very well. The most important factor here is the lack of funding of political parties. Scholars mentioned above have carefully considered the issue of state funding of political parties. Opposition parties feel very strongly about it. Their argument is that they cannot campaign effectively across the length and breadth of the country due to lack of funds. This is a legitimate point.

There is now a general consensus amongst scholars and civil society activists that the state should fund political parties as is the case in several Southern African Development Community countries. The thrust of the argument is that democracy does not come cheap and this study endorses this position. The state must invest in democracy. The BDP government has persistently rejected this proposal for no apparent reason. It has now been revealed that the BDP has been generously funded by De Beers in each general election since 1974. So there is no incentive for the BDP in this proposal. Expediency rather than principle seems to be holding sway.

Party funding, even if agreed to by the government, will not be a panacea for the opposition. For instance, in the run-up to the 2009 elections, Kgalagadi Breweries donated a sizeable amount of money to all political parties contesting the elections. Still, the opposition performed poorly, In fact, party funding is likely to benefit the BDP more than any other political party in the country if the criterion used for sharing the money is each party's share of the popular vote. To sum up, the political opposition in Botswana is fragmented, poorly organised and chronically weak.

This does not necessarily mean it is useless. In fact, the opposition has contributed significantly to democratic politics in Botswana. It has raised political awareness amongst Batswana and taught them about their fundamental freedoms.

The opposition has contributed to the legitimacy of multiparty democracy in Botswana by participating in all general elections since the pre-independence general elections of March 1965. As expected of it, it has acted as a watchdog on the government. Some opposition MPs have raised pertinent criticisms of government policies and programmes, thereby contributing to lively debates in parliament.[38] In one case, an opposition MP tabled a motion that led to the appointment of a commission of inquiry into allegations of improper land allocation in some parts of Gaborone. Not only that: the opposition was instrumental in the introduction of the electoral reforms referred to above. It was the political opposition which demanded these reforms.

It was also the opposition that first raised the issue of the rights of minority ethnic groups in the mid-1980s. Specifically, it was M Dabuta, BNF MP for Gaborone North, who correctly questioned Section 77 and 78 of the Constitution of Botswana which designated the eight Tswana ethnic groups as principal tribes, implying that the rest were minor. The Constitution has since been amended accordingly and the House of Chiefs has been expanded to 35 members in order to accommodate other tribes.

Finally, the opposition has been constructive in its criticisms of the ruling party. Otherwise the latter would not have implemented some of the proposals made by the opposition. In summary, the opposition in Botswana is highly fragmented, bedeviled by factionalism, highly suspicious of one another and very weak. Nonetheless, the opposition has played a positive role in Botswana politics.

Future Possibilities: Pathways to a Strong Opposition in Botswana

Prospects for the political opposition in Botswana are not very encouraging. Data gleaned from Afrobarometer surveys show that the majority of voters are satisfied or very satisfied with the performance of the BDP government. This is why the sub-title of this section is 'pathways to a strong opposition' and not 'pathways to an alternative government'. Individually, opposition parties are just too weak to unseat the BDP. They were also collectively weaker than the BDP in 2009; that is to say, even if opposition unity had materialised in the 2009 elections the BDP would still have had enough seats in parliament to form a government. Judging by the results of the 2009 elections it would appear that voters want a strong opposition that can compel the BDP to be accountable and responsive to citizens' aspirations and needs. However, the political landscape in Botswana has changed considerably with the formation of the BMD.

One variable that has not received sufficient attention in discussions around the political opposition in sub-Saharan Africa is how constraining the social formations are on the chances of opposition parties to win state power in free and fair elections. It is only in a few countries such as Kenya and Zambia where the opposition has managed to unseat ruling parties. In the case of Zambia, the ruling party had been thoroughly discredited by the early 1990s due to, among others, falling standards of living and the authoritarianism of the Kaunda regime. By contrast, the BDP is not a discredited party. Therefore to unseat it will be a tall order. Returning to the theme of peripheral capitalist social formations, the private sector in Botswana is weak because of underdevelopment and dependence. That is why the BDP gets the bulk of its funding from a South African company, De Beers.

It is important to bear in mind that generalised commodity production or capitalist accumulation, for short, has not taken root in many African countries outside South Africa and to some extent in Zimbabwe, before the ZANU-PF government ruined the economy. It's only in South Africa where considerable capitalist accumulation has occurred. Political parties in South Africa can raise money for their election campaigns from rich private sector foundations and big companies such as the Anglo American Corporation, De Beers and Sanlam, to mention but a few. They can also appeal to organised labour for financial support. Botswana's opposition parties do not have that privilege. They operate in a predominantly rural terrain where the vast majority of people are not in formal sector employment. Poor peasants and unemployed urban residents cannot be expected to contribute to the coffers of political parties. They simply do not have the money. The simple truth is that liberal democracy cannot advance further without significant capitalist development, especially the transformation of pre-capitalist agrarian relations into fully fledged capitalist relations.

Opposition parties are severely disadvantaged in weak peripheral capitalist social formations such as Botswana. Their candidates are severely disadvantaged because they have little to offer companies in the private sector. Private companies invariably support the ruling party in dominant party systems because that is where they get their tenders. Such parties must fund themselves by raising money from their supporters or members. But supporters of opposition parties are usually the poor and the unemployed. Of course, opposition parties which have seats in parliament and in councils can require their MPs and/or councillors to contribute a specified sum to the party every month from their salaries, and they have done so. But such opposition MPs and/or councillors are usually very few.

This means that individuals have to dig deep into their pockets to finance their election campaigns. The only way such individuals can recoup their expenses is by winning a seat. If not, they are ruined financially. It is very difficult to convince such individuals to step down from being party candidates in the interest of opposition cooperation or to make way for female candidates. They too want to accumulate and join the ranks of the petit bourgeoisie or even the bourgeoisie proper. That is the principal reason why they will refuse to step down.

It looks as if opposition politics (and politics in general) in peripheral capitalist societies is the 'politics of the belly' – a fondly held misconception by those who erroneously think the defining feature of African politics is neopatrimonialism. It is not. Riding comfortably on a strong rural support base, and increasingly so in urban areas, successive BDP governments could have easily devised schemes and programmes that could enable the rich and powerful – within and outside the party – to enrich themselves at the expense of the nation, according to the logic of neopatrimonialism. But BDP governments did not do that.

Also accumulation strategies by politicians – whether in the opposition or ruling party – need not be kleptocratic or predatory as the notion of neopatrimonialism suggests. The accumulation strategy preferred by politicians in Botswana is one of 'straddling' – one foot in formal political office earning a salary as an MP or councillor and another in farming, business or both.

The first foot is very critical for politicians. Being inside the system and getting to know what government projects are in the pipeline is a great asset to politicians in peripheral capitalist societies, if not all capitalist societies. Political office easily opens avenues of accumulation which were previously unavailable.

Politicians routinely form companies wholly owned by their wives and children to tender for government projects. Such politicians are frequently referred to as 'tenderpreneurs'. They fiercely resist calls for declarations of assets and liabilities by all elected officials. Furthermore, politicians find it easier to obtain credit from commercial banks because a sitting MP or councillor can use their gratuity as security. Opposition cooperation, quotas for female candidates and such like cannot be allowed to take away such lucrative opportunities for accumulation.

Opposition politics (and politics in general) in peripheral capitalist societies cannot be fully understood outside the context of the imperatives of capitalist accumulation. It must be borne in mind that politicians are not altruists or philanthropists. They join partisan politics to serve the public and also to improve their material circumstances. In the majority of cases, individuals who engage in party politics are not already made; they are not rich unlike their counterparts in advanced democracies. They badly need a monthly salary and to make big money by tendering for government projects.

Opposition politicians in Botswana (and their sympathisers) have been left out in the cold in the allocation of tenders, appointments to boards of parastatals and such like. Not surprisingly, they have a strong appetite for accumulation. This is the context within which we must understand opposition politics in Botswana, especially the repeated failures of 'opposition unity'.

As indicated earlier, no opposition party on its own in Botswana can unseat the BDP. It is only by cooperating that the opposition stands a chance of winning enough seats to threaten the BDP, not to oust it from power. What then are the chances of opposition collaboration given what has been said above? From a pragmatic point of view, the first pathway to a strong opposition in Botswana is opposition collaboration. Almost all opposition parties recognise this. What has made opposition cooperation difficult in the past is the conflicting models of cooperation that opposition parties bring to the negotiation table. Some parties such as the BNF favour a model where other parties affiliate to it and use its symbols in election campaigns. Other parties have resisted this model and rightly so because they will eventually lose their identities if they agree.

It appears that the most fruitful model of cooperation between opposition parties is an electoral pact. In this model, each party retains its identity in election campaigns but refrains from attacking fellow opposition parties. All the firepower is reserved for the BDP.

It is important for collaborating parties to agree at the earliest opportunity, preferably before the campaign starts, on how they are going to share constituencies and council seats. A fundamental precondition is that collaborating parties must avoid splitting the vote at all costs. The best way is for such parties to revisit their performance in the previous general elections in constituencies and council seats where they fielded candidates. Seats won by each opposition party in previous elections should as a matter of course be reserved for those parties. For example, all the seats that the BCP won in the 2009 elections should be reserved for it. And likewise for the BNF.

The next criterion could be constituencies and council seats where a given opposition party was number two. These should then be allocated accordingly. The party that came third in the past elections should support the one that was number two, urging its supporters to vote for it. We are aware that this is a very contentious criterion because all parties want to grow. Negotiations are about compromise and the central issue here is to build a strong coalition. But one may ask: what about a party such as BMD? It was only formed after the 2009 elections. Its support base is not known. The best way out is to give it some of the newly created constituencies and council seats.

In Botswana, a population census is conducted every ten years by law. Such a census is due in 2011. After the census, a delimitation commission is appointed to determine how many more constituencies can be created. The report of the commission is final; it is not even debated in parliament. The next step is that the secretary of the IEC demarcates polling districts or council seats with the input of key stakeholders - the political parties themselves through party liaison committees in the various constituencies. There is solid evidence that the opposition could increase its seats in parliament and councils if it adopts this model.[39] The only problem is that by law the opposition will not be in a position to form a coalition government, even if it has more seats than the BDP. But that is not the primary objective. The principal objective is to have a strong opposition in parliament and also in carefully targeted councils.

In the past the opposition failed to demonstrate the capacity to govern in the councils where it was in control, especially the Gaborone City Council. Admittedly, there were some constraints. For instance, the BNF could not change or amend the city's development plan. But there was plenty of room for innovation. What is being proposed here is that the opposition must aim to take control of targeted councils and run them well in order to demonstrate its capacity to govern to all and sundry. Many citizens of Botswana do not think the opposition has the capacity to govern. It is important that the opposition corrects this perception if it is to govern Botswana one day. The opposition must aim at building a positive track record which it can then showcase in the next elections. Only then will the electorate take the political opposition as serious and a credible alternative government in waiting.

All this presupposes that the opposition is able to come up with a consistent, credible and feasible socio-economic programme alternative to that of the BDP; something the opposition has failed to do in the past. This is a formidable task given 'the new international context of development' dominated by pernicious neo-liberal ideas and narrowing ideological differences between political parties, whether in the global south or in advanced democracies. It is neither insurmountable nor impossible, because no condition is permanent. There are always alternatives even to neo-liberal globalisation. Collaborating opposition parties should spell out in clear and unequivocal terms how their social democratic alternative differs from the BDP's pragmatic, mid-way or centre democratic developmental programme and how their programme would combat poverty, generate jobs, revitalise the education system for 21st century labour markets and enhance 'good governance' in ways in which the BDP has not been able to or is incapable of. In other words, they must have a clear ideological position.

The political opposition should stop making unrealistic promises to the electorate; pies in the sky that attract devastating attacks from the BDP. A new type of voter is slowly emerging in Botswana and in significant numbers, especially in urban areas. This is a kind of voter who is not permanently tied to any political party by virtue of family connections, ethnic affiliation, loyalty to chieftainship or ideological correctness. This kind of voter wants to know how they stand to benefit from any of the party manifestos on the table and more importantly whether their preferred candidate would articulate thei concerns and interests in parliament. These emerging voters are not interested in polemics, rhetoric and clichés. They want convincing political programmes that can address their aspirations and anxieties.

To a considerable extent, the current BDP government has given the opposition sufficient space to capitalise on because it is intolerant of dissenting views, even within its own ranks. Otherwise how does one explain the emergence of the breakaway party from the BDP, known as the BMD? The fact that they could coin the new party's name as the 'movement for democracy' implies that democracy under the current BDP government is under threat; an issue that Pilane raised in his open letter to Khama. However, making significant inroads into BDP strongholds in the Central and Kweneng districts, Gantsi East, Barolong Farms and Moshupa will be very hard. It is almost impossible for the opposition to win a single seat in Central and Kweneng districts and in the aforementioned constituencies which collectively account for nearly half of the constituencies in the country.

Finally, reform of the electoral system is another pathway to a strong opposition in Botswana. As we have seen, 'the electoral system over-represents the governing BDP, under-represents the fragmented opposition and fails to provide the space needed for new parties'.[40] Lest we be misunderstood: electoral reform is not just in the interests of the opposition. It will expand and deepen Botswana's democracy and make it more inclusive.

To start with, it should be acknowledged that the current electoral system has served Botswana quite well. It has many advantages. Only a few will be highlighted here.

Firstly, it promotes stability in government because it is rare under this electoral system to have coalition governments. Coalition governments frequently collapse when one of the parties in the coalition withdraws, causing government instability. Israel and Italy (before electoral reform) are good examples of government instability. Secondly, it promotes the accountability of elected leaders to the electorate because almost all MPs (save for ex officio members and Specially Elected MPs) would be representing a particular constituency. The same applies to councillors. Each one of them, except for nominated councillors, represents a particular ward.

But it has one main fundamental deficiency. It has a tendency to exclude the voices of smaller or losing political parties in representative institutions. This is because the allocation of seats in parliament and councils disregards the share of the popular vote obtained by each contesting party in general elections. It therefore follows that eligible voters who voted for losing parties are effectively not represented in parliament. Yet an inclusive representative democracy is what Botswana should be striving for. Democracy is nurtured and expanded by 'matching popular votes to seats to allow for representation of diverse interests in society' in parliament.[41]

A hybrid of FTPT and proportional representation (PR) appears to be the most attractive option for Botswana. A blending of the two similar to Lesotho's electoral system might prove helpful. It has facilitated compromise and conciliation in that country because almost every political party has a stake in the system. A study of countries that use the mixed member system has concluded that 'mixed member systems have largely been successful'.[42] As a start, Botswana might consider using PR in the allocation of seats for nominated councillors. The present system has the trappings of political patronage and to be frank, it is undemocratic. The same applies to specially elected MPs, except that they are few and that most of them have added value to Botswana's democracy. Actually, their number could be increased to ten seats that could then be shared in proportion to the share of the popular vote that each party received in general elections. These are but a few pathways to a strong opposition in Botswana. Other ways in which the opposition can improve its performance have been ably discussed by Matlosa.[43]

It would be remiss of me to conclude this paper without a brief consideration of political developments in Botswana since the ascendancy of Lt Gen Ian Khama to the presidency on 1 April 2008. Concerns have been raised about an impending military dictatorship in Botswana 'masquerading as a democracy'. Some observers believe that 'democracy is under siege' in Botswana. Others are raising alarm bells about 'a culture of silence' that is slowly descending on the nation.[44] In these accounts citizens no longer feel free to discuss politics because they are allegedly being spied on by agents of the newly established Directorate of Intelligence and Security (DIS). The DIS reports directly to the state president. It has replaced two former intelligence services known as Special Branch and Criminal Investigation Department which also reported directly to the state president throughout their existence. In particular, there has been a public outcry against a spate of extra-judicial killings since April 2008.

These concerns are unwarranted as Botswana has never been known for extra-judicial killings of suspected criminals or such suspects dying in police custody.

There has also been a tightening of control of the state media by the government in recent years or attempts to do so via, for example, the notorious Media Practitioners Act.

Just after the 2009 elections, the Department of Broadcasting Services was transferred to the Office of the President. Over the years successive BDP governments have exercised considerable control over state media; i.e. the Daily News, Radio Botswana and Btv. It appears that the government now wants to exercise total control over state media. This move is a potential threat to democracy. Instead of seeking total control over state media, the government should have taken steps to make that department an independent body similar to the BBC or SABC in order to enrich Botswana's democracy. A free flow of ideas is indispensable in a democracy. This cannot be guaranteed when part of the media is under the armpit of the government.

An investigative, critical and independent press is the foundation for any democracy worthy of the name. It is only a free press that can be the watchdog of the public – publishing and broadcasting without fear or favour.

It is a setback for democracy that the state media is under the total control of the government. Of course, one is not saying that the government should not use the state media. Far from it. It has every right to do so because it is a legitimate government. It must have unimpeded access to state media in order to publicise its policies, programmes and activities. But the government has no right whatsoever to interfere with the autonomy of the media – whether public or private. This latest move has undermined the credibility (and possibly the integrity) of the public media.

The rest of the concerns are unwarranted. Botswana held 'free and fair' elections in 2009 under the watchful eyes of domestic and international observers. All of whom declared the elections free and fair.

Not a single opposition candidate was intimidated, harassed or prevented from campaigning. Supporters of the opposition were free to rally behind their candidates openly. In short, citizens continue to enjoy their civil and political liberties just as before. They are free to join any political party of their choice, as evidenced by those who freely left the BDP to join the BMD. The same citizens who are said to be afraid of DIS have been freely discussing their party programmes in annual congresses. Citizens continue to express their views in newspapers, on television and in radio stations freely and sometimes their criticisms of Khama are just personal and out of order. Furthermore, the Khama administration has not tampered with the autonomy of the judiciary. It is hard to escape the conclusion that the fundamentals of Botswana's democracy remain intact.

Conclusion

This chapter has explored the evolution of the political opposition in Botswana since 1965. It used Botswana's political economy as a strategic entry point to explain why the BDP is such a dominant force in Botswana politics. It showed that the dominance of the BDP is derived from the grand coalition of social forces which it forged in the early 1960s and which has remained basically intact since then, rendering the political opposition almost an occasional irritation.

Like many studies before it,[45] it demonstrated that the opposition in Botswana is fragmented, poorly organised and weak. It concluded that the opposition is collectively weaker than the BDP. It also argued that nevertheless the opposition has made significant contributions to Botswana's representative democracy.

It went further than previous studies to contextualise the failure of the politcal opposition to collaborate within the context of capitalist accumulation in the periphery and mounted a brief critique of the notion of neopatrimonialism. It suggested that the imperatives of accumulation have made it very difficult for the political opposition to cooperate during general elections in the past. But it maintained that it is possible for the opposition to cooperate.

It then considered various routes to a strong opposition in Botswana, including an electoral pact amongst the various opposition parties, ideological coherence of the cooperating opposition parties and reform of the electoral system. It noted that the current system of specially elected MPs and nominated councillors is undemocratic and argued that it should be abolished. Finally, it recommended the adoption of a mixed member proportional system similar to Lesotho's current electoral system, not just because it would increase opposition seats in parliament and councils but mainly because that is what is fair and secondly because it would make Botswana's democracy more inclusive and less adversarial.

ENDNOTES

1   Ball, A and Peters BG 2000. *Modern Politics and Government, sixth edition.* London: Macmillan, p96.
2   Somolekae G 2005. *Political Parties in Botswana.* Johannesburg: EISA, p1.

3   Sadie Y 2006. 'Political Parties, Interest Groups and Social Movements' in Venter A and Landsberg C (eds). *Government and Politics in the New South Africa.* Pretoria: Van Schaik Publishers.
4   Beetham D 1994. 'Conditions for Democratic Consolidation'. *Review of African Political Economy*, No 60, p160.
5   Ibid.
6   Munger E 1965. Botswana: *Pan-African Outpost or Bantu Homeland.* Oxford: Oxford University Press.
7   Maipose G 2008. 'Policy and Institutional Dynamics of Sustained Development in Botswana'.Working Paper No 35, Commission on Growth and Development, World Bank. Washington DC: World Bank, p3.
8   Masire QKJ 2006. *Very Brave or Very Foolish: Memoirs of an African Democrat* (edited by Stephen R Lewis). Basingstoke: Palgrave Macmillan.
9   Picard L 1985. 'From Bechuanaland to Botswana: An Overview' in Picard L (ed). *The Evolution of Modern Botswana.* London: Rex Collins.

    Harvey C and Lewis S 1990. *Policy Choice and Development Performance in Botswana.* Houndsmills: Macmillan.

    Samatar AI 1999. An African Miracle: *State and Class Leadership and Colonial Legacy in Botswana's Development.* Portsmouth, NH: Heinemann

    Samatar AI 2002. 'Botswana: Comprehending the Exceptional' and in Samatar AI (eds). *The African State: Reconsiderations.* Portsmouth, NH: Heinemann.

    Acemoglu D, Johnson S and Robinson JA 2003. 'An African Success Story: Botswana' in Rodrik D (ed), in *In Search of Prosperity: Analytical Narratives on Economic Growth.* Princeton, NJ: Princeton University Press.

    Leith C 2005. *Why Botswana Prospered.* Montreal and Kingston: Queen's University Press.

    Maipose G 2008. Op.cit.
10 Bauer G and Taylor SD 2005. *Politics in Southern Africa: State and Society in Transition.* Boulder: Lynne Rienner, p102.
11 UNECA 2008. *The Progress of Good Governance in Botswana.* Gaborone: BIDPA, p191.
12 UNDP 1997. 'Botswana Human Development Report: Challenges for Sustainable Human Development'. Gaborone: TA Publications, p2.

13 Nengwekhulu H 1979. 'Some Findings on the Origins of Political Parties in Botswana'. Pula: *Botswana Journal of African Studies* 1(2).

   Parson J 1984. *Botswana: Liberal Democracy and the Labor Reserve in Southern Africa.* Boulder: Westview.

   Ramsay J and Parsons N 1998. 'The Emergence of Political Parties in Botswana' in Edge W and Lekorwe M (eds). *Botswana: Politics and Society.* Pretoria: Van Schaik Publishers.

   Lekorwe MH 2005. 'The Organization of Political Parties', in Maundeni Z (ed). *40 Years of Democracy in Botswana.* Gaborone: Mmegi Publishing House.

   Somolekae G 2005. *Political Parties in Botswana.* Johannesburg: EISA.

14 Selolwane O 2007. 'Statecraft in Botswana: Renegotiating Development, Legitimacy and Authority' in Agbese PO and Kieh GK (eds). *Reconstituting the State in Africa.* London: Palgrave Macmillan.

15 Du Toit P 1995. *State Building and Democracy in Southern Africa: Botswana, Zimbabwe and South Africa.* Washington, D.C: US Institute of Peace, p36.

16 Picard L 1985. 'From Bechuanaland to Botswana: An Overview' in Picard L (ed). *The Evolution of Modern Botswana.* London: Rex Collins, p19.

17 Tsie B 1996. 'The Political Context of Botswana's Development Performance'. *Journal of Southern African Studies* 22(4), pp604-605.

18 Fatton R 1990. *'Liberal Democracy in Africa'.* Political Science Quarterly 103(3), p460.

19 Lekorwe MH 2005. 'The Organization of Political Parties', in Maundeni Z (ed). *40 Years of Democracy in Botswana.* Gaborone: Mmegi Publishing House, p129.

20 Ibid.

21 Neocosmos M 2002. 'The Politics of National Elections in Botswana, Lesotho and Swaziland' in Cowen M and Laakso L (eds). *Multiparty Elections in Africa.* London: James Curry, p52.

22 Picard L 1987. *The Politics of Development in Botswana: A Model for Success?* Boulder: Lynne Rienner.

23 Samatar AI 2002. 'Botswana: Comprehending the Exceptional' in Samatar AI and Samatar AI (eds). *The African State: Reconsiderations.* Portsmouth, NH: Heinemann.

24 Osei-Hwedie B 2001. 'The Political Opposition in Botswana: The Politics of Factionalism and Fragmentation'. *Transformation* No 45, p59.

25 Parson J 1993. 'Liberal Democracy, Liberal State and the 1989 General Elections in Botswana' in Stedman S (ed). Botswana: *The Political Economy of Democratic*

Development. Boulder: Lynne Rienner, p79.

26 Bauer G and Taylor SD 2005. *Politics in Southern Africa: State and Society in Transition.* Boulder: Lynne Rienner, p97.

27 Ibid.

28 Lodge T, Kadima D. and Pottie D 2005. *A Compendium of Elections in Southern Africa.* Johannesburg: EISA, pp49-50.

29 Molomo M. 2000a. 'In Search of an Alternative Electoral System for Botswana'. *Pula: Botswana Journal of African Studies* 14(1).

30 BCP Manifesto.2009. A Nation at the Cross Roads: Which Way Now; Democracy and Prosperity or Dictatorship and Economic Collapse. Gaborone.

31 Sebudubudu D and Osei-Hwedie B 2010. 'In Permanent Opposition: Botswana's Other Parties'. *South African Journal of International Affairs* 17(1), p88.

32 Somolekae G 2005. *Political Parties in Botswana.* Johannesburg: EISA.

33 Molomo M 2000b. 'Understanding Government and Opposition Parties in Botswana'. *Commonwealth and Comparative Politics* 38(1).

34 Lotshwao K 2010. 'The Weakness of the Opposition in Botswana: A Justification for More Internal Democracy in the Dominant Botswana Democratic Party (BDP)'. Unpublished. Memeo.

35 Pilane S 2009. 'Would Lt Gen Ian Khama Please Stand Down and Make Way for Mr Ian Khama' in Sunday Standard, 1 June 2009.

36 The Telegraph, 14 May 2010.

37 Ake C 1995. "The Democratization of Disempowerment in Africa", in Hippler, J (ed). *The Democratization of Disempowerment.* London: Pluto Press.

Mkandawire T 1998.'Crisis Management and the Making of Choiceless Democracies in Africa', in Joseph R. *State, Conflict and Democracy in Africa.* Boulder: Lynne Rienner.

38 Sebudubudu D and Osei-Hwedie B 2010. 'In Permanent Opposition: Botswana's Other Parties'. *South African Journal of International Affairs* 17(1).

39 Somolekae G 2005. *Political Parties in Botswana.* Johannesburg: EISA.

40 Elklit J and Reynolds L 2002.'The Impact of Election Administration on the Legitimacy of Emerging Democracies.' *Commonwealth and Comparative Politics* 40(2).

41 Sebudubudu D and Osei-Hwedie B 2010. 'In Permanent Opposition: Botswana's Other Parties'. *South African Journal of International Affairs* 17(1), p90.

42 Shugart SM and Wattenberg MP 2001. *Mixed Member Electoral Systems.* Oxford: Oxford University Press, p591.

43 Matlosa K 2005. *Political Parties and Democratization in SADC: The Weakest Link.* Johannesburg: EISA.

44 Pilane S 2009. 'Would Lt Gen Ian Khama Please Stand Down and Make Way for Mr Ian Khama' in Sunday Standard, 1 June 2009.

45 Molomo M 2000b.'Understanding Government and Opposition Parties in Botswana'. Commonwealth and Comparative Politics 38(1).
Lotshwao K 2010. 'The Weakness of the Opposition in Botswana: A Justification for More Internal Democracy in the Dominant Botswana Democratic Party (BDP)'. Unpublished. Memeo.

Sebudubudu D and Osei-Hwedie B 2010. 'In Permanent Opposition: Botswana's Other Parties'. South African Journal of International Affairs 17(1).

CHAPTER THREE
LESOTHO: POLITICAL PARTIES IN A FRAYING POLITY
FRANCIS K MAKOA

Introduction

A multiparty democracy implies the presence of and freedom for all political parties to recruit members and compete for governmental power through fairly contested elections. In this type of regime, political dissent is tolerated not only as legitimate but also as a right. In Lesotho opposition political parties operate in this kind of political climate, and the older ones share the same history; that is, they were originally formed to fight colonialism possibly in order to form the next government. Political parties in Lesotho were formed also as a response to the socio-economic, political and institutional changes – also dubbed 'modernisation' occurring in that country's society beginning in the early 1900s.

The initial modernising force was colonialism, underpinned by a capitalist economy protected by a modern state modelled on that of Britain and which served as the latter's agency for implementing and overseeing its imperialist projects. The political and administrative reforms instituted in the territory by Britain beginning in the early 1900s, though not designed for this purpose, saw the emergence of political parties which later competed in the elections, starting with the 1960 district council elections in colonial Lesotho.

Opposition in multiparty parliamentary democracies means more than losers of elections. It means differing and opposed roles, and opportunities in terms of appointment of the executive or cabinet – hence potential benefits. This political tradition that began during colonial Lesotho had become the norm in the tiny kingdom at independence, although it was interrupted by the cessation between 1970 and 1993 of the holding of regular periodic democratic elections, only to be reinstated in 1993.

Our analysis of political opposition in Lesotho in no way examines the trajectory of political development in that country, although it encapsulates some background to the evolution of modern political parties in Lesotho in order to clear the ground for arguments and assertions made by the author. It sees Lesotho's system of government as a liberal representative democratic regime, albeit with deficits and/or limitations, with multiple parties which freely compete for political power and space. Viewed through the liberal democratic perspective, the system of government in Lesotho thus becomes an arena in which multiple parties actively seek to influence the public policy-making process, election outcomes and each other's political behaviour.

According to this perspective, the key defining features of multiparty democracy are pluralism, freedom of association and of speech, regular political party-based competitive elections and the effective representation of citizens in national decision-making bodies, secured through and underpinned by the right-to-choose principle. It regards all political parties, whether or not currently holding state power, as integral and functional to democracy, even where they sharply differ in their stances and views. It also assumes some rough power parity, bargaining and mutual recognition and tolerance among such political parties and between them and the ruling party.

However, Lesotho's experience with its return to democratic rule in 1993 suggests that the country ought to do more than enfranchise its people, guarantee freedom of association, and ensure the holding of periodic competitive elections. Contemporary Lesotho's multiparty political system is devoid of a strong opposition featuring either a single opposition political party or a coalition of several non-governing political parties roughly matching the ruling party in strength and together constituting an effective bargaining force and a watchdog restraining, when necessary, government in its actions while participating meaningfully in the policy-making process. In sum, Lesotho's democratic rule has not empowered its people or political organisations. Hence a 'bargaining political system' for Lesotho that would prevent unfettered unilateralism by any of the participating units is yet to be achieved.

This chapter looks at national opposition political parties in Lesotho against the backdrop of the widely held view that multipartyism is a *sine qua non* of political representation and participation in the policy-making process.

2. Emergence of modern political parties in Lesotho

Modern political parties, or organisations that fit in with the contemporary concept of a political party, emerged in Lesotho in the 1950s. But these were born into a political arena already carved out nearly four decades earlier by two political movements, namely the Basutoland Progressive Association (BPA) and Lekhotla la Bafo (LLB) or the Commoners' League, both of which were mainly civil rights-cum-protest organisations merely demanding improvements in certain aspects of the administration of the country, such as facilitating the partaking of the chiefs and Basotho elite in national decision-making processes, and non-discrimination in public service employment.

The first of the modern political parties, namely those seeking self-rule for Lesotho and governmental power, to emerge was the Basutoland African Congress (BAC) formed in 1952 and assuming the name, Basutoland Congress Party (BCP), in 1960. The BCP initially recruited mainly former members of the then moribund Basutoland Progressive Association (BPA) and the increasingly moribund Lekhotla la Bafo. Later, it extended its influence over all the sectors of the population, while remaining at least rhetorically a commoners' party. As one writer observed, by recruiting members from among varied sectors of the population, the BCP 'sought to transcend the urban elite and mobilise broad support, temporarily uniting ... the chiefs, and commoners, the Protestants and the Catholics, as well as workers and peasants'.[1] Its stated objectives were to oppose the incorporation of Basutoland into the then Union of South Africa, to fight racial discrimination against Basotho by the British colonial administration, and to achieve self-government for Lesotho,[2] while stressing that power must reside with the people, not chiefs or traditional authority structures and non-elective institutions like the church. Its splinter factions, including the ruling Lesotho Congress for Democracy (LCD) formed in June 1997, have maintained this stance. The LCD rule has attempted to add substance to this by transferring, through the Lesotho Local Government Act of 1997, some of the powers of the chiefs to the people. The LCD has been ruling Lesotho since assuming governmental power in 1998 after winning the general elections held in that year.

Because of their stance regarding traditional authorities, the 'congress parties'– so collectively described here for want of a better descriptive label – can be said to be occupying the centre left of the country's political continuum. But the BCP and its splinter congresses' erstwhile open attacks against the chiefs and the churches have abated or, in some cases, dissipated. On the extreme left of the political spectrum in contemporary Lesotho is the Popular Front for Democracy (PFD), which envisions an egalitarian socio-economic system for Lesotho in which the workers and peasants play a leading role and are the main beneficiaries, and unity or a special economic and political relationship between Lesotho and South Africa.

The other two oldest political parties and the BCP's traditional rivals, the Basotho National Party (BNP) and the Marema-Tlou Freedom Party (MFP), are rightwing organisations, insisting that chieftainship must be retained as part of the Basotho nation-state and repositories of traditional values. The MFP – a result of a merger between the erstwhile Marema-Tlou Party (MTP) and Lesotho Freedom Party (LFP) – and the BNP were formed in 1957 and 1959, respectively, in response to the BCP's leftwards-leaning tendencies manifested in its links with radical international political movements such as the communist parties in China and Eastern Europe. Yet the left/right posture has not seemed a factor behind the parties' relative strengths, as mirrored by their performance in national elections.

Both the BCP and the LCD have suffered further debilitating splits during the period between 2002 and 2010. The BCP's breakaway faction registered under the BCP's original name of Basutoland African Congress, while the LCD's splinter registered as the Lesotho People's Congress (LPC).

The LCD underwent another serious split in September 2006 when Thomas Motsoahae Thabane – who had held several ministerial positions in the LCD government – formed, along with scores of his fellow LCD parliamentarians, the All

Basotho Convention (ABC) that emerged after the 2007 elections as the biggest of the opposition parties in the country, with over 20 representatives in the National Assembly. The BCP and LCD splits thus did not benefit the BNP, which until the end of 2006 was the second biggest opposition party in the country. Nor did these splits benefit the rest of the opposition political parties as a whole in terms of boosting their numerical strength and bargaining power. If anything, the BNP support base, in particular, continued to attenuate and/or atrophy, as it lost members due to the autocratic style of leadership that allowed them no room to debate and to criticise the leadership. In fact, like the BCP, the BNP has experienced splits that saw the formation by its disaffected members of the National Progressive Party (NPP) and the Basotho Democratic National Party (BDNP) in 1996 and 2005, respectively.

The BNP's dwindling support base is borne out by the fact that it won fewer than 30 000 votes in the 2007 general elections, a far cry from its performance in the previous elections in which it had polled more than four times this figure and obtained 21 proportional representational (PR) seats in the National Assembly. Moreover the BNP was supplanted as the main opposition party by the ABC, as noted earlier, and with only three PR members in the 2007-2012 parliament, it ranks among the smallest opposition political parties in Lesotho. The newcomer to Lesotho's political scene, the ABC, has not been spared the splits problem, having seen in 2009 a departure from its ranks of its two prominent members and MPs who formed the Sankatana Party.

Since 2007 Lesotho has had nine parliamentary opposition political parties, less than half of the registered national total of 19. These have a combined total of 37 seats in the National Assembly out of the national total of 120 – 80 seats held by members elected from an equal number of electoral constituencies and 40 allocated to party-listed members under the PR element of the country's mixed-member proportional electoral model(MMP).However, only two of these nine opposition parliamentary political parties hold constituency parliamentary seats, totalling 18, in the National Assembly, while the ruling LCD has 62 constituency seats.

The one-party dominance that characterised Lesotho between 1993 and 2007 has thus been perpetuated through and reinforced by the LCD/NIP's partnership. It survived the 2007 elections and continues to dog Lesotho's political system while assuring the dominant LCD of unchallenged rule over Lesotho society. This is worrying and a threat to the democracy and pluralism that the country so badly requires in order to consolidate its hard-won constitutional democracy. Such one-party dominance has narrowed the democratic space, limited the enjoyment of democracy by opposition-inclined sections of the Basotho people, whilst also rendering meaningless the much vaunted 'right-to-choose-and-participate' principle in the process of governance. It is, arguably,a disenfranchising phenomenon to the extent that it enables the dominant party to hold sway over the citizenry. This is a far cry from the situation witnessed during the period 1965-1970 when the ruling party's parliamentary majority was just two persons. The continuing splits in the opposition which include departures, as stated earlier, by two members of the ABC who formed their own party, the Sankana Party, have further fragmented the opposition and thus benefited the ruling LCD.

Both the BCP and its progeny, the LCD, have faced daunting challenges at different stages during their rule. The former had to contend after its victory in the 1993 elections, with the lingering legacy of the BNP and military rules that together spanned two decades. While beaten by the BCP in the 1993 general elections, the BNP did not accept defeat, resorting instead to acts that destabilised the BCP government. Such acts included instigations by the BNP of public protests that culminated in a march at the end of July 1994 by its members and those of other small opposition parties to the Royal Palace to petition King Letsie III to dissolve the BCP government. The king obliged, staging a coup on 4 August 1994 that ousted the BCP regime and replaced its cabinet ministers with a coterie of his loyalists who included the then BNP leader, the late Retselisitsoe Sekhonyana, who became minister of foreign affairs in King Letsie III's administration.

Meanwhile, the country's armed forces were still sympathetic to the BNP. Together with police and prison warders,they had staged a number of peace-threatening anti-government protests against the BCP between January and August 1994.The apogee included army infighting in January 1994 and the murder in April, 1994 of Selometsi Baholo, then minister of finance in the BCP government, by a section of the army.

The LCD, on the other hand, faced police and army mutinies in 1997 and 1998 respectively, while post-1998 election opposition parties supported violent protests that paralysed its government, forcing Prime Minister Pakalitha Mosisili to appeal to the Southern African Development Community for intervention, as some towns in Lesotho were being looted and set ablaze by opposition-aligned mobs.

Whether these episodes demonstrated the opposition's strength is a moot point. Be that as it may, the LCD government agreed to negotiate a new deal for the nation with the opposition, namely the reformed electoral system, or the MMP electoral and parliamentary model, that has been in use by the country since the 2002 elections.

3. Political economy of dependence and labour migrancy

The emergence of political parties in Lesotho has occurred neither 'as an autonomous self-driving process nor simply a series of events'.[3] Rather it is one of the vicissitudes of the country's labour migrancy-driven political economy, overseen and protected by the colonial state to serve the interests of British mining capital in neighbouring South Africa. Concerned with the promotion and protection of the investment interests of its bourgeoisie in South Africa and expecting that Lesotho would eventually be incorporated into the latter,[4] Britain did little to develop the enclave country, instead turning the tiny territory into a labour reserve for the South African mines and related extractive industries. This policy facilitated the development within Lesotho of an oscillating force of labour migrants-cum-working class with access to a piece of land for subsistence farming back home in its country. But the policy stirred, as one of its dialectics, antipathy towards colonialism.

However, while working in South Africa the Lesotho labour migrants acquired a basic political consciousness – which they took back to their home country – through participation in protests, strikes and related struggles against the oppressive state-supported racial capitalism in that country. The Basotho migrant workers were thus ready to join the budding political movements back home in Lesotho, or even to form their own political parties, drawing upon their experience while involved in working class politics in South Africa. For the BCP which saw the oscillating migratory labour system as the enslavement of the Basotho people, these people became an important source of membership and a support base. In fact, the BCP forged and maintained a special relationship with Basotho migrant workers in the various South African cities, establishing branches that sent delegates
to its annual and special conferences back in Lesotho. The LCD inherited these branches after supplanting the BCP in 1997 as the main 'congress' party, and these branches send delegates regularly to its annual and special conferences in Lesotho.

Lesotho produced surplus food grain both for domestic needs and the emergent market in the South African mines in the 1870s.[5] However the enclave kingdom had become poor by the 1950s due mainly to economic neglect by the colonial government and the loss of fertile arable land to soil erosion and human settlement. Poverty meant a diminished ability for many families in that country to feed, clothe and educate their children. It thus spurred able-bodied Basotho men to seek contract employment in South Africa in large numbers, whilst also further fuelling anti-colonial feelings among the Basotho people, goading them to seek an alternative regime to colonialism. 'At independence there was no economic infrastructure to speak of. Industries were virtually non-existent. Whatever commerce there was, was largely in the hands of South African traders. Former colonial rule was geared to administering the country and was not development oriented.'[6]

Subsistence farming had also atrophied by independence, even though its share of the gross domestic product was as high as 48.1%.[7] It was nevertheless inadequate as a source of income, even though it employed at independence 85% of the resident labour force, and contributed 65% of total exports,[8] while accounting for 65% to total exports.[9] Yet the high participation rate of subsistence farming in the GDP and the domestic economy in general means no more than that there were no alternative sources of employment. In fact, poverty is more entrenched in Lesotho's rural communities for whom subsistence farming is supposed to be a source of income. 'More than half of rural people are poor, and more than one quarter of them are extremely poor.'[10]

Revenue derived by the state from the Southern African Customs Union (SACU), on the other hand, has accounted for the largest chunk of government's budget, that is, 'more than half, in some years, up to 70 percent'.[11] SACU is still a critical source of revenue for Lesotho, notwithstanding the effects of the current global economic problems that have seen a decline in total revenue from the union, contributing 'about 60 percent to the total revenue' in 2009, according to the Central Bank of Lesotho.[12] But revenue from SACU is expected to decline due to the current 'global economic crisis.'[13] The beneficiary of SACU revenues is the ruling party which has the mandate to manage state funds, rather than the opposition parties, to the extent that these are used by the prime minister and his cabinet ministers – all of them in the leadership of the LCD – among other things for organising and holding country-wide political rallies. But the point here is not, however, the irrelevance or otherwise of SACU for opposition political parties. Rather the issue is that Lesotho's opposition parties compete in a political economy that not only favours the ruling party but also offers little if any scope for them to build a sound financial base that is critical to their development and growth.

That said, initially, the political movements and/or parties that emerged in Lesotho were in the main a manifestation of deepening resentment against the policies of the British colonial administration which facilitated the exploitation of adult Basotho males by mining magnates in South Africa, instead of developing their poor enclave country. Yet the drivers of this political development were not only those who formed political movements or parties but also the colonial state. Indeed, one analyst discovered while studying the country's political development that, within Lesotho, the colonial state guided the process of political change, as it unfolded, in accordance with 'the civilized norms and standards of political behaviour as defined by Britain, the colonial power'.[14]

4. The constitutional context and framework for Lesotho's opposition

Lesotho's national constitution guarantees freedom of association and the right to form or belong to an association or organisation of one's choosing, including a political party.[15] It opens governmental power to competition via competitive elections freely contested by all registered national political parties, whatever the size of their membership, and allows individuals to stand as independent candidates. It imposes no restrictions as to the number of political parties that can be formed, registered and contest elections. Neither does it outlaw party coalitions forged to contest elections or created for pursuing other legitimate programmes. The growth in the number of political parties in Lesotho from five to 19 since 1993 after the country returned to constitutional rule was thus in part encouraged by this liberal constitution. However, their increase in number has occurred largely due to party splits or breakaway factions, and does not necessarily imply deepening political polarisation based on ideological leanings within the Lesotho population.

The country's Friendly Societies Act[16] under which political parties register is equally if overly liberal, making it possible for just ten people to form and register as a political party. Undoubtedly, the Act may have also encouraged the formation of many political parties in Lesotho, although the majority seem set to remain insignificant forces. The liberal constitutional and legal environment in which the Lesotho political parties operate does not, however, hinder their growth, for it offers the freedom to recruit members and to field candidates for elections. However, the majority of political parties cannot take advantage of this and build the necessary support bases among the voting population. This is because they do not have the required financial and manpower resources for travelling around the country recruiting members and selling their policies. Lesotho's Independent Electoral Commission's (IEC's) token donations of campaign money amounting to approximately R20 000 offered to each political party having 500 members on registering and contesting elections is not enough to alleviate their poverty.[17] This situation is not inhospitable for the opposition as a whole, but also highlights the challenge facing small political parties in Lesotho in their quest to become competitive units in national elections.

Lesotho has held four general elections, including those of 1993, since returning to constitutional rule. Yet these have witnessed continually poor performances by the opposition. Neither has there been a change of government through elections. The LCD has continued to dominate Lesotho's politics and the legislative process.

Table 1 provides a combined summary of the 1993 and 1998 election results and shows the one-party dominance in both elections. The BCP dominated, as the first column of the table shows, until the LCD came on the scene and took over after winning the 1998 elections, capturing 79 of the country's 80 electoral constituencies. The outcome sparked political protests and violence by opposition party supporters. It is clear from the table that the opposition was by this time very weak and almost non-existent in parliament. The ruling party could do virtually anything that it wanted without fear that this might adversely affect its support base.

However, the defeated parties were able to fight from outside parliament, and it is here that their impact was felt and evoked a response from both the LCD government and the SADC, resulting in all-party negotiations and the electoral reforms that eventually spawned the present MMP electoral model. That saw an increase in National Assembly seats from 80 to 120 by adding to the former the 40 'compensatory' seats allocated on the basis of the parties' percentage shares of the total number of votes in an election, beginning with the 2002 general elections. The original PR parliamentary seats as per the award of an arbitration tribunal appointed with the approval of the negotiating parties amounted to 50, but these were reduced to 40 by the LCD-dominated parliament without consulting or further negotiating with its partners.

The reformed electoral model does not compensate the worst losers as Table 2 shows. It merely ensures parliamentary seats for some of the losers in the elections without boosting their bargaining power vis-à-vis the ruling party, or improving their performance in subsequent parliamentary elections. The LCD-dominated National Assembly's frequent unilateral actions underscore the opposition's weakness. The LCD was still a dominant party as Table 2 shows. Admittedly, though, the thrust of the electoral reforms has neither been to increase scope for the growth of opposition parties in Lesotho nor to improve the prospects of their winning state power. Rather the purpose was to mollify, if control, opposition parties by giving them a stake in the political system.

Table 1: 1993 and 1998 elections results in Lesotho

Party	Votes cast		% Share of votes		Seats won	
	1993	1998	1993	1998	1993	1998
LCD	-	364 290	-	60.6	-	78
BCP	398 355	63 445	74.7	10.6	65	-
BNP	120 686	146 566	22.4	24.4	0	1
CDP	-	1 185	-	0.20	-	0
KBP	417	174	0.07	0.03	-	0
LEP	63	92	0.01	0.02	0	0
LLP	244	-	0.04	-	0	-
LLP/UDP	-	357	-	0.06	-	0
MFP	7 650	7 546	1.43	1.27	0	0
NIP	241	1 644	0.04	0.28	0	0
NPP	-	2 897	-	0.49	-	0
PFD	947	3 077	0.17	0.52	0	0
SDU	-	3 160	-	0.20	-	0
UDP	582	-	0.10	--	0	-
IND	2 753	6 536	0.51	1.10	0	0
Total	532 678	593 955		100	65	79

Table 2: Performance of Lesotho's political parties in the 2002 general election and the number and type of parliamentary seats gained by each

Name of party	No of FPTP seats	No of MMP seats gained	Total no of party votes	Percentage of total electoral votes
BNP	0	21	124 234	22.4
BAC	0	3	16 095	2.9
BCP	0	3	14 584	2.6
Christian Democratic. Party	0	0	1 919	0.3
PFD	0	1	6 330	1.1
Kopanang Basotho	0	0	1 155	0.2
LCD	79	0	304 316	54.9
LPC	1	4	32 046	5.8
LWP	0	1	7 788	1.4
MFP	0	1	6 890	1.2
NIP	0	5	30 346	5.5
NPP	0	1	3 985	0.7
New Les. Freedom Party	0	0	1 671	0.3
Sefate Demo. Union	0	0	1 541	0.3
Social Dem. Party	0	0	542	0.1
United Party	0	0	901	0.2
Independents	0	0	10 363	1.8
Totals	80	40	564 749	100.0

Table 2 portrays the 2002 general election results and the performance by the parties which contested that election. The outcome of the 2002 election did not satisfy all the competing political parties and was rejected by the then main opposition, the BNP. The opposition did not use violence to challenge the outcome. Neither did it boycott parliament. But its reaction to the outcome served as a warning that the electoral and parliamentary reforms alone might not solve Lesotho's political problems. This, in fact, signalled the need for Lesotho to explore other options, such as a shift to a full PR electoral and parliamentary system, although this has not to date seemed attractive to the ruling LCD.

5. Opposition political parties and the MMP electoral model

The MMP system appears to be an effective stratagem for placating the losers in elections who otherwise under the FPTP system seemed to be condemned permanently to an extra-parliamentary opposition. The FPTP system also placed the losing political parties 'beyond the purview and influence of the government',[18] whilst also alienating such political parties from the latter. The MMP was meant in part to overcome this problem. But it has created two sets of parliamentarians who are accorded differential treatment. MPs elected directly from the constituencies via the FPTP have different entitlements from their PR counterparts. The FPTP MPs are, for example, paid a monthly constituency allowance of an undisclosed amount.[19] This segregation benefits the LCD - the financial allowances received by its MPs are an important capacity-building resource, enabling their party to expand and consolidate its support and power base, thus dwarfing its rivals. This exacerbates the existing inequality in strength between the ruling party and its rivals and seemingly undermines the opposition's development, while reinforcing the current single-party dominance that offers no political space for and alienating them, thereby reducing them to irrelevant malcontents. Undoubtedly, it is likely to erode Basothos' confidence in democracy and the current system of government in Lesotho. Democracy is supposed to be a means of increasing people's control over the political environment and their lives.

That the MMP model has not seen political violence since it was introduced suggests, however, that it could be the right antidote for instability that has wracked Lesotho's polity for decades. The MMP is not a restraining force or phenomenon, however, that insures against majority power misuse by the ruling party but rather a formula and a means of expanding scope for representation in the legislature. The LCD used its parliamentary majority to kick the BNP leadership out of the National Assembly on 31st May 2006, for example, thus showing that MMP could be as much a tool of the majority party as was the previous FPTP-based parliament.

The LCD MPs voted on 31 May 2006 to suspend without pay the leader of the BNP and his close party associates for periods varying between six and ten months.
The suspension was issued in response to an allegation by the National Assembly Speaker that the BNP leadership had instigated a march on parliament by its party members in protest BNP MP to participate in a SADC parliamentarians' conference in Botswana, ignoring the BNP leadership's plea that only it should make the appointment.

Table 3: Actual results of the National Assembly elections, 17 February 2007[20]

Party	Total valid votes	Constituencies won by party	Party's allocation of constituency seats	Total no of seats	% party votes	% Seats won (constituency + compensator seats)
Alliance of Congress Parties	20 263	1	1	2	4.6	1.7
Basotho Batho Democratic Party	8 474	0	1	1	1.9	0.8
BCP	9 823	0	1	1	2.2	0.8
BDNP	8 783	0	1	1	2.0	0.8
BNP	29 965	0	3	3	6.8	2.5
ABC	107,463	0	10	10	24.3	8.4
MFP	9 129	0	1	1	2.1	0.8
NIP	229 602	0	21	21	51.	17.6
New Lesotho Freedom Party	3 984	0	0	0	0.9	0.0
PFD	15 477	0	1	1	3.5	0.8
ABC	_**	17	0	17	0.0	14.3
LCD	_**20	61	0	61	0.0	51.3
Totals	442 963	79***	40	119***	100	100

Thus, while more inclusive than the previous FPTP model, the MMP model has been unable to protect civil rights and democracy when such protection was required, and this is because it is not a power-balancing or power-redressing machine but a means of easing entry into parliament. Achieving power symmetry between the ruling and opposition parties is not the goal of the democratic theory of which exponents might, indeed rightly, argue that democracy does not depend on power parity, although this may be desirable. In any case, negotiations and compromise become important precisely because power parity between the units competing for political space is always hard to achieve. Noteworthy is that Lesotho's MMP parliament has so far not been able to engender a spirit of political tolerance among the country's population as well as within the ranks of political parties. Evidence of this is borne out with the assassination in June 2006 of a prominent politician and a BNP MP in the previous parliament, Bereng Sekhonyana, after a long stand-off between Sekhonyana and his party leadership.

The country nevertheless witnessed marked progress in its political development with the emergence in April 2005 of an elective local government operative throughout the country. It is not adequately funded, but this is one of the best ways of devolving power to the lower levels of administration and ensuring some degree of participation by the people in the governance process. By participating in local council elections, the opposition parties can use it as an opportunity to penetrate remote areas of the country and recruit members in order to boost their strength.

The phenomenon of local government has, in fact, brought another new and positive dimension to Lesotho's politics: local parochial loyalties have been broken or weakened by the councils' criss-crossing and straddling of the traditional wards and areas under different chiefs and headmen who, under the country's chieftainship law, in turn, account to different ward and principal chiefs and districts. These loyalties not only impeded the rational delivery of public services, but were also a source of violent inter-ward conflicts over farming and grazing lands and access to other natural resources in the chiefly wards. With their rigidly set physical and political boundaries, the wards administered by chiefs also made difficult collaboration, cooperation, interaction and the sharing of the above resources among the people living within the wards.

The relevant local government elections were, however, held amid a tense political atmosphere involving serious disagreements between the government and the opposition political parties. These disagreements centred among other things on the lack of implementing regulations and the reserving of 30 percent of council electoral constituencies for women or female candidates. Unresolved until the date of election, the disagreements led the opposition to boycott the elections, which registered a low voter turn-out when they were held on 30 April 2005. Nonetheless, they produced the required 129 councils, and more than 50 percent of all elected councillors are women. Without a clear explanation, these local government elections were held under the defunct FPTP model.

Table 4: Hypothetical results of the National Assembly elections, 17 February, 2007[21]

Party	Total valid votes	Constituencies won by party	Party's allocation of constituency seats	Total no of seats	% party votes	% Seats won (constituency + compensator seats)
Alliance of Congress Parties	20 263	1	4	5	4.6	4.2
Basotho Batho Democratic Party	8 474	0	2	2	1.9	1.7
BCP	9 823	0	3	3	2.2	2.5
BDNP	8 783	0	2	2	2.0	1.7
BNP	29 965	0	8	8	6.8	6.7
ABC/LWP	107,463	17	12	29	24.3	24.4
MFP	9 129	0	3	3	2.1	2.5
LCD/NIP	229 602	61	1	62	51.8	51.1
New Lesotho Freedom Party	3 984	0	1	1	0.9	0.8
PFP	15 477	0	4	4	3.5	3.4
Totals	442 963	79***	40	119***	100	100

The LCD still dominates this level of government, however, controlling all the local councils. This means that the local councils throughout the country are essentially LCD instruments. Only a few of the Lesotho opposition political parties have representatives in the local councils. Applying the MMP to local government elections would, as with the national legislature, ensure participation in the councils by more opposition parties.

Lesotho's opposition according to the trade unions, employers union, civil society and political parties

Based largely on empirical data generated through interviews in a 2006 South African Institute of International Affairs-commissioned study, but drawing upon developments and evidence in the last four years, this section shows how some of Lesothos citicitzens view the country's opposition political parties. The broad questions that were that were posed individuals from the above mentioned groups during the study were: how effective are Lesotho opposition political parties in representing people holding views different from those of the ruling party? Have these parties any leverage against the Lesotho political system, have they been able to leverage it, and what mechanisms and opportunities are available to them in this regard? What are constraints on the opposition parties and what are their sources?

The people selected for interview were representatives of trade unions, employers' unions, civil society organisations (CSOs), political party leaders and activists in Lesotho. The positions that these chosen interviewees hold in their respective organisations suggested that they would be more credible and reliable than ordinary Lesotho citizens.

Fairly knowledgeable about their organisations' role in and the nature of the country's political system, the selected groups were indeed able to assess Lesotho's opposition and politics as a whole. They were easily able to identify the problems and challenges facing the opposition say what they thought were its future prospects. But the majority of the party functionaries, at least six out of nine, would not state the number of paid-up party members even though they were aware of the activities of their parties; their reticence was clearly due to the lack of capacity to recruit members and maintain proper records.

The study revealed the oft hidden but important characteristics of Lesotho's opposition political parties, and indeed, a missing element in previous analyses of political parties in Lesotho. It showed that Lesotho's opposition political parties are collectively and individually ineffective, generally without the financial resources required for normal party work – organising, maintaining a members' register, acquiring assets of any type and renting an office, hiring paid full-time staff and operating a bank account. Nor are they able to raise funds needed for supporting their activities.

However, Lesotho's three oldest parties – the BCP, the BNP and the MFP – own buildings which they rent out, even though this may not cover all their operating costs. The ruling LCD seemingly has some financial resources as well and also has an office in Maseru manned on a full-time basis. The ABC appeared to have fairly strong financial strength, as it contested the 2007 elections and has since been able to rent offices and hire permanent staff.

For some of the opposition parties, membership fees are paid annually, but not regularly, with the amounts payable ranging between 50 cents and R1; they are the parties' only sources of income. In some cases, party leaders pay out of their own personal money for the costs of maintaining their party and for campaigning during elections. But this seemingly benign gesture was seen by the interviewees as the cause of intra-party conflicts, as such leaders have tended to cling to power to compensate for their 'investment'. This implies no capacity for some, perhaps a sizable number, of the Lesotho opposition parties to grow and compete in elections.

The PFD and the BNP claimed that they had 4 000 and 106 000 paid-up members, respectively. The BNP's own stated membership of 106 000 registered members was, however, belied by the abysmally small number of votes it won in the February 2007 elections, as Tables 3 and 4 show. Only the BNP and the LCD have been able to place candidates in all electoral constituencies since after the 1993 elections, and only these two parties existed in every part of Lesotho prior to the birth of the ABC in September 2006.

Lesotho's political parties can freely seek financial aid from outside the country, as long as they declare all amounts in excess of R20 000, as required under the National Assembly Election Order of 1992. But not all political parties in Lesotho have been able to attract such aid. This is because potential donors tend to want to support a party that has a clear chance of winning elections. In any case, external aid to Lesotho's political parties has historically had to do with the erstwhile competition between East and West, which involved efforts by the two blocs to influence political events in developing countries. Until well after independence, the BCP and the BNP attracted aid from East and West, respectively, with the BNP successfully endearing itself to and securing recognition and aid from the Eastern communist bloc. Only the LCD is able today to secure some external financial assistance.

While conceding that their political parties are weak, the party functionaries who were interviewed did not see such weakness as irreversible. Yet they agreed that it is because of the this situation that the LCD has been able to maintain its unchallenged grip on the nation since 1997. This group of interviewees see their parties' poor performance in elections as being partly because the LCD is a channel for and distributor of aid destined for ordinary poor citizens, and because it uses state resources for mobilising political support. Indeed, both tangible and intangible aid plays an important role in LCD's patron/client politics by which it inculcates a feeling among the voters that if the voters voted for another party, the LCD government would withhold the existing rights and services.

Although an intangible form of aid, free primary education introduced in Lesotho nearly ten years ago is an integral part of the Lesotho state patronage system, and an important political mobilising tool for the LCD. However, a caveat is that state patronage during its 20-year rule did not increase the BNP's popularity. The BCP's sustained attacks against state patronage turned the electorate away from the

BNP, contributing to the latter's electoral defeat in the annulled 1970 elections and in every subsequent election.

That said, by and large, progressively poor, food insecure and hungry Basotho cannot easily survive without a fair amount of financial assistance and state patronage. Since independence, no more than 49 percent of Lesotho's population has lived above the poverty line,[22] while over 60 percent has had no regular cash income. Food aid has thus been an important source of assistance for many Basotho, roughly one-quarter of them in 2005 being in need of food aid,[23] while their country's economy has not performed well, persistently registering negative growth rates[24] proceeding in tandem with high unemployment.[25]

BNP, BCP and MFP interviewees adamant that their parties could defeat the LCD in a fair election. Yet these two political parties today belong in the category of small opposition parties, if we use Tables 3 and 4 as measures, the BNP having progressively shrunk in size since 1993. The BNP's stable income from its rented buildings has not proven enough to win it votes in the elections held in 2007 or to enable it to maintain its erstwhile position as the second largest political party in the country. Its supporters' optimism regarding the prospects of its winning elections, in fact, seems to be no more than a fantasy. Like the rest of the small parties, the BCP, the BNP and the MFP have had neither clear plans for approaching elections nor effective mobilising strategies for winning votes. It emerged during the study that the BNP in particular needs to shed the image it acquired in 1970, reinforced by its appointment of a former military ruler and dictator as its leader, of being an oppressive machine and a bulwark against democracy.

The ruling LCD and opposition parties ABC and LPC forged alliances, as indicated previously with small parties for the purpose of contesting the 2007 elections. Together with their small alliance partners, these parties benefited from the outcome in the form of PR seats, as the foregoing tables show. The actual allocation of PR seats by the IEC evoked anger from the entire opposition, which accused the ruling party and the IEC of deviation from the principle underlying the MMP electoral model. But this aside, the opposition still lost the elections, winning fewer than one-third of the 80 constituency seats, thanks to the MMP model, without which only three political parties would be represented in the National Assembly. Under the sway of the LCD, the Lesotho parliament offers little scope for the opposition to successfully formulate and pass motions, as revealed by the study. The LCD has blocked all resolutions or motions by the opposition, except those serving its interests. Intra-party conflicts, which have increased with the country's switch to the MMP system, may be contributing to the opposition's weakness, for it is an incentive to jockeying for party leadership positions that have become a gateway to parliament and hence access to a regular cash income.

The decision as to who should be party candidates in an election and in the PR list that has to be submitted to the IEC lies with party leaderships. Thus PR lists have tended to be a divisive issue for virtually all the Lesotho political parties, as those omitted from party PR lists or not placed high enough in such a list in order to stand a chance of entering parliament always allege unfairness on the part of their party leaders. It emerged during the interviews that there is a feeling of a lack of accountability and intra-party democracy in all the Lesotho political parties, paralleled by arrogance, corruption and selfishness among party leaderships, and that this also contributes to the opposition's weakness since it repels potential members, especially the educated youth. Like all other youth, the youth in Lesotho tend to believe in accountability, equality of members, freedom to criticise and of speech, merit in appointment to high office and opportunity for all. These values are either completely denied or discouraged by the Lesotho political parties as a whole. The so called political party youth, whether of the ruling or opposition parties, are not allowed free expression by their parties, let alone criticising or differing with their leadership on any issue.

Most of Lesotho's opposition parties, including those in parliament, rarely hold annual conferences, according to the study. Even when they have held conferences, the leaders have manipulated them and the processes used for appointing executives. This is another issue that undoubtedly does not endear the youth to the political parties. Their largely unenforceable constitutions or an unwillingness by the leaderships to enforce the provisions of their party constitutions when situations demand it have meant that most intra-party conflicts and disputes are invariably the subject of arbitration by the High Court. A drain on the parties' meagre finances, this inhibits the growth of the affected parties.

The study also revealed that regardless of its weaknesses the opposition's presence in parliament is important. Like the governing parties, opposition is the linchpin of multipartyism because it spreads democracy to all sections of the population; it is an alternative to the ruling party and a sounding board for minority voices. In principle the opposition polices government actions. But the general view among those interviewed and our observation is that the Lesotho opposition does not play this role. The study revealed, though, that opposition MPs have attacked or criticised some of the parliamentary bills during parliamentary debates. There is media freedom in Lesotho which the opposition could use for selling its programmes and views. However, weak and not seen as an alternative to the governing party in terms of what it can offer voters, the opposition in Lesotho tends to be accorded little attention by the national media. In any case, saying that the Lesotho opposition is weak and powerless should not be construed as a suggestion that it has not and cannot threaten the state or paralyse the government. The post-1998 election opposition-organised mass demonstrations and stay-aways, noted earlier, paralysed the state and business. However, these occurred outside parliament where the ruling party cannot use its majority to stop the opposition's actions.

Conventionally, though, Lesotho opposition parties can improve their effectiveness by exposing corruption and other weaknesses in governance through the media and during parliamentary debates. Example of corruption in the Lesotho is the fraudulent acquisition at taxpayers' expense of state-owned barely two-year old luxury motor cars by cabinet ministers and top civil servants, who paid the paltry amounts of R4, 000 and R2, 500 respectively.[26]

Recently instituted parliamentary reforms are beneficial for the opposition, enabling opposition parties to exert some pressure on the government and the ruling party. The reforms encapsulate parliamentary portfolio committees which include opposition MPs in each committee, in some cases the chair. Such committees not only scrutinise parliamentary bills; they assess them and suggest amendments where necessary before the bills can be passed as law by the legislature. They also investigate all allegations within the purview of their respective portfolios.

Prospects for the opposition's development and growth

The development and growth of an effective opposition in Lesotho depends, according to the insights provided by the study, on a number of things:

The first is the economic muscle and self-reliance of the voters in terms of the capacity to generate their income independently of the government or the ruling party. This would lessen voters' dependence on government handouts, as independent and self-reliant voters will not easily be manipulated or bought through patronage by the rulers..

Secondly, the opposition parties' concept of politics and political power must change: political leaders must not view their parties as simply an avenue to parliament and, therefore, an access to regular income. It will ensure that party leaders do not cling to power and forestall the growth of conflicts within the parties.

Thirdly, deepening engagement with the nation in general and with civil society will enhance opposition parties' understanding of the problems and challenges facing them and the Lesotho polity, and also market opposition parties to the wider voting population. Lesotho's opposition parties rarely utilise the CSOs' skilled manpower in building their organisational capacity and educating party members.

Fourthly, the opposition parties must ensure intra-party democracy and good governance. With no exception, Lesotho's political parties are generally top-heavy – power lies exclusively at the top – with closed systems offering little scope for members to freely debate issues of concern to them. Some Political parties, are certainly regimented systems discouraging individual member initiatives. This limits popular participation and control over the party, while resulting in leadership unaccountability.

Fifthly, they must introduce civic and political education programmes, teaching members about the system of rule and their political rights. This must proceed in tandem with and be backed up by enforceable national legislation making the violation of democratic norms by political parties a punishable offence.

Conclusion

The Lesotho opposition is weak in terms of influence over policy and law-making. It does not have a significant number of MPs in parliament to enable it to assert itself against the ruling party. Lesotho needs an opposition that is able to exert enough pressure on the government and the ruling party to ensure its accountability. A strong opposition would help deepen parliamentary democracy and ensure greater participation in the legislative process. This is in contradistinction of the mantra that Basotho seem to want a strong or powerful 'Prime Minister with a free hand in passing laws, without worrying what Parliament may think'.[27]

The political space afforded the opposition by the constitution, the parliamentary portfolio or sector committees and the MMP electoral regime are potential bases for power and possible resources for building their support base and increasing their bargaining power vis-à-vis the ruling party. Lesotho's opposition parties must target in their membership recruitment campaigns educated youths who can better articulate party programmes and goals. The parliamentary opposition in Lesotho is not seen by voters as yet as an alternative to the ruling LCD; hence it might take a while for it to attract enough votes to dislodge the latter from power.

ENDNOTES

1 Gill SJ 1993. *A Short History of Lesotho: From the Late Stone Age until the 1993 Elections*. Morija: Morija Archives and Museum, 1993, p 210.

2 Machobane LBBJ 1990. *Government and Change in Lesotho, 1800-1966: A study of Political Institutions*. Houndsmill: Macmillan Lesotho, p 254.

3 Makoa FK 2004. 'Electoral reform and political stability in Lesotho'. *African Journal of Conflict Resolution* 4(2): p 80.

4 Ferguson J 1990.T*he Anti-politic Machine: 'Development', Depoliticisation, and Bureaucratic Power in Lesotho*. Cambridge: Cambridge University Press, p 31.

5 Thabane M 2002. 'Aspects of colonial economy and society', in Pule NW and Thabane M (eds), *Essays on Aspects of the Political Economy of Lesotho 1500-2000*. Department of History, National University of Lesotho, p 106.

6 Ferguson J, op. cit.

7 Ferguson, op. cit., p 42.

8 Bardill JE and Cobbe JH 1985.Lesotho: *Dilemmas of Dependence in Southern Africa*. Colorado: Westview Press, p 31.

9   Bardill and Cobbe, ibid.
10 Rural Poverty Portal.'Rural poverty in Lesotho'.http://www.ruralpovertyportal.org/web/guest/country/hometags/lesotho p 1 [accessed 31 August 2010]
11 van den Bosch, Servas 2010. 'The Story Underneath: Southern Africa Unexpected Low Custom Revenue Causes Budget Shortfalls'. Windhoek: Inter Press Service, March 17, p 1. http://www.ipsnews.net/print.asp?idnews=50700 [accessed 24 June 2010]
12 *CBL Economic Review* 2009.'The Global Economic Downturn: Economic Implications for Lesotho'. 102 January 2009, p 4
13 *Afrol News.*'Lesotho economy stagnating'. http.//www.afrol.com/articles/36263, p1 [accessed 28 July 2010]
14 Makoa FK 2004, op.cit.p 84.
15 The Constitution of Lesotho, section 16.
16 Societies Act No. 20 of 1966.
17 National Assembly Election Order, 1992, section 35.
18 Makoa FK 2005. 'Conflict resolution and peace building through electoral and parliamentary reforms: A note on Lesotho's mixed-member parliament'. *Lesotho Law Journal* 15(1), p173.
19 Makoa FK 2005. 'Strengthening parliamentary democracy in Southern Africa: Lesotho country report'.*South African Journal of International Affairs.*12(1), p73.
20 See K. Matlosa 2008. 'General Election in Lesotho: Managing the Post-Election Conflict'.*Journal of African Elections, Special Issue: Elections and Democracy in Lesotho* 7 (1) June 2008, p 38
21 Ibid, p.39
22 The Kingdom of Lesotho Economy, Economic Overview 2005.Available at http://www.lesotho.gov.ls//sseconomy.
23 Thakalekoala T 2005. 'Food shortage, assistance needed', *Mopheme/The Survivour*, 26 July-1 August, p 3.
24 Ramsamy P 2001. 'SADC: The way forward', in Clapham C, Mills G, Morner AM and Sidiropoulos E (eds), *Reginald Integration in Southern Africa: Comparative Perspectives.* Johannesburg: SAIIA, p 40.
25 World Fact Book 2006, available at https://www.cia.gov/cia/publications/factbook/geos/it.html#Econ[accessed 7 August 2006].

26 See Public Eye 2006, 10, 26, 30 June, p2.
27 Green T and Chikwana, AB 2006.'Changing attitudes towards democracy in Lesotho', Afrobarometer Bulletin, Lesotho, 22 May, p5.

CHAPTER FOUR
MAURITIUS: BEYOND ELITE COMPACTS AND INCESTUOUS POLITICS
SHEILA BUNWAREE

Introduction

More than 30 years ago, Robert Dahl suggested that the extent of political competition in part determines the extent that a regime perceived as democratic. Dahl noted that without political opposition, there is no choice and when there is no choice, people cannot exercise their rule.[1] In a recent contribution, Van de Walle suggests that in Africa the quality of competition and the power of the opposition could go a long way to explain the level of democracy that has developed in these countries.[2] Thus, we need to understand the dynamics of opposition groups, their behaviour and role.

The questions that are therefore posed in this chapter are as follows: do Mauritians really have and exercise a choice on the basis of different/alternative programmes or do they simply sanction one alliance/coalition in favour of another and practise the famous dictum, *donne ene lecon* ?[3]

Although geographically small, Mauritius has a relatively large number of political parties, but the latter usually form coalitions and alliances in order to contest the elections. While ethno-politics dominate the Mauritian political landscape, none of the parties, except perhaps for a couple of very small and insignificant ones, usually associated with some form of extremism, are constituted of particular ethnic groups.

Voter turnout usually revolves around the 80 per cent mark and election outcomes are hardly ever contested by the opposing parties. The conflict-free nature of the post-election period is remarkable and has been commented on in laudatory terms by international and regional observers. This reflects the prevalence of a strong democratic ethos in the country.

Unlike many former colonies which achieved their statehood through wars of national liberation against the colonial powers, Mauritius, like some other parts of the British Empire, achieved its independence by concession from the parent country. Many countries can speak of their independence as being fuelled by nationalist sentiment, but Mauritius experienced a different situation altogether. No nationalist sentiment existed in Mauritius. Anti-colonial feelings were expressed by the Hindu majority but the other ethno/religious groups preferred to maintain ties with the mother country. As independence became imminent, there was some resistance to it and the country experienced a certain amount of turmoil.

The Creole population (i.e. Mauritians of African descent) expressed all sorts of doubts and fears. The Creoles, who had been closely associated with the Franco-Mauritians and dominated the civil service and the mid-level positions in the private sector, feared the emergence of a Mauritian government led by the Indians.

Mauritius was divided as it moved to independence; there was no sense of national unity. In order to reduce tensions and dampen the fears of the different communal parties, the British put forward a plan to establish a new electoral commission to deal with issues of representation. The proposals that emerged continue to shape Mauritian elections even today.

Soon after independence, Seewosagur Ramgoolam, leader of the Labour Party, and Gaetan Duval, leader of the Parti Mauricien Social Democrate (PMSD), decided to form a Government of National Unity. This was perhaps the beginning of a cycle of alliances and coalitions and the diminution of the powers of potentially strong opposition in the country. This development will be discussed more fully in the next section.

The Constitution of Mauritius provides for an opposition. The Westminster parliamentary model makes provision for at least two parties or party alliances to be represented in the National Assembly. The party or alliance having a majority of seats forms the government, while the other party or coalition forms the opposition. Mathur notes that an opposition is a *sine qua non* (which literally translates to without which not) for the successful working of a parliamentary democracy inspired by the British Westminster model.[4]

Section 73 of the Constitution of Mauritius states that the president appoints the leader of the opposition party that has numerical strength over other opposition parties, or if there is no difference in numerical strength, the person designated by consensus by all opposition parties. The office of the leader of the opposition becomes vacant if the leader is no longer an MP or if their party no longer holds a majority in the opposition. It is also possible for the president to revoke the leader of the opposition on grounds that they do not control a majority or that the other leaders of opposition parties do not accept their leadership.

Mauritius has had eight elections since independence and on a few occasions it has run the risk of ending up with a parliament void of an opposition as a result of its electoral system. This chapter argues that there is an urgent need for electoral reform as well as a new political culture in the country. Electoral reform will help to palliate the most important democratic deficits of the country – the under-representation of women and the biased electoral winner-take-all system. Elections based on a proportional representation (PR) system can help to reconfigure the Mauritian landscape by giving more of a chance to smaller opposition groups, redefining the way alliances and coalitions are made, and in the same vein making the choice that Mauritians exercise more meaningful.

Outline of opposition in post-independence Mauritius

Mauritius' post-independence political landscape has been dominated by four political parties – the Labour Party, the Mouvement Militant Mauricien (MMM), the Mouvement Militant Socialiste Mauricien (MSM) and the Mauritian Social Democratic Party (PMSD), which had, just a few months before the 2000 general election, split into the PMSD and the Mauritian Party of Xavier Duval (PMXD). Although rather small, not so dominant and generally perceived as representing the interests of the Creole groups, recourse was often made to the Mauritian Social Democratic Party (PMSD) and the PMXD to help enhance the country's politics of recognition and representation. The Mauritian Social Democratic Party (PMSD) and Mauritian Party of Xavier Duval (PMXD) re-united and reverted to the name of PMSD one year before the May 2010 elections.

Mauritius has had four prime ministers and nine opposition leaders. The former includes Sir Seewoosagur Ramgoolam, first leader of the Labour Party, Sir Aneerood Jugnauth, leader of the Militant Socialist Movement (MSM), Navin Ramgoolam, son of Sir Seewosagur Ramgoolam and current leader of the Labour Party, and Paul Berenger, leader of the Mouvement Militant Mauricien (MMM). Leaders of the opposition include Sir Gaëtan Duval, Maurice Lesage, Sir Aneerood Jugnauth, Paul Berenger, Prem Nababsing, Sir Satcam Boolell, Navin Ramgoolam, Nicolas Von Mally and Nando Bodha. The small number of prime ministers – Paul Berenger, Navin Ramgoolam and Sir Aneerood Jugnauth – highlights the fact that power in Mauritius has been concentrated in the hands of very few people, and that the alternation of government is only between the dominant parties and particular leaders.

Table 1 (overleaf) shows the election results for the period 1982 to 2010. It highlights the disproportionality between the percentage of votes won in an election by a party and the number of seats eventually obtained in the National Assembly. In some cases, the landslide victory of an alliance/coalition meant that the opposition received no seats.

Please note: The table does not take into consideration the split after each election and the formation of a new opposition. The party or alliance which has won the majority of seats forms the government.

Table 1: General election results in Mauritius, 1982–2010

Year	Party	% of votes	Elected seats	Best Loser seats
1982	MMM/PSM	64.16	60	-
	PAN	25.78	0	2
	PMSD	7.79	0	2
	OPR	-	2	-
1983	MSM/LP/PMSD	52.2	41	5
	MMM	46.4	19	3
	OPR	-	2	-
1987	MSM/LP/PMSD	49.86	39	5
	MMM	48.12	21	3
	OPR	-	2	-
1991	MSM/MMM/MTD	56.3	57	-
	LP/PMSD	39.9	3	5
	OPR	-	2	-
1995	LP/MMM	63.7	60	-
	MSM/RMM	19.3	0	-
	OPR	-	2	-
	PGD	-	0	1
	Hezbollah	-	0	1
	MR	-	0	2
2000	MSM/MMM	52.3	54	4
	LP/PMXD	36.95	6	2
	OPR	-	2	-
	MR	-	0	2
2005	Alliance Sociale	48.8	39	3
	MMM/MSM/PMSD	42.6	21	3
	OPR	-	2	-
	MR	-	0	2
2010	Alliance PTR-PMSD-MSM	50.7	41	4
	Alliance MMM-UN-MMSD	42.88	18	2
	Front Solidarite Mauricienne	2.59	1	
	OPR	0		1
	MR	2		

Source: Compiled from the Electoral Supervisory Commission database.

Factors influencing the nature and extent of opposition

The Electoral system and the silencing of alternative voices

Elections and political parties are the lifeblood of democracies, but the Mauritian electoral system does not provide for a broad spectrum of representation.

The first-past-the-post (FPTP) system, with its associated best loser variant, has the potential of wiping out an opposition altogether. The Mauritian electoral system suffers from certain aberrations. The FPTP system in three-member constituencies frequently produces results which are grossly disproportionate to the share of votes won by the different parties. At times, although obtaining a substantial percentage of votes, the opposition is either completely, or nearly completely, eliminated. Thus, in 1982 and in 1995, the result was 60-0, while in 1991 and 2000 the presence of the opposition barely reached representative levels. The other main problem is that the FPTP system lacks gender sensitivity, which will be addressed later in this chapter.

Mauritius, a multiparty parliamentary democracy based on the Westminster model, has been independent for almost 40 years but it is still stuck with an electoral system which it inherited from its colonial rulers. Despite the fact that it became a republic in 1992, no changes have been brought to the electoral system. The unicameral national legislature is made up of 62 members directly elected by free and fair elections every five years. More specifically, the Mauritian electoral system distinguishes itself with two unique features.

First is the splitting of the country into 20 constituencies in which each voter has to vote for three candidates, with the three candidates receiving the most votes being elected (there are two additional members from the island of Rodrigues). There is no legal imposition of vote blocking in Mauritius; theoretically, in this system, people vote for individual candidates regardless of their party affiliations.[5] Voting records in Mauritius, however, show that most
voters usually vote for three candidates from the same alliance or select two candidates from one alliance and one from the other.[6] In some cases, the opposition is completely undermined and weakened, such as in 1982 and 1995. In such circumstances, the opposition tends to be merely symbolic and cannot play its watchdog role fully. The quality of democracy suffers enormously under such conditions.

The best loser system constitutes the second feature of the Mauritian electoral system. The best loser seats are given to those candidates belonging to underrepresented ethnic groups and who get the highest percentage of votes after the first three who have been elected. The rationale of the best loser system, which is endorsed in the Constitution, was to ensure a secure and adequate representation of minority communities in parliament. Allocation of best loser seats does not alter the net result of the election.

Section 5 of the first schedule of the Constitution states:
> In order to ensure a fair and adequate representation of each community, there shall be 8 seats in the Assembly, additional to the 62 seats for members representing constituencies, which shall so far as is possible be allocated to persons belonging to parties who have stood as candidates for election as members at the general election but have not been returned as members to represent constituencies.
> The first 4 of the 8 seats shall, so far as is possible, each be allocated to the most successful unreturned candidate, if any, who is a member of a party and who belongs to the appropriate community [ethnic group] regardless of which party he belongs to.[7]

Section 5(4) spells out who the next four seats should go to. It states:
> When the first 4 seats (or as many as possible of those seats) have been allocated, the number of such seats that have been allocated to persons who belong to parties, other than the most successful party, shall be ascertained and so far as is possible that number of seats out of the second 4 seats shall one by one be allocated to the most successful unreturned candidates (if any) belonging both to the most successful party and to the appropriate community or where there is no unreturned candidate of the appropriate community, to the most successful unreturned candidates belonging to the most successful party, irrespective of community.[8]

The best loser system has provoked considerable debate in the country. Some commentators such as Mathur,[9] Bibi[10] and Lallah[11] argue that it institutionalises communalism in the country, while others such as Mohamed[12] believe that it is an important safeguard for the protection of minorities. Bunwaree[13] argues that if the best loser system is to be maintained, it should be completely de-ethnicised and de-racialised and instead should be genderised. In other words, all the best loser seats should be reserved for women irrespective of ethnicity and race.

In the 60-0 'configuration', section 5(4) cannot be applied for two obvious reasons: first, the winning parties have obtained all the seats provided in the FPTP system; and second, the losing parties have no elected MPs and cannot be considered as per section 5(4) of the Constitution. In this case, parliament consists only of 66 members instead of 70 as provided by the Constitution.

The Sachs Commission report on constitutional and electoral reform 2001/02 states that: 'There was also widespread acceptance of the necessity to correct the gross under representation of opposition parties produced by the electoral system.'[14] The Sachs report recommended that the electoral system be reformed to allow for a compensatory PR formula, which would ensure that a party obtaining at least 10 per cent of the vote could be represented in parliament – thereby creating a stronger opposition. The system proposed by the commission is focused on correcting under-representation of the opposition without challenging the undisputed right to form the government of the party or alliance that gains a majority under the FPTP system. But despite the propositions made, no action has been taken so far.

Coalitions and alliances

All elections except for the 1976 poll have been contested by parties which engaged in pre-electoral alliances or coalitions. In many ways the formation of such coalitions, coupled with the nature of the Mauritian electoral system, reduces the possibility of the emergence of a strong opposition. Perhaps the only time when there was a strong opposition in the country was from 1976 to1982, the period during which the left-leaning, radical MMM was contesting the policies being implemented by the ruling party of the time and was interrogating the inequitable relationships of power as well as the different forms of oppression that large segments of the population were subjected to.

Despite the fact that the Labour Party and the PMSD entered into a post-election coalition, the coalition remained weak and was no match for the MMM team in parliament. The 1976-1981 parliament saw the erosion of the Labour government. Kadima and Kasenally note that:

"dogged by internal division and a slim parliamentary majority, it encouraged some members of the MMM to cross the floor for ministerial and other office. The leadership was undermined by fractious groups either calling for reform or jockeying for power. On two occasions (1979 and 1980) the opposition filed motions of censure against the government, which were only averted after certain members of the opposition sided, for opportunistic reasons, with the government."[15]

It is generally argued that political parties do not differ much in ideological terms in contemporary Mauritius, and that the differences that may exist are more at the level of the culture of the political parties, style and general management. The dominant political parties believe in and propound social democracy and are more or less at the centre-left.[16] The absence of ideologies, according to some research respondents, facilitates the formation of coalitions and alliances. One respondent described contemporary Mauritian politics as 'being very cheap and without character or dignity. People are thirsty for power and any formula that can lead to some form of power sharing which is satisfactory to the key leaders of two major blocs can easily form an alliance.'[17]

When parties are about to enter into an alliance or coalition, they choose the most popular party to engage with since no political party wants to be with a loser. In order to avoid all risks of losing and to ensure that they get the best partner, political parties are prepared to get into high level negotiations on various aspects of governance, including the sharing of power itself – as evidenced by the MMM-MSM Med Point accord where it was agreed that Paul Berenger (a non-Hindu) would be prime minister from 2003 to 2005, while Aneerood Jugnauth would become president, and Jugnauth's own son would become the deputy prime minister. One respondent noted that such coalitions 'constitute various kinds of gymnastics to satisfy the immediate desires of the principal politicians and real issues take second position'.[18]

Since Mauritian politics is largely determined by coalitions and alliances, the dynamics behind such alliances imply that the smaller and less popular parties are left on the fringes. They often only revive at the time of elections and their role as some kind of opposition between elections is insignificant.

Dynastic politics, leadership and the reproduction of a political elite

Mauritian politics is heavily influenced by dynastic politics: Sir Seewosagur Ramgoolam was followed by his son Navin Ramgoolam; Pravind Jugnauth became the leader of the MSM after his father became president, as noted above; and Xavier Duval, currently one of the deputy prime ministers of the country, took over the PMSD which was led by his father, Sir Gaetan Duval.

In addition to these, we have cases of other sons, nephews, brothers of senior ministers, current and past, who have joined the political elite. Examples include: Arvin Boolell, son of Sir Satcam; Anil Gayan, nephew of Sir Satcam and Kushiram, son-in-law of Sir Satcam. Ashok Juganuth, a former minister of health, is the brother of Aneerood Jugnauth; Rajesh Bhowon, a former parliamentarian, is a nephew of Aneerood Jugnauth. Others such as Raj Ringadoo, Anquetil and Seeneevassen, who were offered tickets, ran for the 2005 elections but were not elected.

Some of the respondents interviewed for the study describe Mauritian politics as being heavily dominated by cronyism, patronage and clientelism. It is argued that dynastic politics combined with ethno-politics provides very little space for a new political class and culture to emerge in the country. The absence of new charismatic figures and of ideology, as well as limited opportunity structures, makes it possible for the prevailing dynastic politics to go unchallenged. The reproduction of the same political elite therefore implies that opposition continues to remain weak in the country. Commenting on the nature of Mauritian politics, one respondent noted:

"We cannot speak of a democracy in Mauritius. Politics is reduced to a family affair. You find brothers, sons, nephews, sisters-in-law etc all belonging to one party or the other. There is little scope for others to penetrate the political arena. You need to belong to certain clans and groups."[19]

Another respondent referred to the 'clientelistic relationships with the state'. He noted that,

"There is a lot of cronyism and patronage ... it is not a politics of ideals and values and defending a particular cause ... there is no ideology; if anything it is the ideology of the market which dominates and within such an ideology there are a number of arrangements that people make to suit their own needs and interests."[20]

The above echoes Darga's views when commenting on the engagement of civil society with parliament. He notes:
"One can highlight two factors that appear to contribute to this state of affairs: first, political culture in Mauritius has become predominantly clientelistic; civil society members as individuals therefore interact with MPs or groups of MPs more to seek personal material reward than to influence policies. The second factor may be a culture of fear (particularly among the petty bourgeoisie and the intelligentsia) to speak out against the power resulting from patronage and clientelism, as well as the retribution practised by all parties when they are in power."[21]

On the surface, political parties in Mauritius tend to operate in a very democratic manner, but the reality is that excessive power is vested in the hands of the leaders of political parties. One observer of Mauritian politics argued that: 'There exists no democracy within political parties, things are handled in a top-down manner, there is only a semblance of interaction, but in fact the latter remains very limited ... .'[22] Others noted that 'leaders are often the sons of past prime ministers and are treated as some kind of *culte de personalité* or demigods. Songs are composed around their personalities.' Leadership has not changed for years within the dominant parties and there seems to be very little preparation for succession. Interestingly, ethnicity and caste are key factors in the determination of leadership positions. The two largely Hindu-based parties – the MSM and the Labour Party – have always had a Hindu of the Vaish caste as their leaders.

Mauritius is still a nation in the making. The country lacks a sense of Mauritian-ness and has not been able to achieve a Mauritian identity.[23] Lehembre writes: 'In Mauritius one rarely feels Mauritian, one is either Indian or Catholic or Muslim or Chinese or Tamil but rarely Mauritian.'[24]

Mauritius' relatively successful management of its diversity so far can be attributed partly to the economic diversification of the country in the 1970s and 1980s. As the economy diversified and expanded, more opportunities were created for everyone and there was an improvement in the standard of living of all citizens. But now that the economy is experiencing a painful decline and unemployment is rising, frustration and alienation is growing among certain segments of society, as reflected by the riots of February 1999.

The growing asymmetry in the distribution of entitlements can easily provoke a rise in identity politics. The revival of identity politics and its relationship with ethnic-based parties may not augur well for multi-ethnic Mauritius. So far there are only a few and rather insignificant ethnic-based parties in the country, but it is important to remember that the potential for growth exists.

Candidates are largely chosen by leaders in line with the ethnic profile of the constituency. Some constituencies are much larger or smaller than others. For example, constituency number three has only some 25 000 electors, while constituency number 14 has approximately 40 000 electors, but they all elect the same number of representatives to the National Assembly. Most of the leaders are hesitant to suggest redrawing these boundaries and revisiting the number of representatives to reflect the size of the constituency out of fear that this may upset their party's ethnic logic. Moreover, redrawing boundaries can also impact on election results and can consequently change the nature of the opposition which emerges.

Party funding and financial resources

Access to resources is a decisive factor in electoral contests and party existence. It impacts on the quality and extent of opposition as well as on gender representation, since women tend to be the least resourced citizens of the country.[25] The amount of funding available determines the quality of campaigning as well as the level of communication that the party has with the voters.

Party funding is becoming a crucial issue in the contemporary Mauritian landscape. It is generally argued that entering the political arena has become very costly and therefore excludes a wide section of Mauritians who may be interested in running for office, but are at the very outset excluded since they do not have the necessary resources. The lack of financial resources is therefore a major barrier and hampers the opening of the political space to a greater diversity of representation. The chances of an opposition emerging become slimmer as the political venture becomes more costly.

Public funding of political parties does not exist in Mauritius. Many politicians admit that their parties obtain funds from what they call 'well wishers'.[26] Darga adds:
> "Parties mobilise funds either through some direct corruptive practices during tenure of office or through what are diplomatically termed 'donations', mainly from private sector companies, such donations always being unofficial and unacknowledged."[27]

The phenomenon of what is commonly known as the 'bases' in local political arlance is also very costly and yet has become essential. The 'bases' are a sort of regional office structure set up during electoral campaigns to liaise with voters.

Some respondents alluded to this as the 'commodification of politics' and argued that only big political parties which 'have the support of big firms, "well wishers" and/or who have amassed money during previous mandates can afford to set up these "bases" and compete on the same level as the other strong and big parties'.[28] It is therefore clear that smaller parties and individuals who want to run as independent candidates and who lack resources cannot compete on a fair basis. Women, who are the least resourced, find it very difficult to enter the political arena, let alone overcome the other barriers that they have to surmount in order to do so.

Floor crossing and dissidence

Mauritius does not have floor-crossing legislation. The political history of the country shows that this phenomenon happens from time to time and has an impact on the opposition, as revealed by the dissenting elements of the last MMM/MSM government. Just a few months prior to the 2005 elections, stalwarts such as minister Baichoo left the MSM to form part of the Alliance Sociale. Together with Baichoo, parliamentarians Chamroo and Ramloll, also of the MSM, left the party, thus weakening the government.

Other examples include Labour MPs Glover, Sajadah and Ghurburrun who joined the MSM when the prime minister, Sir Aneerood Jugnauth, sacked Sir Satcam Boolell of the Labour Party from his government. Sir Satcam joined the ranks of the opposition but without his followers. Party hopping can have serious implications on the numerical strength of an opposition party or the government, and it is perhaps time for modern Mauritius to look into the possibility of formulating legislation to minimise this problem.

The demise of a left ideology

The absence of a clear ideological divide has also weakened the opposition. In the 1970s, when the MMM was rapidly rising to popularity, it had a very different and alternative view of development and society compared to now. The slogan was: 'One people, one nation, unity in diversity'. Yet soon after they came to power in 1982 'Berenger was clearly drawing back from the 1982 campaign promises; his rejoinder was that no socialist programme was remotely possible until the economy was released from [International Monetary Fund] dependence'.[29] Over time the MMM increasingly embraced the ideology of the market, like most other dominant political parties in the country. Only small and politically insignificant parties such as Lalit continue to espouse a communist orientation.

Carroll and Carroll characterise Mauritius as an elite-dominated democracy, noting that party ideology has gradually become less important than ethnicity, personality and 'office seeking' as the three major parties – the Labour Party, MMM and MSM – shift and vie for the centre. In many ways, this absence of conflicting ideologies and the kind of subtle consensus that emerges make the formulation and implementation of policies easier and provide for continuity in a number of programmes and projects.[30]

Weak culture of opposition

The very fact that some political parties in Mauritius are born within the corridors of power implies that they do not possess a culture of opposition. For instance, the MSM was born when the MMM/PSM coalition government collapsed in 1983. Jugnauth has through a series of alliances and coalitions managed to retain the reins of power for more than 13 years, although he lost the elections in 1995.

When parties which are born within the corridors of power are ousted from office, they have very little knowledge of how to oppose democratically. Contrary to parties which have a rich historical past in terms of observing, criticising the wrongdoings of those who rule and offering alternative solutions, the MSM has hardly ever had the opportunity to engage in opposition politics. When Aneerood Jugnauth lost the elections in 1995, he felt let down by the Hindu population and rather uninterested in politics. According to one respondent, he then became more motivated by his personal ambitions and that of his family. This triggered him into accepting the MED Point accord of power sharing.[31]

The factors discussed above highlight how the dynamics of politics, particularly the opposition, play out. Governments change not because of a strong and viable opposition but rather as a sanction against governments for their wrongdoings. Additionally, the need for change is well entrenched in the Mauritian psyche. The *donne ene lecon* syndrome mentioned earlier is embedded in the system.

Other factors that impact on the nature of the opposition are the ageing of political leaders, the absence of efforts towards renewal, the absence of any form of preparation for succession, and the poor representation of women and youth in Mauritian polity. The latter two categories – women and youth – could go a long way in transforming the functioning of the political system and making a difference to the human condition, but this has unfortunately not been the case so far.

Gender and political parties

The Mauritian political space has been largely monopolised by males. Despite having ratified the Convention on the Elimination of All Forms of Discrimination against Women, the Beijing Platform of Action and the Southern African Development Community (SADC) protocol of a 30 per cent quota for women in parliament, Mauritius continues to lag behind many SADC countries regarding the representation of women in the legislature. Some of the factors responsible for this state of affairs include the gender-insensitive FPTP electoral system, socialisation patterns, the shrinking of potential female space resulting from male-dominated alliances and coalitions, lack of financial resources and general resistance to any form of affirmative action whatsoever.[32] Very few women are nominated as candidates by political parties, and a lack of pressure by civil society to bring change has contributed to the strengthening of males' appropriation of the political space.

For the first time in the political history of Mauritius, a small women's group called Federaction took to the streets a few months before the 2005 general elections, contesting for more women in parliament. It was backed by some women's groups such as Media Watch, a non-governmental organisation (NGO) which works for the promotion of women in and through the media, le Parti de la Majorité, a newly created female-only political party, and other women NGOs. In some ways, this awakening of civil society contributed to the political parties nominating more women as candidates.

Interestingly, 12 of the 16 women presented as candidates by the dominant parties were elected in the last general elections. This quantum leap of a 200 per cent rise in gender representation as compared to the 2000-2005 legislature does not, however, guarantee the maintenance of a rise in the numbers of women in the legislature. There is an urgent need to move towards a more gender inclusive electoral system such as PR, accompanied by some other positive discriminatory measures in order to obtain some feminisation of the political space.

Civil society, trade unions and the media

Civil society, in its most abstract sense, can be conceived as an aggregate of institutions whose members are engaged primarily in a complex of non-state activities.[33] These institutions engage in economic, cultural and voluntary activities, and preserve and transform their identity by exercising a myriad of pressures, or controls, upon state institutions. Civil society thus relates to a non-state sphere comprising a plurality of public spheres – productive units, voluntary organisations and community-based services – which are legally guaranteed and self-organising. Haddenius and Uggla refer to civil society as a certain area of society which is dominated by interaction of a particular kind:

"The area in question is that public space between the state and individual citizens (or household). Civil society is further distinguished by the fact that activities contained therein take an organised and collective form. When we speak of civil society, it is to groups arranged in social networks of a reasonably fixed and routinised character that we refer to."[34]

Issues that have been central in debates concerning civil society – its broad role, its internal democracy, its relation with the state and participation in the political process – also inform discussions on civil society organisations in Mauritius. While it is true that the opposition usually refers to political parties which contest and challenge the views of government, especially when they feel that the latter is not acting in the best interests of the public, there are other institutions which can act as an opposition force and be somewhat of a watchdog. These institutions include civil society, the media and trade unions. The latter two are sometimes considered to be part of the broader society, but because of their own peculiarities and distinct nature, and also because civil society in Mauritius has generally been restricted to the NGO world, the media and trade unions are often treated separately.

Carroll and Carroll, in an article on civic networks in Mauritius, argue that 'most of the Mauritian groups that participate in the civic network are led by members of the middle class, but few have leaders who come from working class backgrounds'. For Carroll and Carroll, the civic network is 'the consultation between government and this broad civil society in the form of an open but organised network'. They argue that successful interaction between government and civil society (and the success of civil society in Mauritius) depends on five factors, one of which is that 'groups must be sufficiently independent of government [so] that the public will view the process of interaction as legitimate'.[35] However, civil society groups are not independent, nor do they have much capacity to influence and shape the policies of the country.

According to records at the Registry of Associations in Port Louis, 519 organisations had already been officially registered by the time Mauritius gained independence in 1968. Miles goes on to add that given the great numbers of NGOs in Mauritius, 'one is tempted to characterise Mauritius as a "supercivil society"'.[36] But what strength does this supercivil society have? Does it make its voice heard on key issues, or is it tantamount to certain socio-economic groups defending their immediate interests and concerns? Many of the NGOs are grouped under an umbrella association called the Mauritius Council of Social Services, which is affiliated to the Ministry of Social Security and is dependent on the state for funding.

Commenting on Mauritian civil society, Bunwaree notes that it remains fractured, dependent on the state and has no advocacy or lobbying culture.[37] The weakness of Mauritian civil society has been put forward as a principal reason to explain the country's inability to complete the African Peer Review Mechanism (APRM) exercise in time. Mauritius, together with Rwanda, Kenya and Ghana, signed up for the APRM in 2003. The other countries completed the process within a few years but Mauritius, which projects itself as a model of democracy, has taken more than six years to produce its APRM report. Which was completed in the first half of 2010.

Trade unions and political parties

The trade union movement played a very important role in post-war labour relations. Members of the Labour Party criticised the various forms of oppression and injustices that the population was subject to. They campaigned intensively for the introduction of social legislation and changes in the franchise to include workers' representation in the colonial executive council. The refusal of the white sugar plantocracy to entertain these demands led to a labour strike in August 1937 in the districts of Flacq and Grand Port, where five workers were shot dead.[38] The government was then compelled to revise labour conditions and to set up a commission of inquiry. The commission condemned the abuses of the sugar planters and supported the setting up of a labour department as well as legislation on trade unions. In short, the Labour Party sought political reforms, broader representation in the Council of Government and better laws.

The rise of the MMM and the powerful support base of the unions

As mentioned earlier, the MMM gathered increasing support in the early 1970s and even won a by-election for a vacated seat in Ramgoolam's home constituency of Triolet. The MMM candidate won 70 per cent of the votes. Very quickly, the leader of the MMM changed the party's discourse from a revolutionary one to one guided by moderation. He acknowledged that a revolution was not possible and that it was necessary to embrace the country's progressive and democratic elements.

In the 1970s, the Labour Party started experiencing a sense of discomfort with the rising popularity of the MMM and reacted immediately to the victory of the MMM in the by-election. The government amended the Constitution to delay the next general elections, moving the elections from 1972 to 1976, and to abolish by-elections. At the end of 1971, the government also declared a state of emergency, arresting many union and MMM leaders without charges, closing down Le Militant, the MMM's newspaper, and banning most union and political activity. Ramgoolam described the emergency powers as: 'armouries of a democratic government, and they must be there to be resorted to swiftly and without delay when required. They are not intended against the people, but against those who are out to uproot our liberal institutions, for which all Mauritians have struggled over the years'.[39] Ramgoolam used the argument that the MMM were communists using subversive action to bring dictatorship and chaos to the country. Meanwhile, the MMM had realised that Mauritians were not generally inclined towards revolution and that the route to power lay in electoral politics.

At the time of its conception, the MMM attempted to modify political thinking from a communal one, to a class one: class politics was elevated over ethnic politics and the slogan – 'One people, one nation, unity in diversity' – referred to earlier attracted much support and contributed to the landslide victory of the MMM in 1982. To give credence to its class politics, the MMM focused its energies on building and developing a power base with the trade unions; dockers and sugar and transport workers rallied in great numbers around the radicalism of the left-leaning MMM party. From September to December 1971, Mauritius was hit by MMM-supported strikes in several major economic sectors: transport, sugar, docks, public service and electricity. The strikes were very disruptive and led to various kinds of economic and social problems, including mounting violence in the country.

Before the 1982 election, the MMM went into an alliance with Boodhoo's PSM in order to ensure the support of the rural Hindus. During the campaigning period, the Labour Party was taken to task for high levels of corruption, nepotism and mismanagement of public funds. In large rallies throughout the country, the MMM-PSM alliance accused the Labour Party of having favoured and supported the white sugar plantocracy. Promises were made to redesign the tax system, and to re-examine wealth distribution and make it more equitable.

Although trade unions played a critical role in the early development of the two-party dominant political parties of Mauritius, trade unions no longer have the same influence. But now that the country is facing a number of important economic challenges and sustaining livelihoods is becoming increasingly difficult, trade unions may begin to organise better and impact more effectively on political thinking and policy-making.

Trade unions in contemporary Mauritius

The history of both the MMM and the Labour Party has been largely infused by trade union activities, but unions' links with political parties have been greatly reduced. Their power is largely eroded and the domain that they mostly engage in is centralised wage bargaining. Mauritius is often cited as a country where tripartite negotiations work rather well. Negotiations take place among government, trade unions and the business sector and, for many years now, the main area of these negotiations is the indexing of salaries/wages to the cost of living and compensation for workers. On most occasions, some kind of consensus is reached. There is an increasing level of debate about the need to index salary increases to productivity, but this has not been implemented.

The relatively low rate of unionisation during the 1980s and 1990s can perhaps be explained by the fact that work conditions had substantially improved by the 1980s and the diversification of the economy had made it possible for people to enter emerging work sectors, some of which did not encourage union membership.

Trade unions in modern Mauritius do not have the right to strike. Unions resent the fact that their most basic right of withdrawing labour is trampled upon and have not stopped demanding a revision of the Industrial Relations Act of 1975. This Act was passed in response to the wildcat strikes which paralysed the economy in the late 1960s and early 1970s. When political parties are in opposition, they often promise that they will review and revise the legislation, but once in power they conveniently forget about it. For Cuttaree, chairman of the select committee that was instituted in 1982 to revisit the Industrial Relations Act, this Act is 'based on fundamentally anti-democratic options' and was a 'piece of repressive legislation'.[40]

Although trade unions no longer have the same links with political parties as in earlier periods, they still play a relatively important role in trying to contain the vulnerabilities that some workers experience. The biggest employer in Mauritius is the civil service, currently employing some 100 000 people, representing 10 per cent of the labour force. Each time attempts are made to create a leaner civil service by retrenching workers, the unions have acted vociferously and have prevented this from happening. Unions have also prevented the privatisation of certain sectors and the loss of jobs that this may entail, but they do not have much influence on macro-economic policy-making and on the resulting labour dynamics. What is more worrying is that there are no trade unions defending the rights of workers in the informal sector, which is becoming a major absorber of labour.

Table 2 shows the trade union density rate between 1981 and 1996. Data for more recent years is not available but it is common knowledge that the union density rate has been falling continuously over time. It revolves around 20 per cent at the moment.

Table 2: Trade union density rate and industrial stoppages in Mauritius, 1981--1996

Year	Union membership	Unionisation rate (%)	Year	Total man-days lost in 1000s
1981	70 478	20.9	1987-1988	16.5
1983	83 202	23.0	1988-1989	22.2
1986	102 317	24.0	1989-1990	5.4
1989	113 160	28.9	1990-1991	0.3
1992	104 311	32.2	1991-1992	1.8
1994	107 659	22.5	1992-1993	4.1
1996	108 106	21.8	1993-1994	1.4
			1994-1995	2.7

Note: Values for 1981-86 and 1989-96 are from different sources and may therefore not be completely consistent with each other.
Sources:
  Ministry of Labour and Industrial Relations, 1988 for union membership and unionisation rate for 1981-1986. MEF Annual Report 1997 for union membership and unionisation rate for other years. Ministry of Labour and Industrial Relations, 1998, unpublished data for industrial stoppage data.

Table 2 shows the trade union density rate between 1981 and 1996. Data for more recent years is not available but it is common knowledge that the union density rate has been falling continuously over time. It revolves around 20 per cent at the moment.

The role of the media and the recent liberalisation of the airwaves

Both the print media and the recently liberalised airwaves contribute to debates and dialogues on key societal issues. The print media is a powerful institution in Mauritus, with four dailies and about ten weeklies. Newspaper circulation is in a ratio of about 74 per 1 000 inhabitants. The two main dailies, Le Mauricien and L'Express, are very powerful opinion shapers and also have the potential to act as watchdogs on various aspects of Mauritian society. This is due to their perceived independence and high degree of professionalism, yet sometimes they are influenced by their own ideological biases, particularly that of the middle class and the coloured community. The media is often seen as being 'too dominated by the light-coloured Creole group who have their own complexes and can even be racist'.[41]

Despite such biases, it can be safely argued that Mauritian media has, over the years, played a very important watchdog role on issues of pertinence to Mauritian society. It has contributed to denouncing major scandals such as the Mauritius Commercial Bank/National Pension Fund scandal,[42] the Amsterdam drug affair,[43] and the Air Mauritius scandals,[44] to name but a few.

The liberalisation of the airwaves has in more ways than one provided a space for a plurality of voices. But despite the fact that there is greater potential for alternative views and analyses, during electoral campaigns incumbents tend to abuse the airspace for their own ends, leaving little possibility that opposition groups (especially the smaller and weaker parties) might make their voices heard. There is no official provision made by state-owned media for coverage of political party campaigns, but it is common practice that all political parties are granted some air time for their campaigns during the pre-electoral period. The only difference is that the incumbent government often abuses its power in accessing much more time on state-owned media than its rivals can.

The media do, however, contribute to providing some kind of checks and balances. The fact that they uncover a number of dark issues related to law and order, corruption and the protection of human rights means that the media have a major role in promoting and consolidating democracy in Mauritius.

Conclusion

The findings of this chapter confirm the view of a United Nations Economic Commissionfor Africa expert panel survey undertaken in 2002, which states that the influence of the parliamentary opposition remains weak in Mauritius.[45] Unless genuine efforts are made to review and revisit the electoral system, the funding of political parties and voter education, democracy in Mauritius will continue to suffer from relatively weak opposition.

Hopes were raised when South African Constitutional Court Justice Albie Sachs was invited to advise on the need for reform, but little has happened since. The government set up a parliamentary committee comprising parliamentarians from both the ruling parties and the opposition to examine the commission's report and recommendations to introduce a measure of PR into the electoral system, but the 'select committee appears, however, not to be in agreement and the proposed reforms have been delayed'. [46] More recently, the Institute of Social Development and Peace, in collaboration with EISA and the Institute for Democracy and Electoral Assistance, organised a workshop on the theme 'Moving towards an inclusive democracy – Electoral reforms in Mauritius' in an attempt to reopen the debate around the question; but once more the debate has not been sustained.

Mauritius therefore continues to live with two major deficits: an electoral system which often results in a very weak opposition; and the under-representation of women in parliament. It is clear from the above that the opposition, which is supposed to be the bearer of hopes and aspirations of the population, does not play its role adequately. Democracies are never static, but are constantly in a state of flux. For a political party to remain relevant it has to be prepared to shift with the attitudes of the population. The shift is not necessarily an ideological or policy one, but a shift in the way that political parties engage with issues that affect the micro-realities of the citizens of the country. The major problem in contemporary Mauritius is that there seems to be no room for a new political party to emerge and yet the country badly needs new blood and new ideas.

Mauritius has been referred to as a mature democracy and a model for the rest of Africa, but one is tempted to ask what sort of model it can be if opposition parties, which are the essence of modern and well functioning democracies, remain small, weak and inadequate. Moreover, Mauritius does not have any term limits regarding the mandates of parliamentarians, there is very little direct engagement of civil society with parliament, and most political debates are carried out in English or French, which remain a barrier to large segments of the population. Civil servants and intellectuals can vote, but do not have the right to stand for election unless they resign from their posts. Interestingly, the current prime minister speaks of Mauritius as not needing to promote democracy. In an interview with the Financial Times in 2006, Navin Ramgoolam notes:

> "Mauritius is paying the price of its success ... Here is a paradox. We are saying, Europe is saying and other countries are saying, we have to write off debt of poor indebted countries and we have to promote democracy, you have to promote good governance and all of this. You don't have to promote democracy in Mauritius – it already exists. We have good governance, we have institutions ... we have not gone with a begging bowl all over the place. We have used the advantages that we have ... and now we are going to be – I don't know whether I can use the word 'punished' but punished for our success."

To think that there is no need to promote democracy implies a very restrictive view of democracy. While it is true that Mauritius has a number of achievements to its record, numerous democratic deficits persist. And unless there is a habitus – a predisposition of the mind, to borrow a term from the French sociologist Pierre Bourdieu – to understand that democracy and democratisation are unfinished agendas, there is a risk that development itself is threatened. Democracy is about the participation and empowerment of the people as well as the creation of space for alternative voices and views. These are essential ingredients for the deepening of democracy and making governance more meaningful.

ENDNOTES

1   Dahl R 1971. Polyarchy: Participation and Opposition. New Haven: Yale University Press.
2   Van Walle N 2002. 'Elections without democracy: Africa's range of regimes'. Journal of Democracy 13(2), pp66-80
3   The term 'donne ene lecon' refers referred to by various respondents to explain that Mauritians do not tolerate the wrong doings of any government and they sanction the latter by voting en masse for the adversarial bloc if and when they feel that the incumbent government does not deliver.
4   Mathur H 1991. Parliament in Mauritius. Rose-Hill, Mauritius: Edtions de l'Ocean Indien.
5   Reynolds A and Reilly B 1997. The International IDEA Handbook of Electoral Systems Design. Stockholm: International IDEA.
6   Bunwaree S and Yoon M 2006. 'Women and the Mauritian Legislature: A grave democratic deficit". Journal of Contermporary African Studies 24(2).
7   Constitution of Mauritius, Section 5(3). Port-Louis, Mauritius.
8   Ibid.
9   Mathur H. Op.cit
10 Bibi JC 2006. 'The Best Loser System – Rights of Citizens and the Ethno Religious Logic'. Paper presented at the Institute of Social Development and Peace conference on 'Electoral Reform – Moving towards an Inclusive Democracy'. Port Louis, Mauritius, 17-18 February.
11 Lallah R 2006. 'The Best Loser System – Transformation of Democratic Political Votes into Communal Ones'. Paper presented at the Institute of Social Development and Peace conference on 'Electoral Reform – Moving towards an Inclusive Democracy'. Port Louis, Mauritius, 17-18 February.

12 Mohamed Y 2006. 'The Best Loser System – Protecting Minority Rights'. Paper presented at the Institute of Social Development and Peace conference on 'Electoral Reform – Moving towards an Inclusive Democracy'. Port Louis, Mauritius, 17-18 February.
13 Bunwaree S 2006. 'Elections, gender and governance in Mauritius'. Journal of Elections 5(1).
14 Sachs et al 2001/01. 'Report of the Commission on Constitutional and Electoral Reform'. Prime Minister's Office, Port Louis, Mauritius. Available at http://www.gov.mu
15 Kadima D and Kasenally R 2005. 'The formation, collapse and revival of political party coalitions in Mauritius', in Kadima D (ed.). The Politics of Party Coalitions in Africa. Johannesburg: EISA.
16 Bunwaree S 2005. 'The ballot box and social policy in Mauritius'. Paper presented for the social policy and democratisation project of UNRISD, Geneva.
17 Interview with respondent.
18 Interview with respondent
19 Interview with respondent
20 Interview with respondent
21 Darga LA 2005. Strengthening Parliamentary Democracy in SADC Countries: Mauritius country report. Johannesburg: SAIIA.
22 Interview with respondent
23 Bunwaree S 1994. Mauritian Education in a Global Economy. Rose-Hill, Mauritius: Editions de l'Ocean Indien.
24 Lehembre B 1984. L'ile Maurice. Paris: Karthala.
25 Bunwaree S 2006. Op. cit.
26 Bunwaree S and Kasenally R 2005. Political Parties and Democracy in Mauritius. Johannesburg: EISA.
27 Darga LA 2005. Op. cit.
28 Interview with respondent.
30 Carroll B and Carroll T 1999. 'The consolidation of democracy'. Democratization 6(1), pp179-197.
31 Interview with respondent.

32 Bunwaree S and Yoon M 2006. Op.cit.
33 Keane J 1998. Democracy and Civil Society. London: Verso.
34 Haddenius A and Uggla F 1996. 'Making civil society work, promoting democratic development: What states and donors can do'. World Development 24(10).
35 Carrol B and Carroll T 1999. 'Civil networks, legitimacy and the policy process'. Democratization 12(1).
36 Bunwaree S and Yoon M 2006. 'Women and the Mauritian Legislature: A gravedemocratic deficit". Journal of Contermporary African Studies 24(2).
37 Bunwaree S 2006. 'The Role of Civil Society in the APRM Process'. Paper presented at the Banjul meeting on the APRM, June 2006.
38 Mannick AR 1979. The Development of a Plural Society. Nottingham: Russell PressLtd.
39 Ramgoolam S 1973. Extracts from Council Debates. No 18 of 1973, pp1301-1309.
40 Cuttaree J 1982. Extracts from Council Debates. No 16 of 1982, pp1205-1220.
41 Interview with respondent.
42 Large sums of money were embezzled by certain people from the National Pension Fund, implicating some top executives of the Mauritius Commercial Bank.
43 The Amsterdam Drug Affair refers to the arrest of four Mauritian male MPs who were found in possession of hard drugs at Amsterdam airport while travelling on diplomatic passports.
44 The embezzled money that constituted the 'black funds', free tickets and various other perks totalling hundreds of millions of rupees, distributed to political parties and other people over two decades, represents the core component of the Air Mauritius scandal.
45 IUNECA Expert Panel Study on Governance in Mauritius 2003. UNECA: Addis Ababa.
46 Darga LA 2005. Op.cit.

CHAPTER FIVE
MOZAMBIQUE FROM CIVIL WAR TO LOYAL OPPOSITION:
FIVEJOÃO C.G. PEREIRA, SANDRA MANUEL AND CARLOS SHENGA

Introduction

From 1977 to 1992 Mozambique suffered under a devastating civil war and an authoritarian regime. FRELIMO (Front for the Liberation of Mozambique) was in power and RENAMO (the Mozambican National Resistance Movement) was in the opposition. RENAMO was a movement created by then-Rhodesia (1976-1980) and later supported by South Africa's apartheid white minority government (1980-1990), out of fear that the Marxist regime in newly independent Mozambique (under FRELIMO) would support the guerrillas fighting to overthrow the Rhodesian and apartheid regimes.[1]

The prerequisite for democratic elections in Mozambique was an end to the civil war and a change of the political system. From 1986 to 1992 the Mozambican government led by Joaquim Chissano slowly introduced political reforms aimed at transforming socialist Mozambique into a more pluralistic society. Those efforts culminated in the enactment of a new Constitution in November 1990 which provided for a multiparty political system with regular, presidential and parliamentary elections and a market-based economy.

The 1990 Constitution created basic rights: freedom of association, expression and the formation of political parties. Article 77 of the 1990 Constitution states that all citizens shall have the freedom to form and participate in political parties; and that party membership shall be voluntary and shall derive from the freedom of citizens to associate on the basis of holding the same political ideas.

Following the end of the civil war and the enactment of a peace agreement and constitutional guarantees for a multiparty political system, political activity increased and the number of political parties in the country soared.[2] From 1990 to the third general elections held in December 2004, 42 political parties were registered in Mozambique. The first to be registered – on 19 August 1991 – was FRELIMO, which had ruled the country for 28 years. RENAMO, the former rebel movement, was registered on 22 August 1994 – the year of the first multiparty general election – when 16 other parties were registered. Before the general election of 1999 eight more parties were formed.

In Mozambique, political parties are grouped into different categories. Using some of the political party typology developed by De Brito,[3] Sitoe et al[4] political parties in Mozambique are grouped into five categories[5] based on their leaders' socio-economic and political trajectories. The first group are those organisations whose leadership comprise of former FRELIMO members. This group includes the Liberal and Democratic Party (PALMO), established by former FRELIMO students trained in eastern European countries; the Social Liberal and Democratic Party (SOL), formed after a split in PALMO; the National Democratic Party (PANADE), set up by a former FRELIMO member jailed in the early 1980s on charges of spying for the CIA; and the Democratic Party of Mozambique (PADEMO), formed on the initiative of a Foreign Ministry cadre and former guerrilla soldier in FRELIMO's armed struggle.

The second group consists of two parties led by political figures from the opposition to the colonial regime who did not join FRELIMO at independence and instead spent many years in exile in Portugal. They are the United Front of Mozambique (FUMO), led by Domingos Arouca, and the Mozambican National Democratic Movement (MONAMO), headed by Maximo Dias. Both political leaders are trained lawyers.

A third group of parties has emerged from the mobilisation of young people educated at Mozambican universities following independence. These include the National Convention Party (PCN) and the Patriotic Action Front (FAP). A fourth is a group of parties with origins in the long-standing communities of Mozambican emigrants in East African countries such as Kenya. This group includes, among others, the Democratic Liberal Party (PADELIMO) and the Mozambican People's Progress Party (PPPM). The final entity is a party led by political figures who were formerly part of RENAMO but who left the party because of internal problems. The Party for Peace, Democracy and Development (PDD) is led by Raul Domingos, a peace negotiator and former top member of RENAMO.

Coalition formation

By the time of the run-up to the first multiparty elections in 1994, leaders of some of the so-called small political parties had realised that the existence of a minimum electoral threshold of five per cent of the national vote in parliamentary elections for a political party to gain representation in the National Assembly would make it difficult for them to get into parliament. They therefore entered into pre-election coalitions. Since then the country has seen the formation of about a dozen political party coalitions, nearly all of which cease to function between elections.[6]

In the 1994 election, two electoral coalitions were formed:

- the Patriotic Alliance (AP), comprising MONAMO and the FAP; and
- the União Democrática – Democratic Union (UD), comprising three parties advocating a federalist system of government – PALMO, PANADE and Mozambique National Party (PANAMO).

In the second general elections in 1999, the political arena in Mozambique presented the following coalitions:
- the RENAMO-Electoral Union (EU), comprising 11 political parties: RENAMO, PPPM, Democratic Renewal Party (PRD), FAP, Independent Alliance Party (Alimo), National United Party (PUN), PCN, MONAMO/Social Democratic Party (PMSD), United Democratic Front (UDF), FUMO/Democratic Convergence Party (PCD) and Mozambique National Union (UNAMO);[7]
- the UD coalition, which by then was reduced to two parties following PALMO's defection;
- the Mozambican Opposition Union (UMO) comprising Mozambique Democratic Party (PADEMO) and Democratic Reconciliation Party of Mozambique (PRDM).

The number of party coalitions increased further ahead of the 2004 general elections:
- the RENAMO-EU, based on 11 political parties - RENAMO, PPPM, PRD, FAP, ALIMO, PUN, PCN, MONAMO/PMSD, UDF, FUMO/PCD and UNAMO.
- the Union for the Salvation of Mozambique (USAMO), comprising the Democratic Alliance for Social Restoration (PAREDE), the Socialist Party of Mozambique (PSM), and Union Changes (UM);
- the United Front for Change and Good Governance comprising the Mozambique National Union (UNAMO) and Party of All Mozambican Nationalists;
- the Broad Opposition Front (FAO), comprising the Liberal Front (FL) and African Conservative Party (PAC).

Of the many coalitions created since 1994, only RENAMO-EU has managed to survive. According to Kadima et al[8] several reasons explain RENAMO-EU's ability to remain intact after seven years in opposition politics. First, the parliamentary representation of the opposition has been enhanced by leaders of the small parties finding a place in parliament and by the fact that the RENAMO leadership saw the need to reach an agreement with leaders of the small parties in order to avoid dispersing votes and to enhance Dhlakama's chances of winning the presidential election. Second, the RENAMO-EU coalition gives the leaders of the coalition partner parties financial security and provides some funds for their parties. Although the affiliated parties have complained that their share is too small, these funds would not have been accessible to them had they not entered into a coalition with RENAMO.

The third reason is that the coalition allows RENAMO to be perceived as an open party which accepts and is accepted by others. The RENAMO leader has been prepared to compromise by accepting the sacrifice of sharing parliamentary seats, often at the expense of the party's own members. Finally, the RENAMO-EU coalition has survived because Dhlakama's leadership has never been disputed. (Despite the combined 13 per cent of the total valid votes in 1994, which would have secured the smaller parties a considerable number of seats had they been in a coalition, their leaders were unable to agree on who should lead a coalition.)

However, several factors pose challenges to RENAMO-EU's continued survival. These include the lack of internal democracy within the coalition, inadequate organisational capacity, resistance among RENAMO members to the coalition itself, in-fighting over resources, and discontent about the selection of parliamentary candidates and appointments to positions such as the National Electoral Commission (CNE).

Social base of opposition parties

Lipset et al[9] argue that cleavage structures determine the number of political parties in a given polity. For Lipset et al, social divisions that emerged decades earlier left a significant mark on European nation-states, and these traditional cleavages had powerful effects on the creation of political parties. Political parties are thus seen as products of cleavage lines generated by the effects of the great 'revolutions' which took place during the processes of state- and nation-building. The authors distinguish among four basic sets of cleavages that underlie the party systems of Western countries, namely:
- subject vs dominant cultures;
- church(es) vs state;
- primary vs secondary economies; and
- workers vs employers.[10]

In Europe, the most common cleavages among those presented by Lipset et al[11] centre on class, religion, regionalism, urbanisation, church-state, and centre-periphery (dominant and subject culture) divisions.

The introduction of multiparty competition in Mozambique has led to the establishment of a plethora of political parties and political organisations, all clamouring to represent the interests of significant social groups. Which social groups do the various opposition parties in Mozambique actually represent?

RENAMO

RENAMO was able to draw upon strong internal dissatisfaction with in FRELIMO to garner some support among local populations. In other words, the social base of RENAMO lay in a level of discontent provoked by the policies of the post-independence government which the population regarded as inappropriate to their socio-cultural universe. However, its base also lay in socio-political and ethnic animosities, either historic ones or those that emerged under colonisation and were sharpened during the national liberation struggle and in the structuring of the independent Mozambique state.

Generally, RENAMO's support has come from peasants and traditional chiefs who were the most affected by FRELIMO's socialist project. As a party-state, FRELIMO served its own cadres and those who in some way had close links with the state, rather than the mass of peasants who faced additional difficulties due to the war, particularly from the early 1980s.[12] RENAMO's support base is predominantly in the rural areas, whereas FRELIMO enjoys majority support in most of the urban areas.[13] However, RENAMO considers its traditional support base in the rural areas to be seriously threatened by the FRELIMO government's recent efforts to provide some form of legitimacy to traditional chiefs.

The core of RENAMO's ideology in its dealings with the peasants was expressed in a religious idiom rooted in traditional African ancestor worship. The central political propaganda refrain of the RENAMO military commanders in the field was that the war they were waging was a 'war of the spirits' – a crusade – in which FRELIMO was painted as a traitorous organisation which forced people to abandon their ancestors and accept foreign 'communist' ideas, whereas RENAMO was allied to ancestral spirits who wanted to return Mozambique to its traditions and ancestral ways. This neo-traditional religious discourse permeated all aspects of social and military life in RENAMO-held areas. RENAMO became an outspoken defender of traditional rules and leadership, of religious beliefs and of (especially non-southern) rural communities. In other words, RENAMO sought to be seen as a protector of all those who had been penalised or marginalised under FRELIMO's rule.[14]

In addition, RENAMO has successfully managed to get support from the Islamic elite and other groups from the central and northern parts of the country, particularly among the Ndaw, Sena and Makwa ethnic groups. RENAMO's initial tribal base was among the Ndaw and it still enjoys strong support through the middle belt/ central region of the country. The first president of RENAMO, André Matshagaissa, the recent president of RENAMO (Afonso Dhlakama) and most of its senior represent- atives are Ndaw, Sena or Makwa. In summary, RENAMO draws its political support from those who consider themselves marginalised and excluded from the centres of power, and who are associated with Maputo city and the southern areas of the country.[15]

The other opposition parties

Instead of reflecting or articulating the interests of social groups, 'the emerging party system appears to be reflecting the fault lines, fissures and fads among political elites'. Using Bratton et al's argument, many of these political parties are vehicles to promote personal bids for power.[16] An examination of their actual strategies (as opposed to their rhetoric) reveals that the goals pursued by party leaders vary widely – from grabbing a few crumbs of the 'national pie' to gaining a role in the everyday operation of government.

Social actors in Mozambique do not understand what those who compete in elections are promising to their voters, or what economic and social interests they represent. As one peasant in Dondo (Sofala Province) stated:

"When these opposition parties came here during the elections we did not know what they would do for us. They did not tell us how they were going to build hospitals, schools and companies. They all speak the same language, they say they are going to increase our standards of living; but when we look at them they are like us. They are poor and without anything to offer us. All they want is to share the cake with FRELIMO. We know that all the political parties, including FRELIMO, want power to make their families rich and us poor… ."[17]

Another peasant in Nhamatanda (Sofala province) explained how he sees the opposition parties in Mozambique:

"We do not know where all these opposition parties come from … who created them … why there are many political parties which talk in the name of the people, while they are a group of friends and relatives. What all these parties want is money which is available during election time. When the elections come we see their leaders driving nice cars and talking in the name of the people – the people they talk about are only from Maputo, not from all Mozambique. It is in Maputo where most of these opposition parties have their headquarters. They do not visit Nhamatanda, Mafambisse, Beira or Chimoio after elections. They stay in Maputo and talk in the name of Mozambicans. Maputo is not Mozambique. Mozambique is a country with ten provinces …."[18]

As in many other African countries, the Mozambican party system is faced with a rise of what scholars term 'catch-all' parties. The defining characteristic of instant, catch-all parties is that they try to appeal to all of the people, at all times using:

- a drastic reduction of the party's ideological baggage;
- a strengthening of top leadership groups;
- a downgrading of the role of the individual party member;
- a de-emphasis of specific denominational clientele in favour of the recruitment of voters among the population at large; and
- access to a variety of interest groups to secure electoral support via interest group intercession.

Owing to their fundamental non-committal nature as parties, catch-all parties retain much flexibility in terms of what actual policies they choose to campaign on, what policies they adopt once in power, and leeway in deciding precisely how to develop, as parties, in the future.

Hierarchical structure and leadership and succession

Parties require organisational capacity in order to perform their duties, and party organisations engage in a variety of activities. These include conducting election campaigns, maintaining contact between leaders and activists between elections, and mobilising public support on various issues. All these activities require financial, human and organisational resources. Organisationally, most political parties in Africa have a caucus (branches/cells/militia) spread across regions.[19] Do opposition political parties in Mozambique have well-developed party structures, and how good or bad are these structures at different levels?

RENAMO

RENAMO maintains an effective organisation that was built over two decades of civil war and that is now proving its relative efficacy in a multiparty context. In fact, RENAMO's organisational set-up has remained largely unchanged, both at national and local levels. Representatives can be found in remote places and to some extent receive communications through a hierarchy. According to Carbone,[20] RENAMO branches on the ground are often little more than a flag on a member's house. Nevertheless, the party has long benefited from networks of support and, in particular, from the sympathetic role of the many traditional leaders who have supported it.[21] This has allowed the party to expand its support by keeping in touch with the population in spite of FRELIMO's more efficient organisational structures.

Although featuring some organisational structure, RENAMO – like many political parties in Africa – has always worked in a top-down fashion and has retained the highly personalised, centralised and hierarchical structure inherited from the guerrilla war. Upon changing from a liberation movement to a political party in 1994, RENAMO was disorganised, the roles of officials were not clear, and even small decisions were taken by Dhlakama. Even with the changes that came out from the Congress, the re-structuring of the party was marred by confusion and an over-concentration of power and, once again, the personal whims of the party leader overruled formal regulations.[22]

Dhlakama himself still embodies the core of the party; he is the unifying centre of a network of different groups which hardly communicate with each other: groups such as the resistance fighters who were in the bush (including the likes of Vicente Ululu, Jose de Castro and, until recently, Raul Domingos); those from the cities who had either been clandestinely active until 1992 or joined the party at that time; the former expatriates, also known as the Lisbon group, who supported the guerrillas from abroad; and the demobilised soldiers, as well as those who joined the new Mozambican army and who still see RENAMO as their political referent. This sense of 'personal party' is shared by members of civil society. As one member of a Mozambican non-governmental organisation (NGO) commented:

> "The leader of the main opposition party rules his party in a non-democratic manner. Who can guarantee us that if he gets to power he will change his ways? And it is amazing the fact that opposition parties simply do not communicate with [civil society organisations] CSOs..."[23]

The other political parties

The other political parties have reasonably coherent structures on paper, but not on the ground. The only parties that have relatively sound national and local structures in the field and can boast representatives in some remote places are the PDD and Mozambique Independent Party (PIMO). For a nascent political organisation, the PDD looked well financed and well organised during the 2004 elections.

As is the case with many small opposition parties throughout Africa, the other opposition parties in Mozambique are top heavy and dominated by a few individual party elites. Strong individual personalities, usually termed 'founding fathers', who invariably treat the parties as personal fiefdoms have dominated the political party process. Decisions are made at the top, to be executed without question by the lower echelons of the party. According to Patel[24] the top-heavy approach of the party can be linked to the common notion that power is associated with the executive branch of government and not with the legislature. If the legislature was seen as the organ of the people and therefore the real power house in democracy, then the party structure would also be different and could possibly catalyse a bottom-up approach.

Apart from being heavily dependent on their leaders, the opposition parties have weak internal structures and lack internal democracy, transparency and accountability. These conditions have weakened their capacity for policy formulation, the articulation of broad-based interests, representation and membership mobilisation. If opposition parties in Mozambique hope to survive they need to build internal structures and vibrant branches and must mobilise their members. For a branch to be vibrant it has to offer its members:

- involvement in meaningful local issues and stimulating national debates;
- information and education, which lead to developing an analysis and understanding that members find useful;
- empowerment, which makes members feel that they have developed as human beings;
- entertainment – the branch work must also build members' social lives.
- reward – since most people gain no money or power from being involved, members must be given recognition and social status for their efforts.

Intra-party democracy is a key prerequisite for strengthening political parties as it enables parties to renew their leadership and build communication channels within the party hierarchy. Internal democracy requires a set of impersonal rules and procedures to avoid the arbitrary control of internal elections and party functioning by individuals or cliques. In this way intra-party democracy helps the masses to be heard.

The more the members exercise power the greater the institutionalisation and strength of a democratic party. In most cases, well-drafted party constitutions or regulations are largely ignored in practice, thereby impacting negatively on intra-party democracy. Conventions or national conferences are not held regularly, and positions in the party's highest executive body are held for prolonged periods of time by officials who do not account to anyone in the party except the high command. Most members of political parties in Mozambique therefore have little reason to believe that they have the power to influence party decisions. The party elite sets agendas for them and uses them to serve their ends. As one journalist in Maputo stated:

"Members of any opposition party in Mozambique are like small fish; they do not have the power to decide about anything related to their political parties' policies ... They are there only to follow what their leader wants ..."[25]

Members of the National Reconciliation Party (PARENA) in Maputo noted that they do not have a voice inside the party to decide on the party's policies or agenda:

"We do not have power to decide which direction the party has to go. Few of us have been consulted about our party policy. The party leaders do not organise Congress or consult us regularly. They sit in Maputo and talk in the name of members. Our leaders [have not established a] mechanism that would give us a voice to decide about our party ..."[26]

Intra-party democracy in Mozambique is yet to mean more than something cosmetic; an empty concept devoid of concrete meaning.[27] Internal rules have little relevance to the working of some parties.[28]

Two things were noted about intra-party democracy in Mozambique. First, parties are divided into two factions, supporters and loyalists, and the party presidents only deal with the latter. As a result, those who occupy high positions inside the parties are those who are loyal to the president; and even the few financial resources that the parties might have are filtered to the loyalists, rather than to the supporters or down to the grassroots party structures. The second issue is that intra-party democracy (or the lack thereof) is characterised by high levels of corruption. Members with financial resources and high levels of education are better able to occupy high positions.

The absence of internal democracy also contributes to poor communication inside party structures, whereby members at grassroots level do not know what is happening at national, provincial, district or village level. Members at grassroots level who work hard to keep their political parties alive claim that they are forgotten about except during election campaigns when party leaders send messages regarding the planning for campaigning.

Finances and resources

The availability of appropriate party funding is critical in all democratic countries. Parties need funds to carry out their functions of representation and articulation, which includes running election campaigns, distributing manifestos and campaign messages, placing advertisements in the media, conducting membership mobilisation and organising party structures.

There are two common sources of political party funding: private funding and public or state funding. Private funding of political parties is by far the most widespread form of party financing in the world. Under private funding, finance is derived from membership card sales, individual and corporate donations and fundraising activities. Membership card sales and private donations are the largest source of party funds in established democracies. In Africa, private sources of party funds can be limited due to the high levels of unemployment and low per capita income in many countries. With the collapse of the vast parastatal sector and the massive job losses in the 1990s and early 2000, few Africans are able to make regular contributions to party activities. This has left political parties at the mercy of a few powerful individuals. According to Simutanyi the narrow funding sources of political parties and the potential for them to be 'hijacked'[29] by powerful interests have some people advocating for public funding.

Public funding of political parties involves formal government support for political parties by legislation.[30] Pottie argues that public funding of political parties is intended to enable parties to increase their institutional capacity and to play a role in the democratic process by ensuring fair political competition among the contending political actors. Opposition parties are at a huge disadvantage in countries where the ruling party is dominant and abuses state resources and facilities. This has led to calls for public funding in order to level the playing field.[31]

There are two compelling arguments for public funding of political parties: first, public funding of parties may contribute to the promotion of democracy; and second, public funding promotes a diversity of representation. Those opposed to public funding of political parties argue, among others, that state funding of political parties, especially in the developing world, is not desirable because:
- it would enrich a few opposition party leaders;
- it would lead to the mushrooming of political parties;
- it would undermine initiatives to engage in vigorous fundraising activities;
- funds would not be properly accounted for by opposition party leaders;
- there are many needy areas where public funds could be well spent; and
- politicians are perceived as being corrupt and untrustworthy.

The experience in Africa, particularly in southern Africa, shows that there is a movement towards public funding of political parties. Out of 13 Southern African Development Community (SADC) countries, eight have introduced public funding of political parties legislation, namely: Lesotho, Malawi, Namibia, Mozambique, Seychelles, South Africa, Tanzania and Zimbabwe.

The source of funds for political parties in Mozambique is stipulated in the Political Parties Law No 7/91 of 1991. According to this legislation, political parties can mobilise financial resources through membership, voluntary contributions, the political party's investments, donors (donations), legacies and grants. With regards to state funds, the political system stipulates two types of modalities. The first modalities can be called electoral process funding. This system funds political parties for election campaigning and is done through the National Electoral Commission (CNE). The second can be called the funding of political parties on selective criteria. This system operates when the electoral process is over and only parties with representation in parliament are funded by the state. The process is based in proportion to the number of seats in parliament won by each party.

According to Nuvunga[32] political parties in Mozambique have done very little to develop a culture or mechanism of accountability within party structures and with the state or public. In 1994 three parties were represented in parliament: FRELIMO, RENAMO and the UD. None of these accounted for the funds they had received, nor did any of them publish their accounts. In 1999-2004, the only parties in parliament, FRELIMO and RENAMO-EU, also failed to account for the funds they had received or to publish their accounts as required.[33] The lack of accountability is against the spirit of Political Parties' Law No 7/91: Article 20(2) of that law states that 'the accountability procedures for these amounts ... are identical to those used for public administration' and Article 19(2) states that 'the accounts of the political parties are to be published in the Republic Gazette and in one of the newspapers with highest dissemination in the country'.

With regard to political party funding for election campaigns, Article 35(1) of Law No 7/04 lists the following sources of political party funding:
- contributions from candidates;
- voluntary contributions by Mozambican and foreign sources;
- proceeds from activities related to campaigning (such as selling of electoral materials);
- contributions from national and international friends or parties;
- contributions from national and international NGOs.

Article 35(2) of that law states that 'the state must allocate amounts to fund election campaigns' and Article 35(3) states that 'neither foreign governments and government organisations nor national public institutions and companies may fund political parties'. Article 35(4) provides, however, that 'the entities referred to in Article 35(3) may fund election campaigns through contributions to the general state budget'.

The law also makes clear that it is within the competence of the CNE to approve the criteria for the distribution of public funds for presidential and legislative elections, taking into account that for legislative elections, consideration must be given to the proportional representation (PR) of the parties with seats in the legislature.

RENAMO

The sustainability of RENAMO in terms of financial resources is based mainly on public funding and membership fees, but with greater emphasis on public funding. Senior party members and MPs are also asked by the leader to contribute to the running costs of the party. RENAMO, like most opposition parties in Africa, is hamstrung in its operations by a lack of resources. It is unable to rely on party membership fees as most of its members are poor. Apart from reasons of poverty, it should be noted that the collection of party membership fees has never been done in a consistent way, notably because the party has never had a tradition of a fee-paying membership. Thus, the amount of money raised through these means is insignificant for RENAMO's activities. Commenting on the lack of financial resources raised through membership fees, a RENAMO district delegate in Mafambisse stated:

"... It was very easy for us to mobilise peasants to provide food or water to RENAMO guerrillas. But now it is very difficult to mobilise them to pay fees to RENAMO. Some peasants here are always asking why RENAMO needs money. Others complain that they have already helped RENAMO so much, but they do not see benefits. Our children die of hunger and they cannot go to school because we are poor – how can we pay fees if we are poor ..."?[34]

Other peasants believe that RENAMO should be an agency through which they could get benefits from the state apparatus. For example, a peasant in Dondo said:

"My family and I joined RENAMO because we wanted to get benefits the way FRELIMO members get them. During the war we helped RENAMO with food and we were expecting that when the war was finished we would benefit with something from RENAMO. But it seems that they still want to exploit us, They asked us to contribute money. I will not contribute money until they fulfil their promises to us ..."[35]

Apart from public funding and membership fees, RENAMO has benefited directly and indirectly from overseas support through donations, gifts and grants. These donations and grants are given in cash and in kind; for example, several NGOs have supported RENAMO programmes such as voter education, election monitoring, party seminars and conferences, study visits and technical assistance. Specific organisations that have in one way or another supported RENAMO capacity-building programmes include the Konrad Adenauer Stiftung (KAS) and the Netherlands Institute for Multi-Party Democracy (NIMD). It should be noted that the NIMD works with political parties in Mozambique (ruling and opposition) without discrimination, while KAS works mainly with RENAMO and the Friederich Ebert Stiftung works mainly with FRELIMO.

The other political parties

Political parties not represented in parliament rely financially on a handful of patrons, usually their leaders/founders or various other individuals.[36] They are therefore susceptible to attempts at building personality cults and internal structures of patronage. Many of these political parties are not able to raise funds from membership fees and annual contributions because their members live in poverty. A former member of PCN in Beira said:

"When I was in PCN we tried to collect membership fees, but only a small number of PCN's members could contribute monthly. Because we could not raise a significant amount of money via membership we had to depend on our leaders in Maputo. But in Maputo they also were facing the same situation. As a result our activities were only concentrated in Beira city rather than other districts of the province. Only during election times are we able to contact our grassroots structures ...."[37]

But this financial dependence comes at a price since the individual or group of individuals who are bankrolling a party tend to want to dominate the party. Their domination is often manifested in the general orientation of the party, the formulation of policy and programmes, party elections, the choice of party candidates for elections or even for seminars or workshops, the party's organisational structure and reporting systems, etc. Some members and party leaders tend to resent this situation and feel their scope of activities and responsibilities are at the mercy of the party president or a group.

The other opposition parties have also benefited directly or indirectly from overseas support through donations, gifts and grants. Several NGOs, for example the NIMD, have provided assistance to these political parties in such areas as voter education, election monitoring, leadership workshops, strategic planning, party seminars and conferences, study visits and technical assistance.

The absence of financial grants and a clear vision regarding how to expand party activities and develop better mechanisms to mobilise voters forces some political parties to concentrate their primary activities in Maputo. They are therefore less effective in mobilising public opinion in the rural areas. One opposition leader in Maputo explained the difficulty in reaching rural areas:

"We only have money during the campaign because we receive money to develop our activities. When the campaign is over we do not have money to reach the rural areas; we concentrate our activities in Maputo. We know that by using these approaches we are not going to have seats in parliament but what can we do if we do not have money to develop our activities? People like leaders with money.

When you meet the population, they like you to organise parties and pay for traditional beers. When you do not have money it is hard even to mobilise members of your own political party. This is politics of survival rather than ideas ..."[38]

Financial resources seem to shape the modus operandi of the opposition parties in Mozambique. This view is shared by members of civil society who commented that:

"The opposition parties do not have money to organise themselves and work properly; that is probably a major handicap. However, sometimes they do not strategise well. They should have active and prominent members who are academics, who are able to think of a plan of action that can satisfy people."

Policy differences

Even after a decade of democratic transition, political parties in Africa are primarily personality-based with very weak ideological foundations. It has been argued by some that the end of the Cold War has upheld the liberal democracy model as the sole model applicable for all states. Some African scholars share this opinion, saying that in Africa where the issues and challenges are more or less the same, there is no need for diversity. However, it can be argued that where problems are daunting and options are few, the need for ideology is great.[39]

Opposition parties in Mozambique, as in many African countries, are separated by the diverse trajectories and social origins of their leaders. In fact, analysis of the political programmes of these parties (where they exist) and the public statements of their leaders might suggest that there are few fundamental differences between them, and that the most significant line of political cleavage is between those who defend a unitary state (FRELIMO) and those who advocate the establishment of a federal state (PADEMO, PPPM).

With regards to the establishment of a federal state, De Brito (2003)[40] noted that even on this point, closer observation reveals that the federal proposal put forward by some parties is vague and appears more like a move for the politico-administrative decentralisation of the FRELIMO state, which is dominated by 'southerners', than the expression of a real federalist current of thought. Ten years after the formation of most of the minor parties, these federalist references have disappeared.

The question of decentralisation – as an expression of the desire to put an end to the hegemony of the southerners – is not a concern restricted only to the groups that formed federalist parties. In reality, the entire movement to create new political parties shows the fundamental and historic cleavage between Mozambican elites and the expression of opposition to the hegemony of FRELIMO[41] by a marginalised elite primarily from the country's central and northern provinces[42]. Many of Mozambique's minor parties are thus merely factions whose leaders have been historically excluded from positions of power in the economic and state apparatus and who, motivated by a desire to gain access to power and have 'a piece of the cake' (as described by a leader of one such party), have mobilised politically to contest FRELIMO's power.[43]

According to Barany[44] ethno-regional mobilisation does not occur in a vacuum; it needs a number of prerequisites in order to succeed. These are, in descending order: political opportunity; ethnic identity and its formation; leadership; organisational capacity; ideology, profile and programme; financial resources; communications; and symbols. Opposition parties in Mozambique have not fulfilled these requirements. Their poor insertions into the political scene, low social representation, lack of ideology, profile and programmes, internal divisions and splits, and organisational and financial difficulties have prevented them from mobilising voters based on ethno-regional discourse and have stopped them from competing with the two major parties.

Lack of substantive debate and consensus around policy options also creates confusion as to how policies advocated by different political parties can effectively improve material existence. The elections process in Mozambique can be described as 'elections without policy choice'. Under these circumstances the party system offers electoral accountability but not policy accountability, since the electoral system is capable of getting rid of parties but not of shaping policies in critical areas of government. During elections, voters are probably asking which party is more likely to provide them and their communities with loans, food, agricultural instruments and other needs rather than what policies Party A or Party B is advocating.

Commenting on the lack of policy debate, one political scholar states:
> "It is difficult to argue that policy preferences account for the pattern of polarisation observed in Mozambique: political attitudes within groups are diverse, embracing a wide range of options, and there is little evidence of policy preference polarisation between different groups. Most groups seem to agree that the primary policy of any Mozambican government should be to increase employment opportunities as well as reduce poverty. Political parties also have the same kind of song. All this reduces the power of policy debate ..."[45]

According to Nuvunga[46] most of these political parties can be seen as electoral organisations often headed by a single personality and not able to make a meaningful contribution to the consolidation of democracy. Since there is no policy difference, if the opposition were to win power, the only difference would be that the new group in power would expect to participate in the distribution of official resources and enjoy the fruits of patronage.

Opposition parties' performance

Opposition parties have a critical role to play in the governance process and are a key element in monitoring government performance and mobilising citizens to participate in public life. There are different ways to measure parties' performance. Among the most important indicators of parties' performance in a multiparty democracy are the electoral results that each party obtains during elections.

Eighteen political parties, alone or in coalitions, were registered for the first multiparty National Assembly elections in the history of Mozambique, held on 27 October 1994. Not all of them stood in all the constituencies. Those parties were FRELIMO, RENAMO, FUMO, UNAMO, the Labour Party (PT), Democratic Congress
Party (PACODE), The Independent Party Of Mozambique (PIMO) and the UD coalition (PALMO, PANADE and PANAMO). The Labour Party (PT) of Miguel Mabote, Democratic Renewal Party (PRD) of Manecas Daniel, National Convention Party (PCN) of Lutero Simango, and the UD coalition only stood in the parliamentary

elections and not the presidential election. The parties that presented lists for constituencies were: FRELIMO, RENAMO, AP, UD, SOL, PCN, PPPM, PACODE (all constituencies); and UNAMO, PT, FUMO, PIMO and PADEMO (some constituencies).[47]

Despite the proliferation of political parties, two parties took 82 per cent of the total valid votes for the parliamentary elections: FRELIMO with 44 per cent and RENAMO with 38 per cent – proving the polarisation of Mozambican political life. No other political force obtained a majority of votes in any of the 148 districts that comprise the 11 provinces in Mozambique.[48] Although the PR system established by law does in principle favour the possibility of smaller parties winning parliamentary representation, only the UD broke through the legal threshold of five per cent and it was the second most popular at district level south of the Save River. The establishment of a multiparty National Assembly created a new political elite in Mozambique: 129 seats went to FRELIMO; 112 to RENAMO; and nine to the UD. Table 1 show the percentage of votes won by each party or coalition in the 1994 legislative elections.

Table 1: Percentage of votes won by each party or coalition in the 1994 legislative elections in Mozambique

Party/coalitions	Number of Votes	% of Votes	Number of Seats (250)
FRELIMO	2,115,793	44.33%	129
RENAMO	1,803,506	37.78%	112
UD	245,793	5.15%	09
AP	93,031	1.95%	-
SOL	79,622	1.67%	-
FUMO-PCD	66,527	1.39%	-
PCN	60,635	1.27%	-
PIMO	58,590	1.23%	-
PACODE	52,446	1.10%	-
PPPM	50,793	1.06%	-
PRD	48,030	1.01%	-
PADEMO	36,689	0.77%	-
UNAMO	34,809	0.73%	-
PT	26,961	0.56%	-

Table 2: Percentage of votes won by each party or coalition in the 1999 legislative elections in Mozambique

Party/coalitions	Number of Votes	% of Votes	Number of Seats (250)
FRELIMO	2,005,713	48.54%	133
RENAMO-UE	1,603,811	38.81%	117
PT	111,139	2.69%	-
PALMO	101,970	2.47%	-
SOL	83,440	2.02%	-
UMO	64,117	1.55%	-
UD	61,122	1.48%	-
PADELIMO	33,247	0.80%	-
PIMO	29,456	0.71%	-
PANAOC	24,527	0.59%	-
PPLM	11,628	0.28%	-
PASOMO	2,153	0.05%	-

The second multiparty election in Mozambique in 1999 featured a coalition between the main opposition party, RENAMO, and ten small parties, known as RENAMO-EU. Other coalitions were the UMO and UD. Apart from these coalitions, eight parties also stood for this election: FRELIMO, PT, PALMO, SOL, PADELIMO, PIMO, National Workers and Peasants Party (PANAOC), Progressive Liberal Party of Mozambique (PPLM) and Mozambique Social Broadening Party (PASOMO). However, Mozambique's dominant party, FRELIMO, was again the overall winner, taking most seats in the National Assembly (133). RENAMO-EU won 117 seats, with FRELIMO and RENAMO-EU sharing the nine seats formerly belonging to UD (see Table 2).

In the 2004 elections, RENAMO and other opposition political parties were not able to gain additional seats. RENAMO's performance in fact declined and the party won only 90 seats in the 2004 election (see Table 3).

Table 3: Percentage of votes won by each party or coalition in the 2004 legislative elections in Mozambique

Party/coalitions	Number of Votes	% of Votes	Number of Seats (250)
FRELIMO	1,889,054	62.03%	160
RENAMO-UE	905,289	29.73%	90
PDD	60,758	2.00%	-
PAZS	20,686	0.88%	-
PARENA	18,220	0.60%	-
PIMO	17,960	0.59%	-
PASOMO	15,740	0.52%	-
PT	14,242	0.47%	-
SOL	13,915	0.46%	-
PE-MT	12,985	0.40%	-
MBG	11,059	0.36%	-
UD	10,310	0.34%	-
PVM	9,950	0.33%	-
PALMO	9,263	0.30%	-
PAREDE	9,026	0.30%	-
USAMO	8,661	0.29%	-
FAO	7,591	0.25%	-
PADELIMO	3,720	0.12%	-
CDU	1,252	0.04%	-
PPD	448	0.01%	-

On 28 October 2009, simultaneous polling was held for three elections (presidential, legislative and provincial assembly elections). The legislative elections were contested by the following political parties and coalitions: FRELIMO, RENAMO, Party for Liberty and development (PLD), Party of Freedom and Solidarity (PAZS), Democratic Patriotic Movement (MPD), ECOLOGISTA-MT, PARENA, Mozambique Democratic Movement (MDM), ALIMO, PT, UDM, UM, PDD, Green Party of Mozambique (PVM), PANAOC, PRDS, PPD (parties) and UE, Democratic Alliance of Veterans for Development (ADACD)- (coalitions).FRELIMO saw its legislative majority grow dramatically in the 2009 elections, from 160 (62 per cent of the seats) to 190 seats. Its absolute

majority surpassed the two-thirds majority required to amend the Constitution and enabled it to govern alone and uncompromisingly. The opposition performed poorly in the 2009 elections, decreasing its share from 29.7 per cent to 17.6 per cent of the seats (see Table 4).

Table 4: Percentage of votes won by each party or coalition in the 2009 legislative elections in Mozambique

Political parties and coalition	No of votes	Percentage of total valid votes cast
FRELIMO	2 907 335	75.66 %
RENAMO	688 782	17.6%
MDM	152 836	3.93%
PLD	26 929	0.70%
PDD	22 410	0.58%
PVM	19 577	0.50%
ADACID	17 275	0.44%
PAZS	16 626	0.43%
ALIMO	14 959	0.38%
UE	6 786	0.17%
ECOLOGISTA-MT	5 267	0.14%
PARENA	5 160	0.14%
MPD	2 433	0.06%
UDM	2 190	0.06%
UM	1 641	0.04%
PT	1 239	0.03%
PANAOC	852	0.02%
PPD	712	0.02%
PRDS	399	0.01%

FRELIMO's victory across the country was also confirmed in the provincial assembly elections, an unsurprising fact in light of the large number of districts where the party did not face any opposition at the polls. It won 86.6 per cent of the 807 provincial assembly seats available and acheived overwhelming majorities in all ten assemblies. The seat distribution in the new assemblies for FRELIMO was: Inhambane and Gaza 100 per cent, Niassa 94.2 per cent, Tete and Maputo province 93.7 per cent, Cabo Delgado 90.1 per cent, Nampula 85.7 per cent, Manica 76.2 per cent, Sofala 73.7 per cent and Zambezia 63.3 per cent. The MDM won 20 seats in Sofala (25 per cent) and two seats in Niassa and Nampula each. PDD won two seats (2.2 per cent) in Zambezia. The remaining 82 seats (10.16 per cent) were won by RENAMO[49].

The electoral results illustrated in Tables 3 and 4 reveal the lack of support that many opposition parties face in Mozambique. Some political commentators and journalists suggest that this trend is an indication either that opposition parties (particularly RENAMO) are becoming increasingly fragile, or that FRELIMO is slowly becoming more and more the dominant party in Mozambique. According to Sitoe et al,[50] however, this trend is more indicative of voter apathy among potential opposition voters than real decreased support for RENAMO. FRELIMO may have been more successful in getting its captive electorate to vote, thus creating the impression that RENAMO's electoral base is in decline.

Despite the minimal support for the small parties, their existence cannot be completely ignored. These parties tend to have a 'disturbance effect' on the political system, especially due to the dispersal of votes caused during elections. This dispersal has damaged RENAMO and its presidential candidate, whose image is less well known among the population than FRELIMO's. This was evident in the 1994 presidential elections when there were 12 presidential candidates, and in 1999 when only Afonso Dhlakama and Joaquim Chissano competed.

As already mentioned, electoral law through the five per cent threshold of the national vote effectively prevents the representation of small political groups; however, their participation is facilitated by the fact that Mozambique does not require a monetary deposit recoverable on positive results, which is common in many electoral systems and is used to keep out less serious candidates.[51] Ultimately, the effect of this law in Mozambique is that artificial coalitions are created which contribute little, if anything, to consolidating national political life in the country.

There are numerous possible explanations for the poor performance of opposition parties at the polls. First, opposition parties are relatively new and their activities are focused primarily in the urban areas, whereas the older parties have solid organisational structures in rural areas and enjoy huge support there. Second, there is a lack of strategic vision among the opposition parties in terms of how the country should be ruled. For example, the 1994 and 2004 campaigns centred on personalities,[52] the reconstruction process, ethnicity, regional asymmetries and war, rather than on alternative economic policy. FRELIMO's campaigns have focused on RENAMO's past and the civil war that destroyed most of the country's socio-economic infrastructure. Armando Guebuza and his party have chosen a campaign approach based on promises of community goods, notably in the form of social services. Dhlakama and RENAMO, however, have sought aggressively to use the ethnic factor, regional asymmetries and political freedom to the party's advantage. In Dhlakama's discourse during the 1994 campaign, his rhetoric was much simpler: 'He spoke very rarely of "Mozambican" but rather with ethnic groups as Macua or Muanes, particularly in the central and northern areas of Mozambique. In others words, he called people by their ethnic identity, by what had been barred from the nationalist discourse for years.'[53]

Apart from the ethnic discourse, Dhlakama also reminded the voters about FRELIMO's villagisation programmes, re-education camps, the marginalisation of traditional leaders and the lack of political freedom that existed during the one-party era.[54] In general, Dhlakama adopted a vague populism during elections and pitched RENAMO's campaigns around the party's opposition to the lack of political freedom and general promises of a better future.[55]

A third possible reason for the poor performance of opposition parties at the polls is that all opposition parties speak the same development language. Foremost among the national issues that have formed part of their agendas is the need to develop the economy, eradicate poverty, create jobs, and fight crime and corruption. The parties clearly have difficulty in articulating their overall vision with more practical approaches that could show voters how their personal economic conditions would change if an opposition party were in power.

Fourth, RENAMO has revealed signs of losing direction. It is deeply divided into several factions. From one election to the next, people who played key roles in mobilising support are discarded in favour of new people with no persuasive capacity. Moreover, RENAMO has neither the capacity nor the infrastructure to control its militants; and this certainly seemed to be the case in the 2004 election when the party failed to get its supporters to the polling stations.[56]

Conventional wisdom suggests that the lack of credible alternative governing parties is the main reason for the dismal performance of opposition parties in Mozambique. The parties lack cadres and have poor capacity to organise and evolve internally. In addition there is a great weakness in urban implementation and in mobilising intellectuals to their ranks, contributing to their poor capacity for political analysis and to the dominant, rather unfavourable, image in the urban areas (including among diplomats) that the opposition is highly unpredictable and short on competence.[57] It should be noted that RENAMO (the main opposition party) is dominated by a single charismatic person, Dhlakama, whose mercurial style has inhibited the emergence of a broader-based leadership or a coherent political programme.

Fifth, the opposition parties do not enjoy a level playing field. Publicly funded media organisations and various arms or apparatuses of the state are deployed against the opposition parties and their activists, particularly during election time. And finally, the incumbents reluctantly conceded to a multiparty framework but then proceeded to weaken, obstruct, harass and divide the opposition.[58]

Conclusion

This chapter has attempted to examine the various issues and obstacles facing opposition political parties in Mozambique, including the constitutional provisions for opposition politics, electoral systems, the characteristics of opposition parties, policy options and party performance, support bases and party funding. The results reveal that opposition parties in Mozambique:
- have weak bureaucratic organisation, including unreliable membership data and poor funding bases;
- lack human resources;
- are dominated by informal relations such as patronage and clientelism as well as strong personalities;
- lack intra-party democracy and regular communication within the party hierarchy;
- have a dysfunctional hierarchy;
- have a high degree of factionalism;
- have weak formal links to citizens;
- lack strong ideologies and articulate policies;
- are predominantly based in Maputo; and
- operate in a difficult environment characterised by a high level of poverty and lack of trust from citizens.

If the opposition political parties wish to play a significant role in the democratic process in Mozambique, they need to: build good internal structures and vibrant branches; mobilise members; increase their financial resources by improving the collection of membership fees; formulate better policies; and follow leaders who embrace the ideals and practice of democracy.

ENDNOTES

1   Vines A 1991. RENAMO: Terrorism in Mozambique. York: Centre for African Studies, University of York. See also Vines A 1996. *RENAMO: From terrorism to democracy in Mozambique.* York: Centre for African Studies, University of York.

2   According to Gentili A 2005. 'Party, Party Systems and Democratisation in Sub-Saharan Africa'. Paper presented at the Sixth Global Forum on Reinventing Government, Seoul, Republic of Korea, p11. The number of parties that appeared

with the advent of democratisation in sub-Saharan Africa is not a demonstration of increased participation, but rather of the fragmentation and therefore the weakness of the party systems. Many of the parties which appeared after multipartyism was reinstated are irrelevant, and the introduction of multipartyism has not defeated the single-party culture. Single parties are far from being defeated since many of them, some with different names, were the only ones that had some kind of penetration in society and have been able to maintain relative internal discipline and act as unitary forces to stay in power. Few are the cases in which opposition parties have been able to form coalitions which have become dominant, and in all cases this has been achieved through the personal charisma of a leader, or of a strongly personalised leadership. The fragility of coalitions also often depends on the resources that the leadership can deliver to their ethnic or local constituencies.

3   De Brito L 1996. *Political Actors in the PALOPs Countries*. Maputo: UEM-Texto de Apoio. See also De Brito et al 2003. *Moçambique: 2003-Avaliação do potencial de conflito*. Maputo: CEA.

4   Sitoe E et al 2005. *Parties and Political Development in Mozambique*. EISA Research Report No 22. Johannesburg: EISA.

5   It should be noted that the first four categories used by Sito are the same categories developed by De Brito.

6   Kadima D and Matsimbe Z 2006. 'RENAMO-Electoral Union: Understanding the longevity and challenges of an opposition party coalition in Mozambique', in Kadima D (ed), *The Politics of Party Coalitions in Africa*. Johannesburg: EISA/KAS, p149.

7   According to Kadima D and Matsimbe Z, ibid., p164, after losing the 1994 presidential election to FRELIMO by about 20 per cent, and with small political parties together having received a total of about 13 per cent of the popular vote, RENAMO realised that if it joined forces with these small parties the opposition would stand a better chance of winning the presidential election in 1999. In addition, the success of the joint boycott of the 1998 local government elections by RENAMO and many of these small parties (which had resulted in an unprecedented, low voter turnout of about 15 per cent) confirmed that, arithmetically, RENAMO and these parties could make a difference should they come together in a pre-election coalition. The small parties, for their part, wished to be represented in parliament and were aware that if they continued to contest elections individually or in weak alliances they would not achieve the minimum five per cent threshold and would continue to have wasted their efforts. Moreover, they were conscious that RENAMO needed them more than

FRELIMO did. A pre-election coalition became of paramount importance for both RENAMO and the small parties.

8   Kadima D and Matisimbe Z, op. cit., pp174-175.
9   Lipset MS and Rokkan S 1967. 'Cleavage structures, party system and voter alignment: An introduction', in Lipset MS and Rokkan S (eds). Party Systems and Voter Alignments: *Cross-National Perspectives*. New York: Free Press.
10 Lipset MS and Rokkan S, ibid., suggest that there are three specific connotations to the term 'cleavage'. First, a cleavage involves a social division that separates people by at least one key social characteristic such as occupation, status, religion or ethnicity. Second, groups on either side of a cleavage must be conscious of their collective identity and be willing to act on that basis. And third, a cleavage must have an organisational component that gives formal institutional expression to the interests of those on one side of the division. Also Rokkan S 1970. *Citizens, Elections,* Parties. Oslo: Universitetsforlaget.
11 Lipset MS and Rokkan S, op. cit.
12 De Brito L 1996. 'Voting behaviour in Mozambique's first multiparty elections', in Mazula B (ed), *Mozambique: Elections, Democracy, and Development*. Maputo: Elo Grafico; Pereira J 1997. 'As primeira eleições multipartidárias e o comportamento eleitoral no distrito de Marromeu', *Boletim do Arquivo Histórico de Moçambique*, 21. Maputo: AHM; Pereira J 1999. 'The Politics of Survival: Peasants, Chiefs and RENAMO in Maringue district, Mozambique, 1982-1992'. MA dissertation. Johannesburg: University of the Witwatersrand.
13 FRELIMO won 59 per cent of the urban vote at a national level, while RENAMO won 29 per cent (De Brito L, op. cit.)
14 Carbone G 2003. 'Emerging Pluralist Politics in Mozambique: The FRELIMO-RENAMO Party System'. Crise States programme Working Paper no 23. London School of Economics/Development Research Centre, 2003; Geffray C et al 1986 'Sobre a guerra na provincia de Nampula', *Revista Internacional de Estudos Africanos* 4, 5, ; Geffray, C 1991. *A causa das armas em Moçambique: Antropologia de guerra contemporanea em Moçambique*. Porto: Edições Afrontamento.
15 FRELIMO in contrast seems to draw political support from its long-established and socially connected political networks that are based both in urban and rural areas, including substantial support from Cabo Delgado, Nampula and Niassa and the south.

16 Bratton M et al 1994. 'Neo-patrimonial regimes and political transition in Africa'. *World Politics* 46.

17 Interview with M Folinda, Dondo, 18 April 2005.

18 Interview with L Julienta, Nhamatanda, 20 May 2005.

19 Wole O 2003. 'Political parties and multi-party elections in Southern Africa'. *SADC Insight*, IV, p1.

20 Carbone G 2003. 'Developing Multi-Party Politics: Stability and Change in Ghana and Mozambique'. Crise States programme Working Paper no 36. London School of Economic School/Development Research Centre, p13.

21 Roesch O 1992. 'RENAMO and peasantry in Southern Mozambique: A view from Gaza province'. *Canadian Journal of African Studies*, 26.

Roesch O, 1993. 'Peasants, War and Tradition in Central Mozambique'. Paper prepared for the symposium 'Symbols of change: Transregional culture and local practice in Southern Africa'. Germany: Free University of Berlin;

Geffray C et al. 'Sobre a guerra na provincia de Nampula', op. cit.;

Geffray, C, *A causa das armas em Moçambique: Antropologia de guerra contemporanea em Moçambique,* op. cit.;

Pereira J, 'As primeira eleições multipartidárias e o comportamento eleitoral no distrito de Marromeu', op. cit.;

Pereira J, 'The Politics of Survival: Peasants, Chiefs and RENAMO in Maringue district', op. cit.;

Carbone G, 'Emerging Pluralist Politics in Mozambique: The FRELIMO-RENAMO Party System', op. cit. During the war, an alliance between traditional chiefs and RENAMO developed in central Mozambique, largely as a result of FRELIMO's marginalisation of traditional leaders and of the forced resettlements of villagisation policies. The implicit contract between RENAMO and chiefs, who invited RENAMO to set up bases on their land, was that RENAMO would block government interference with their way of life and enable them to remain on their land. In return, the chiefs would serve as administrators for RENAMO, taking the RENAMO title of *mambos* and mobilising the population to provide food and collaborators to serve as *majubas* (Pereira J, 'The Politics of Survival: Peasants, Chiefs and RENAMO in Maringue district', op. cit.)

22 Cahen, M 1998. 'Dhlakama e maningue nice: An atypical former guerrilla in Mozambique electoral campaign'. Transformation, 35: pp1-48 ; Cahen, M 2002. *Les Bandits: Un historeie au Mozambique, 1994.* Portugal: Fundacao

Colouste Gulbenkian; Carbone G, 'Developing Multi-Party Politics: Stability and Change in Ghana and Mozambique', op. cit.

23 Interview with A Julio, Maputo, 20 May 2006.
24 Patel N 2005. 'Political Parties as an Institutional Building Block of Democracy in Africa: Consolidation or Fragmentation?' Paper presented at the regional conference on political parties and democratisation in East Africa. Arusha, Tanzania.
25 Interview with M Forindo, Maputo, 18 May 2006.
26 Interview with A Julio, Maputo, 20 May 2006.
27 Carbone G, 'Developing Multi-Party Politics: Stability and Change in Ghana and Mozambique', op. cit., p14.
28 For instance, while a party congress should be organised every two years, in RENAMO none was held between 1994 (when a small general meeting took place in Maringue) and 2001. In October 2001, Congress re-elected Dhlakama as party president against two hopeless contestants, meant to show a facade of internal democracy.
29 Simutanyi N 2005. 'Funding Political Parties in Zambia: Challenges and Opportunities'. Paper presented to the Netherlands Institute for Multiparty Democracy regional conference on rules of engagement between ruling and opposition parties and funding for political parties. Livingstone Zambia: NIMD, p6.
30 Pottie, D 2003. 'Party finance and politics of money in Southern Africa.' *Journal of Contemporary African Studies*, 21(1), pp5-26.
31 Simutanyi N, op. cit.
32 Nuvunga A 2005. 'Multiparty Democracy in Mozambique: Strengths, Weakness and Challenges'. EISA Research Report no 14. Johannesburg: EISA, p70.
33 Nuvunga A, ibid.
34 Interview with V Lecastro, Mafambisse, 15 May 2005.
35 Interview with A Juliao, Dondo, 21 May 2005.
36 This method is unsteady and unreliable. Political party leaders also do not necessarily have much money themselves, and they are unable to guarantee a substantial percentage of revenue needed by the political parties.
37 Interview with A Juliao, Beira, 25 March 2006.
38 Interview with J Fendiasse, Maputo, 20 March 2006.
39 Patel N, op. cit.

40 De Brito, L et al 2003. *Moçambique: 2003-Avaliação do potencial de conflito*. Maputo: CEA.

41 From the end of the 1990s FRELIMO appears to be much less 'southern' than it was during its Marxist-Leninist period or early period of independence.

42 One of the reasons why the minor parties are notoriously weak is doubtless the fact that Mozambican intellectuals and, in general, the bureaucratic elite which grew in the shadow of the FRELIMO party-state are in a phase of re-conversion and installation into the world of business and of the nascent national business class. For this, their main capital is precisely their links with FRELIMO and its state. It is this stratum – which includes, for instance, army officers from the time of the armed struggle – who have benefited most from the privatisation of companies and services that were once under state control, as well as from bank credits granted with no expectation of being repaid, or at insignificant interest rates.

43 De Brito L, op. cit.

44 Barany Z 2002. 'Ethnic mobilisation without prerequisites: The East European gypsies'. World Politics 54.

45 Interview with J Jose, Maputo, 10 May 2006.

46 Nuvunga A, op. cit., p.60.

47 Lundin L 1996. 'Political parties: A reading of the ethnic and regional factor in the democratisation processes', in Mazula B (ed), *Mozambique: Elections, Democracy, and Development*. Maputo: Elo Grafico, p40.

48 De Brito L, op. cit.

49 EU 2009. 'European Union Observation Report: Presidential, Legislative and Provincial Assembly Elections'. Maputo: EU.

50 Sitoe E et al, op. cit., p23.

51 In the first elections, all the parties obtained money from a trust fund. This was justified at the time because it was not possible to guess how well each party might fare.

52 According to Ihonvbere, African politics suffer from 'leadership fixation'. In this case personality parties such as most that emerged in Mozambique as well as in many African countries do not care very much about presenting clearly distinguishable policy platforms, but rather emphasise the ability of the party leaders to run things better. On this point see, Ihonvbere, JO 1998. 'Where is the third wave? A critical evaluation of Africa's non-transition to

democracy', in Mkabu John Mukum and Ihonvbere Julius O (eds.) *Multiparty Democracy and Political Change: Constraints to Democratization in Africa*, Aldershot: Ashgate; Chabal P et al 1999. *African Works: Disorder as Political Instrument.* Oxford: James Currey.

53 Cahen 1998: 19. The campaign approach used by RENAMO and its leader Afonso Dhlakama is similar to that used by parties in other African countries. In fact, in many African countries election campaigns have been conducted almost entirely on the basis of personal and ethno-regional appeals for support. Ottaway has argued that the political transformation that occurred after the end of the Cold War, which is characterised by the absence of ideology, left ethnicity as the main factor for mobilisation of party support. The absence of ideological or programmatic differences left ethnicity as the major characteristic by which various parties could differentiate themselves: Ottaway, M 1998. *Ethnic politics in Africa: State, conflict and democracy in Africa.* Boulder, Col: Lynne Rienner.

54 Pereira J, 'The Politics of Survival: Peasants, Chiefs and RENAMO in Maringue district', op. cit.;

Harrison, G 1996. 'Democracy in Mozambique: The significance of multi-party elections'. *Review of African Political Economy*, 67, pp19-34;

Harrison, G 1999. 'Mozambique between two elections: a political economic of transition'. *Democratization*, 6. London: Frank Cass;

Harrison, G 2000. *The politics of democratization in rural Mozambique: grassroots governance in Mecufi.* New York: The Edwin Mellen Press

Vines, A 1991. RENAMO: *Terrorism in Mozambique.* York: Centre for African Studies, University of York.

Vines, A 1996. RENAMO: *from terrorism to democracy in Mozambique.* York: Centre for African Studies, University of York.

55 A similar approach is used by many of the opposition parties in Africa. Ideological differences have been minor across parties, and debates about specific policy issues have been virtually non-existent. Although opposition parties may criticise the government's management of the economy or the implementation of structural adjustment programmes, party platforms diverge little and campaign speeches rarely discuss policy issues (Van de Walle N 2002. 'Presidentialism and clientelism in Africa's emerging party systems'. *The Journal of Modern African Studies*, 41, p6).

56 Nuvunga A, op. cit., p65

57 This negative image is strengthened by the treatment it receives from most of the national media.

58 This is the case in most countries where the transition to multiparty politics did not bring about a change of government, but rather a continuation of the former one-party rule, albeit under a new guise. Even in those countries where a change of government took place, the new incumbents resorted to the same tactics of weakening the opposition by luring their members and disrupting their electoral campaigns.

CHAPTER SIX
NAMIBIA: OPPOSITION PARTIES STUCK IN THE SAND
ANDRÉ DU PISANI AND BILL LINDEKE

Introduction

This chapter seeks to examine the genesis, nature and performance of political opposition in postcolonial Namibia through an exploration of the country's recent political history, its constitutional provisions for opposition politics, electoral systems, party performance, support bases and party funding. It addresses the Namibian case in an attempt to shed light on the factors that explain the seeming contradiction of consolidating democracy combined with insignificant opposition. The chapter will advance both structural and informal explanations that account for the present non-competitive, dominant party system and the attendant weakness of political opposition, despite the open and democratic environment that Namibia provides.

Namibia's 1990 Constitution has been broadly praised as being among the most liberal in Africa, if not the world. It is widely respected in the country and has not been subjected to endless tinkering that might reduce its symbolic importance. Among the many admirable elements in the constitution is the embedding of individual rights in Chapter Three. Included in these rights, which cannot be reduced or diminished by government action, are freedoms of speech, opinion, organisation (political party) and media. These values are essential to the effective functioning and consolidation of democracy in Namibia. The courts have been active in defending these and other principles to make sure that they are not just words on a page. Over time the public has come to embrace the Constitution and democracy as its own. Lindberg[1] has suggested that democratic performance has a cumulative reinforcing impact.

Namibia has now experienced 15 elections at three different levels of government that include different electoral features: majority-elected executive president; proportional representation (PR) (with lowest remainder), party-list at the national and local levels; and a constituency-based regional government election system, whose councils then each select two members to the National Council. With one exception at the regional and local level in 1998, all of Namibia's election turnouts have been impressive (see Table 1) and, as with South Africa, the majority received by the succeeding presidential candidate (Pohamba, Mbeki) exceeded that of the founding president (Nujoma, Mandela). As was the case in Botswana, succession elections require or create the conditions for a higher turnout for legitimation and symbolic purposes compared to continuity elections. The 2004 succession election saw an 85 per cent turnout compared to just 61 per cent in 1999 (see Table 1). In the hotly contested 2009 election, turnout was over 70 per cent, although nine opposition parties challenged the results all the way to the Supreme Court, seeking a nullification of the results (outcome pending).[2]

An archetypical Namibian desert environment experience is to find one's car stuck in the sand. This seems an apt metaphor for the circumstance of Namibia's opposition parties. The engines are revving, the tyres are spinning, work is being done, but they can't get any traction. There is no momentum towards their goals. How can this situation be explained?

Table 1: Voter turnout in Namibian elections, 1989–2004

Year	Registered voters	Votes cast	Turnout %
National Assembly			
1989	701 483	680 787	97
1994	654 189	497 508	76
1999	879 222	541 114	61
2004	977 742	829 269	85
2009	1 163 000**	811 143	70
Presidential			
1994	654 189	497 508	76
1999	879 222	545 465	61
2004	977 742	833 165	85
2009	1 163 000**	812 233	70
Regional Council			
1992	470 006	381 041	81
1998	534 278	213 789	40*
2004	977 742	523 746	54*
2010	1,180,925	Not completed	38.2***
Local Authority*			
1992	156 663	128 973	82
1998	188 302	63 545	34*
2004	363 548	163 999	45*
2010	417,111	Not completed	***

Source: LeBeau and Dima, 2005: 48

Explination of the * on Table 1 Voter turnout in Namibian elections, 1989-2004
* Many SWAPO strongholds have no opposition, hence lower voter turnouts.
** Part of the electoral court case involves disputes over the voters' roll, which featured four different totals released by the Electoral Commission and many constituencies unexpectedly achieved over 100 per cent turnout in the two-day election. Voters could cast their ballots outside their place of registration with 'tendered ballots'. 2010 results are not completed as of press time, but some results have been posted and estimated, see www.ecn.na.

Opposition parties in Namibia have been held to less than 30 per cent of the vote in the elections following the United Nations' supervised election in 1989. Despite the revival of older parties and the appearance of new ones, the fate of Namibia's opposition parties has not improved and shows no prospects of doing so in the near term (see Table 2).

To some extent the explanation for the weakness of opposition parties is to be found in the history of Namibia's independence struggle, which elevated the South West Africa People's Organisation (SWAPO) in 1976 to international recognition as the 'sole and authentic' representative of the Namibian people at the UN and afforded it support from the Organisation of African Unity, the Non-Aligned Movement and the Frontline States of Southern Africa. Such external validation and material support significantly increased the legitimacy of SWAPO's cause both inside and outside the country.

The ethnic structure of Namibian society, the 'nationalist' leadership of the independence movement, and the evolving convenience of international borders[3] coincided with these external influences to make SWAPO the leading force in the struggle. At 50 per cent of the population (and 90 per cent SWAPO supporters), Oshivambo speakers make up the core of SWAPO voters, creating one of the most ethnically based African ruling parties, while other population groups only account for populations in the single digits, forming a weak basis for large party mobilisation. Nonetheless, SWAPO has been identified as a nationalist party by virtue of its diverse top leadership and its programme of action. As the main liberation movement, SWAPO and its armed wing, People's Liberation Army of Namibia (PLAN), could take advantage of the Angolan border for recruitment and infiltration from bordering Oshivambo areas. The 1989 election for a Constituent Assembly (the body that drew up the Constitution) under the supervision of the United Nations Transition Assistance Group (UNTAG) following UN Security Council Resolution 435,[4] confirmed that SWAPO was the dominant political force in Namibia.

Table 2: Votes received by party in elections, 1989--2004 (%)

Party	1989 CA Constitutional Assembly	1992 RC Regional Council	1992 LA Local Authority	1994 PE Presidential Election	1994 NA National Assembly
APP All People's Party					
CoD Congress of Democrats					
DTA Democratic Turnhalle Alliance	28.6	22.1	33.3	23.1	20.5
DPN Democratic Party of Namibia					
MAG Monitor Action Group					0.8
NDMC Namibian Democratic Movement for Change					
NDP Democratic Party of Namibia					
NUDO National Unity Democratic Organization					
RDP Rally for Democracy and Progress					
RP Republican Party					
SWANU South West Africa National Union			1.5		0.5
SWANU/ WRP formerly known as the **Workers Revolutionary Party**					
SWAPO South West Africa People's Organization	57.3	74.7	58.0	74.5	72.7
UDF United Democratic Front	5.7	3.2	5.9		2.7
WRP/ Communist Party formerly the **Workers Revolutionary Party**			0.1		0.2

Source: Hunter 2005: 20 and original sources cited there and www.ecn.na for 2009, 2010.

1998 LA Local Authority	1998 RC Regional Council	1999 PE Presidential Elections	1999 NA National Council	2004 PE Presidential Election	2004 NA National Assembly	2009 NA (PE) National Council (Presidential Election)
						1.33
		10.6	9.9	7.1	7.2	0.66
23.9	15.7	9.6	9.5	5.0	5.1	3.13
						0.24
			0.7	1.1	0.8	0.58
					0.5	0.22
						0.15
				4.2	4.2	3.01
						11.16
				1.9	2.0	0.81
0.2					0.4	0.62
			0.4			
60.4	80.4	76.9	76.2	75.1	74.8	74.29
6.7	3.9	3.0	2.9	3.8	3.7	2.40
0.1						0.10

Assembly after the election, and the unfolding Namibian political process in both formal structural and informal procedural developments since independence, will capture both the aspects of SWAPO dominance and opposition party weakness.

To some degree the party system is a captive of the structural features of Namibian politics: state and executive dominance, ethnic structures and traditional values, the electoral system, and a changed global environment. Other factors that influence the relative power distribution among parties include features that are to a degree more open to choice and control by the participants, such as electoral strategies, ideology, policy choices, personalities, organisation and leadership. We shall now explore the structure, ideology, policy platforms and performance of a number of the larger opposition parties.

Rally for Democracy and Progress – A new opposition hope?

In late 2007 several dissatisfied SWAPO members, led by former foreign affairs minister (and defeated SWAPO presidential aspirant) Hidipo Hamutenya and former deputy ministers and ambassadors, formed a new party: the Rally for Democracy and Progress (RDP). These leaders and others felt sidelined and targeted by factions within SWAPO. The new party created the possibility of breaking the dominance among voters from the north-central areas, since many of the new party's leadership were from the Kwanyama tribe. President Hifikepunye Pohamba is also from this group, the largest of the eight Oshivambo subgroups in Namibia. The RDP leaders were targeted with stinging rhetoric from SWAPO leaders, vengeful dismissals, and the most serious collective violence since independence during some by-elections. The slogan for the new party was 'Together, we can do better!' Its aspirations were to be the official opposition and a national (rather than tribal) party after the 2009 elections.

The structure of the party did not break from Namibian practice. Although the party's manifesto attempted to target specific policies where SWAPO might be vulnerable, they mostly campaigned as not being the same as SWAPO. After an initial burst of energy, the party failed to attract any significant defections from either SWAPO or other opposition parties. In the end they managed to capture over 11 per cent of the vote to become eligible to take on the official opposition mantle. However, together with eight other opposition parties, the RDP tried to have the election results nullified in the courts. The High Court rejected the appeal on the technical grounds that a submission was filed 90 minutes late. The appeal of this ruling then went to the Supreme Court, which disagreed and sent the case back to the same High Court Judges, who should in the near future announce their final ruling.

Congress of Democrats – Reviving opposition in parliament

The Congress of Democrats (CoD), a previous defection from the ruling party, was formed on 23 March 1999, almost a decade after independence, following CoD leader Ben Ulenga's exit from SWAPO. Ulenga resigned his post as high commissioner to the United Kingdom in October 1998. He advanced three principal reasons for his decision. These were: SWAPO President Sam Nujoma's plan to run for a third term; Namibia's participation in the Democratic Republic of the Congo (DRC) war in 1998;[5] and the neglect by government of former PLAN combatants. The CoD was the first opposition party that evolved out of SWAPO, and for this reason many local analysts had high hopes for it.[6]

By the time of the launch of the party, Ulenga had been joined by Tsudao Gurirab (a former permanent secretary), and former South West Africa National Union (SWANU) members Nora Schimming-Chase and Kaveri Kavari. Shortly before the 1999 national elections, SWAPO deputy minister of information and broadcasting, Ignatius Shixwameni, joined the CoD.

Although SWAPO saw the CoD as a potential electoral threat and ran a campaign in the party's newspaper, *Namibia Today* to discredit the CoD and its leader Ulenga,[7] the newly formed party took its votes from other opposition parties, principally the Democratic Turnhalle Alliance (DTA) of Namibia. The CoD won seven seats in the National Assembly with 9.94 per cent of the vote, second only to SWAPO. The party performed well in the Caprivi Region[8] and Rehoboth, again mostly at the expense of the DTA.

Claims by the CoD to the Electoral Commission of Namibia (ECN) that its party functionaries were being harassed, particularly in the north-central regions where several election rallies were called off, were dismissed by the ECN. In late 2003 Moses Katjiuongua, formerly of the Democratic Coalition of Namibia and the National Patriotic Front, joined the CoD. In the 2004 local authority elections, the CoD managed to get over 30 candidates elected, although there had not been a significant rise in their support since the 1999 national elections. The party's level of support remained at around ten per cent of the vote.[9]

In the 2004 National Assembly elections the CoD increased its support by just over 6 000 votes but did not make inroads into SWAPO's support base, especially in the northern regions. The CoD captured five seats in the National Assembly and became the official opposition. The party, with the support of the Republican Party (RP), challenged the counting process in court, claiming there had been a series of irregularities. The court ordered a recount in March 2005, but the process produced a similar result to the original one. In the 2004 National Assembly elections, the party lost significant support in Caprivi – with its share of the vote going down from 37 per cent to 13 per cent – and performed best in the southern regions of Hardap and Karas. In the same year, the party failed to win a single seat in regional council elections despite gathering the most votes after SWAPO, underscoring the diffuse nature of its support and the fact that the party did not yet have a national reach.

An internal battle for leadership in 2007 nearly destroyed the party. A complete split among activists led to a court challenge in the leadership election. During the drawn-out affair, some leaders left the CoD while others passed away or retired from party politics. In the 2009 elections the party was only able to hold onto one seat in parliament. It barely held two local authority seats in 2010.

Policy manifesto

The CoD policy manifesto mirrors many of the core values of a social democracy. The three core virtues are: equal opportunities, poverty eradication and social welfare for all citizens. The party supports a basic income grant for all Namibians. At the heart of the CoD's economic policy are poverty eradication, employment creation, and integrated, sustainable land and agrarian reform. The party also proposes free, state-funded education, and affordable health services and housing. Gender equality is another key element of the party's human rights and social policy. On governance, the party proposes zero tolerance of corruption and good governance at all levels of the state. Finally, the CoD supports public sector reform to meet the principal development challenges of the country.[10]

All Peoples Party - New ethnic parties mushrooming in 2008

Ignatius Shikwemeni and some other members of CoD created a new Kavango-based party in 2008 that tried to challenge the ruling party from a more progressive policy stance. This was the most successful of a new batch of parties with narrow ethnic support trying to create new opportunities for reducing perceived group marginality and elite empowerment. The All Peoples Party (APP) was the most successful of these efforts as it gained a seat in the 2009 National Assembly for Shikwemeni. Attempts by these smaller parties to expand to national support did not succeed. In all, nine parties fit this category in 2009, creating some concern about rising ethnic threats to national unity. Such concerns seem to be misplaced.

DTA of Namibia

The DTA of Namibia grew out of the South African-backed Turnhalle Constitutional Conference, a key part of Pretoria's strategy to control Namibia's transition to independence and to neutralise SWAPO's popular appeal. The Turnhalle Constitutional Conference met from September 1975 to October 1977.[11] The DTA took its original name – Democratic Turnhalle Alliance – from the name of the building where the constitutional conference took place. The DTA was spawned by Turnhalle participants who walked out of the conference's constitutional committee in 1977 in protest at the National Party's insistence that some racially discriminatory legislation remain in force.

Since its formation the DTA has essentially been a coalition of ethnic parties – most of which served in the second-tier ethnic administrations set up by the South African-appointed administrator-general in 1980. Therefore, the DTA was tarred with an ethnic brush and was seen widely as a stratagem of the colonial power, South Africa. DTA chairperson Johan de Waal suggested that this remains the major hindrance to the party's effectiveness.[12]

Herero Chief Clemens Kapuuo, an advisor to the legendary Hosea Kutako, became the first president of the DTA until his mysterious assassination in March 1978. Chief minister of the Owambo government, Cornelius Ndjoba, took over as president in August 1978 but resigned in October 1980 and was later killed by a landmine explosion in 1983. Leader of the National Democratic Party Peter Kalangula then became president, but left the DTA in February 1982 to set up the Christian Democratic Action (CDA). Initially the alliance consisted of the following ethnic parties: National Unity Democratic Organisation (NUDO), Rehoboth Baster Association, Labour Party, Republican Party, SWA People's Democratic Front, Nama Alliance, the National Democratic Party, Caprivi Alliance Party, Bushman Alliance and Tswana Alliance.

The DTA played a key role in two initiatives aimed at reaching an internal settlement in Namibia without the involvement of the UN and SWAPO. These were a National Assembly established following internal elections in 1978 and the Multi-Party Conference of 1983. The first initiative ran into the ground after a clash with the South African-appointed administrator-general, and the second established a transitional administration that lasted until 1989, the year of implementation of the UN Transitional Plan for Namibia.[13]

In December 1978 the DTA won an election for a 50-member Constituent Assembly with over 82 per cent of the vote. The election, which was boycotted by SWAPO and other parties, was widely discredited and did not win international credibility for the DTA. In 1979 the Constituent Assembly was transformed into a National Assembly, and in the following year DTA member parties took control in several of the second-tier authorities following elections held along ethnic lines under the apartheid transitional rules of the South African imposed AG8 legislation.

In 1983 the administrator-general abolished the National Assembly and its Ministers Council. The DTA then participated in a new attempt to seek international acceptance – the Multi-Party Conference of 1983 that culminated in the formation of the Transitional Government of National Unity in 1985. The Transitional Government of National Unity, in which the DTA held three cabinet posts, remained in power until it was dissolved in 1989 following the implementation of the UN independence process.[14]

At the UN-supervised independence elections in 1989 the DTA consisted of 12 predominantly ethnic parties. These were: Bushman Alliance, Christian Democratic Party, Democratic Turnhalle Party of Namibia (formerly Nama Alliance), National Democratic Party, National Democratic Unity Party, NUDO, Rehoboth DTA Party, Republican Party, Seoposengwe (formerly Tswana Alliance), SWA People's Democratic United Front (Swapduf), United Democratic Party and United Party of Namibia.

The DTA did fairly well in the 1989 independence elections. The alliance won in electoral districts in the southern, eastern and central areas but faced a crushing defeat from SWAPO's 94 per cent victory in the populous north-central regions of the Oshivambo-speaking community. The first regional and local elections in 1992 showed that the DTA (which had consolidated into a single party a year earlier) was not making any inroads into SWAPO's strongholds. The DTA took 27 per cent of the vote in the regional council elections and 33% in the local authority elections.

By 1994, the national elections brought the DTA support down to 20 per cent, while DTA president Mishake Muyongo polled only 23 per cent support in a showdown with Nujoma for the presidency. Low turnouts (below 50 per cent) in the 1998 regional and local elections saw the DTA losing further support, down from 33 per cent to 24 per cent in the local election, and from 27 per cent to 24 per cent in the regional vote. The lack of a serious challenge to SWAPO may have reduced turnout on all sides with a bit of apathy setting in. The major electoral collapse came in 1999 – the year attempts were made to secede the Caprivi Region – when support sank to 9.48 per cent and the newly formed CoD finished marginally ahead in the popular vote. Since then several of the DTA's affiliate parties – NUDO, NDP, and the RP – have broken away, making future election prospects even more meagre as they only held two seats after the 2009 elections.

In retrospect one has to recognise that in the 1989 independence elections, the DTA received considerable financial backing from South Africa. SWAPO had to face the detainee issue. Following that, the DTA has had to contend with several untested presidents and the involvement of one of them in the aborted Caprivi separatist cause in 1998/99. The party also lost its competent administrative secretary in 2002, while both the RP and NUDO, two constituent parties, left the DTA in 2003. The departure of NUDO and the RP left the DTA in a parlous state and not surprisingly in the May 2004 local authority elections the party lost control of nine local authorities and gained only one. Some of the whites who chose not to join the RP formed a new DTA affiliate body in November 2003 called Action for Democratic Change (ADC), which included party chairperson Johan de Waal and former DTA MP Hans-Erik Staby.

In 2000 the DTA entered into a parliamentary coalition with the United Democratic Front (UDF) in a successful attempt to save its official opposition status. This arrangement came to an end in 2005 and failed to consolidate the DTA as the official opposition. The party slumped to just five per cent of the vote in the 2004

National Assembly elections. As a result, the DTA returned to the National Assembly with only four seats and lost its official opposition status to the CoD. The DTA won only two seats in the 2004 regional council elections – Opuwo and Epupa in the Kunene Region. By the 2009 elections the DTA had lost all momentum to other opposition parties and saw a further spilt of earlier constituent groups. Only two National Assembly seats were won in 2009, and some of the strongest and most popular officials of the party were left out. The party suffered further losses in 2010.

Policy platform

For the 1999 National Assembly elections, the DTA manifesto offered 'Ten commitments for the people of Namibia'. These included access to a better standard of living, equal opportunities in health and education, a fair and well-managed government, human, social and cultural development, a lasting democracy and 'optimum living and working conditions for all our people'.[15]

In the 2004 National Assembly elections, the DTA made the state of education in the country a central plank of its election manifesto. The party blamed what it termed 'the collapse of education' on the introduction of the Cambridge System, inadequately trained teachers and poorly equipped schools, among other factors. Apart from education, health and social services came in for criticism. The party proposed a 'master plan' for this sector before restructuring and decentralising health provision in the country. On the politically contentious issue of land redistribution, the party also proposed a 'master plan' that would address issues of financial and technical support to new farmers, identifying land available for resettlement and determining the rate at which resettlement should be executed. The economic policy of the party provides for strict control over government spending, reducing the cabinet to 12 ministers, an increase in old age pensions, the privatisation of unproductive state assets, and employment creation especially for the youth.[16]

National Unity Democratic Organisation (NUDO)

NUDO left the DTA in late 2003 and subsequently registered as a political party with the Directorate of Elections. With a solid base of urban and rural Herero speakers, the party has survived electorally since then (three seats in 2004 and two seats in 2009). NUDO was originally formed by the Herero Chiefs' Council (HCC) in September 1964, after the former parted company with SWANU over its more radical agenda. Founding members included Clemens Kapuuo and Mburumba Kerina, who left for the United States in 1966. Kapuuo became paramount chief of the Herero on the death of Hosea Kutako in 1970. He led NUDO until his assassination in March 1978, after which Chief Kuaima Riruako took over the leadership.

Initially NUDO joined the National Convention with SWAPO and other parties and campaigned for a UN settlement in Namibia. In 1975 the party joined the South African-supported Turnhalle constitutional talks. Two years later, NUDO became a member of the DTA with Kapuuo as the Alliance's first president. He was assassinated six months later. The party participated in the Multi-Party Conference of 1983, which led to the formation of the Transitional Government of National Unity two years later.

The party participated under the umbrella of the DTA in the 1989 independence elections and NUDO chairperson Katuutire Kaura and the party's legal advisor, Fanuel Kozonguizi, were among the DTA's 21 MPs in the first National Assembly. As indicated above, NUDO broke away from the DTA in late 2003 (on the grounds that it always retained its own identity as a party). The party was soon recognised by the Directorate of Elections as a separate party.[17]

In the local authority elections of May 2004, NUDO gained nine seats countrywide in seven different towns, with its best performance in Okakarara, a Herero stronghold. The party captured three seats in the 2004 National Assembly elections – with four per cent of the national vote. In the following regional council elections of 2004, NUDO took two seats in Omaheke and one in Otjozondjupa, both predominantly OtjiHerero-speaking regions. In 2009 and 2010 the party held most of its support-base.

Party platform

In 2004, the party released a policy paper entitled 'Federalism or Unitarism: Which of the two is viable for Namibia?' where it came out in favour of national unity in values and federalism in structure. NUDO supports a minimum wage for domestic workers and favours more investment in small and medium-size enterprise (SME) development. The party also supports affordable primary health care and views HIV/Aids as the most serious challenge facing the country. The party supports the provision of anti-retroviral drugs to all expectant mothers who have tested HIV-positive.[18]

The party proposes free and compulsory education for the first 12 years and pledges to provide more classrooms, libraries, laboratories, teachers, resource centres and computers, especially to rural schools. For NUDO, the school curriculum should include more science, technology and commercial subjects. NUDO favours a policy of 'zero tolerance' in respect of crime and supports a better trained, better equipped and better resourced police force.

On land reform, the party supports an approach that would make communal land 'tradeable' so as to free up capital currently invested in land. The party also supports land reform and land ownership, particularly for those living on communal land. The party favours expropriation of land owned by absentee landlords, as well as any underdeveloped or underutilised land. Finally, the party proposes the privatisation of all public enterprises, including public utilities, and the outsourcing of selected government functions.

United Democratic Front

The United Democratic Front (UDF), like many other political formations in the country, was formed in 1989 in anticipation of independence. The party draws the bulk of its support from Damara voters, who provide a small, but stable, base of support. Although originally an alliance of six parties, the leading role was played by Justus Garoëb's Damara Council. The other constituent parties of the UDF at its founding in February 1989 were the Labour Party, Caprivi Alliance Party, Original People's Party of Namibia, Namibia National Independence Party and the Caprivi African National Union-UDF. The Workers' Revolutionary Party (WRP) and the Patriotic Unity Movement (PUM) joined in August 1989. In the words of one analyst 'The UDF alliance was a curious hotchpotch of tribal interests, hard line socialists, Caprivian politicians, and former SWAPO detainees who had formed the PUM'.[19]

In the 1989 independence elections the UDF won four seats in the Constituent Assembly. Predictably, the UDF achieved its best results in Damaraland (which was an electoral district in 1989), gaining an absolute majority (52 per cent). Damaraland provided 20.7 per cent of the UDF's overall vote, while the five electoral districts in the west of the country provided another 17.4 per cent of the vote, highlighting the party's ethnic support base.

By 1989 it was apparent that most of the UDF's support lay in what are now the Erongo and Kunene regions and a sprinkling of other towns where there were significant Damara populations. Despite having two Caprivian parties in its alliance, the UDF only managed 556 votes (two per cent) in Caprivi.

The WRP left the UDF in February 1990. Three years later the UDF transformed itself into a unified party and since then it has not managed to extend its power base beyond the Damara community. In the 1994 National Assembly elections the UDF won 21.03 per cent support in the Kunene Region and 10.61% in the Erongo Region, while its support in other regions remained insignificant. The party's share of the vote went down from 5.65 per cent to 2.68 per cent, which gave the party just two seats, occupied by Justus Garoëb and Eric Biwa.

In the 1999 National Assembly elections the party gained 2.93 per cent support, which was enough to maintain its two seats. Again its support came principally from the Kunene and Erongo regions. The first time Garoeb stood in presidential elections he gained three per cent of the vote, trailing Katuutire Kaura of the DTA, Ben Ulenga (CoD) and Sam Nujoma (SWAPO). The UDF entered into a parliamentary coalition with the DTA in 2000 and became part of the official opposition since the two parties had nine seats against the CoD's seven. The pact came to an end in 2005.

In the 2004 local authority elections, the UDF emerged in control of two small towns in the Kunene Region, Khorixas and Uis, and gained a seat for the first time in Windhoek – with 26 councillors in 14 towns – up from 25 in 13 towns in 1998. The party increased its number of seats in the National Assembly to three after the 2004 National Assembly elections and took five seats in the Erongo and Kunene regional council elections. The party's secretary general, Dudu Murorua, was chosen as the governor of the Kunene Region. In 2009 the party retained two parliamentary seats by gaining most of its votes from its core western and north-western constituents.

Policy considerations

The UDF is the only political party that proposes the idea of paying reparations to citizens who lost loved ones during the liberation struggle as a contribution towards social peace. The party supports a policy of decentralisation and proposes that different ministries should be headquartered in different regions of the country. On economic policy, the UDF proposes raising income and property taxes on the affluent by ten per cent so as to raise additional revenue for poverty reduction. The party also proposes spending N$1.2 billion with a view towards creating 100 000 new jobs over four years.[20]

The template of independence

Several decisive elements of Namibian politics can be attributed to the founding 'moment' of Namibia's republic that seemingly have locked in a combination of factors which serve to reinforce, for the foreseeable future, the key dynamics of one-party dominance.

One major factor is the 'independence honeymoon' that SWAPO maintains as the leading liberation movement. Not only do voters repeatedly recreate the 1989 election at all levels of government, but the emotional and symbolic features of liberation and independence are to the advantage of SWAPO. Maintaining such a dynamic is clearly to SWAPO's benefit. Indeed, one of the opposition parties has repeatedly challenged the way SWAPO has transformed national days and events into party political celebrations (at taxpayers' expense with massive state media coverage).[21] When convenient, SWAPO leaders can and do remind the voters and the nation of the colonial past, the racism and oppression of apartheid, imperialism, land alienation, resource exploitation, military conquest and the like to reinforce and keep alive the 1989 moment. The nationalist anti-colonial movement dominates even local elections, where candidates are chosen or vetted by the central party leadership and even removed at will by national leaders.[22] SWAPO has not needed to resort exclusively or excessively to this strategy due to other successes on which the party can campaign and govern.

At the same time SWAPO also emphasised the theme of national reconciliation

which was a major policy of the independence period. Mindful in the early 1990s of the potential for racial and ethnic conflicts to deny the fruits of independence, as had happened in Angola and Mozambique (in contrast to early reconciliation success in Zimbabwe), SWAPO leaders led by Nujoma and Prime Minister Hage Geingob repeatedly called on Namibians to 'forgive and forget'. Nujoma also repeated earlier calls from Botswana and Zambia in their
independence rhetoric, with a plea for 'one Namibia, one nation'.

Elements of this sentiment were encapsulated in the Constitution with entrenched human rights provisions, the protection of property rights and the existing body of public servants' protected employment status (Article 141). Namibia's Council of Churches, perhaps the second most influential force in Namibian society, gave active support to this policy during and after the independence transition. The policy has remained a powerful symbolic moderating tool for a post-conflict heterogeneous society.[23] Together with the commitment to democracy and independence, reconciliation insulates government, SWAPO, and the political leadership from excessive criticism, lest the critiques be seen as opposing these fundamental components of the Namibian experience.[24]

Thus SWAPO is able to wrap itself in the flag of patriotism, independence, democracy, reconciliation, mixed economy and even the policy of international co-operation. SWAPO's anti-colonial nationalist project has packaged these components effectively to insulate the party against criticism. The whole project incorporates the UN Security Council Resolution 435/UNTAG process and the Constitution/democracy compromises. An attack on SWAPO then takes on an appearance of disloyalty to this whole constellation of values.[25]

Namibian political analyst Joseph Diescho argues that the liberation movement also promoted a 'culture of silence' and a 'culture of fear' that has reinforced a negative attitude towards opposition as disloyalty.[26] Afrobarometer data for Namibia suggest that this remains a strong feature of Namibian politics, with 46 per cent of respondents in 2008 (59 per cent in 2006) saying that people have to be careful what they say about politics 'often' or 'always' despite high levels of interest in politics (59 per cent in 2008 and 77 per cent in 2006) and strong satisfaction with existing Namibian democracy (67 per cent in 2008).[27] One could argue that the whole nation-building project, which is necessary and successful, has also reinforced the insulation of SWAPO and consolidated a one-party dominant political process alongside the consolidation of democracy process.[28] In a sense, then, it could be said that SWAPO has co-opted most of the political space, leaving the opposition with seemingly few options save small, narrow, dead-end paths.[29]

In addition to this cultural/historical structure disadvantaging the opposition, other political components of the independence template have also disfavoured opposition forces. The international community, while providing some support to civil society processes and groups, remains mostly concerned with state-building processes during transition processes.[30] Opposition parties are largely off-limits for such support. International support for democratic institutions, practices and values can be seen as support for the choices of SWAPO at independence. The special status that Namibia achieved in the successful, peaceful transition to independence, and all of the international attention that was embedded in that process and what followed, has primarily benefited the ruling party. The end of the Cold War and the democratic reforms that swept across Africa after 1990 only reinforced the direction already taken by SWAPO. The global political environment was warmly embraced by SWAPO and reciprocated in kind with respect and inclusion.

Namibia's choice to pursue a mixed economy model of post-independence development also gained favour, if not resources. Namibia joined the world economy at the height of globalisation in trade and investment. Economic policies adopted by government generally favoured engagement with all sides - North and South, East and West. Such policies found favour internationally with both private and government partners. This was especially true in the dominant fishing and mining industries.

Domestically, the constitutional commitment to private property rights and mixed-economy policies neutralised or won over most of the business sector. Nujoma was particularly popular and accessible to business interests foreign and domestic. This role conformed to the economic development and reconciliation policies adopted by government at independence. Thus a major potential source of support for the opposition was largely neutralised by the openness and attention paid them by government and the lack of better options available through a different government. Trade encouragement, new market access, tax reform and other economic policies adopted at independence or shortly after, continued the process of courting the economic players that SWAPO had initiated in the few years prior to independence. Although the apartheid tradition of protectionism for local businesses was relaxed, occasional protection was still used (e.g., against Castle Brewers of South Africa infringing on the domestic market of Namibia Breweries, the largest private employer in Namibia).

As a new, insecure state, Namibia took some steps against the potential rivalry from traditional authorities that had often plagued newly independent African states. In part there was an understanding of previous difficulties in Africa, but SWAPO also saw many of the traditional authorities as puppets of the apartheid regime. Many leaders had been appointed by the South African colonial authorities precisely for supporting the separatist policies of apartheid. Most of the 40 political parties active in the 1989 elections were apartheid South Africa's attempts to create ethnically based political units (partly to fragment votes away from SWAPO). Many of the traditional leaders lacked legitimacy among their ethnic kin for collaboration and being imposed by the colonial authorities. But SWAPO moved cautiously because these were not universal or tested loyalties.

SWAPO asserted, but did not immediately challenge, ownership of communal lands by the unitary state. The first test came only in the isolated case of Rehoboth, where the Baster community claimed separate treaty-based sovereignty over their lands south of Windhoek. State resources against the tiny minority were decisive and supported by a Supreme Court decision. SWAPO moved slowly and cautiously to assert dominance over traditional authorities beyond the initial independence template.[31] During the 2009 elections, unspecified traditional leaders (presumably in the north) were admonished by SWAPO leaders to stay out of party politics.

Finally, the independence template includes, most importantly, the end of violence in the northern part of the country that had been occupied by South African troops. The tenth independence anniversary government publication from the Office of the Prime Minister sought to emphasise the peace and stability theme in its title 'Namibia: A Decade of Peace, Democracy and Prosperity 1990-2000'.[32] This sentiment reflects the general concerns of late-stage African development policy around the New Partnership for Africa's Development that without peace there would be no development. Voters in the North Central Oshivambo-speaking areas frequently claim that the end of terror by South African and Koevoet troops in their villages and homesteads was sufficient to win their lifetime voting loyalty. Thus far no other party has been able to break the 95 per cent majority for SWAPO among these voters, ensuring a SWAPO electoral majority all by itself.

Independence, peace, a mixed economy and reconciliation make for a powerful template of factors that constrain and close political space for opposition parties. Certain other structural features of the Namibian political and governmental scene also weaken the prospects of opposition. These are examined below.

Structural features supporting one-party dominance

Several features of the government conspire against a vibrant opposition. The electoral systems from party list to constituency-based at different levels alternate the benefits of concentrated or dispersed support and thus do not consistently benefit any of the smaller parties. With limited resources a party might be stronger in one arena but not in others. In the end this fragments and weakens opposition effectiveness. In the most powerful elected body, the National Assembly, a largest remainder election system encourages a proliferation of smaller parties (see Table 3).[33] Parliamentary seats are allocated on the basis of 1/72nd of the valid votes per seat until no party reaches that level. Then, the remaining seats are allocated to parties based on the largest remaining votes necessary to beat the other parties until all the seats have been allocated. A party could gain a seat with only a few thousand votes.

Hence, Namibia's party system has maintained numerous smaller parties at the expense of potentially more effective grand coalitions of a two- or three-party system. Party leaders of these smaller parties are satisfied to be 'big fish in a small pond'. An additional consequence of such a fragmented party system is an under-representation of women in the smallest parties in parliament, holding Namibia under the 30 per cent female representation threshold established by Southern African Development Community (SADC) leaders for 2005. The continuation of this set of electoral systems seems to favour SWAPO and disadvantage the establishment of a more effective opposition.[34]

Table 3: Allocation of National Assembly seats using PR 'largest remainder method' 2009

Party	Total NA votes	Seats per 11 265 votes	Votes not allocated to a seat	Seats to parties with largest remainder	Total number of seats
APP	10 795	0	10 795	1	1
CoD	5 375	-	5 375	1	1
C P	810	-	810	-	-
DTA	25 393	2	2 863	-	2
DPN	1 942	-	1 942	-	-
MAG	4 718	-	4 718	-	-
NDP	1 187	-	1 187	-	-
NDMC	1 770	-	1 770	-	-
NUDO	24 422	2	1 892	-	2
RDP	90 556	8	436	-	8
RP	6 541	0	6 541	1	1
SWANU	4 989	0	4 989	1	1
SWAPO	602 580	53	8 310	1	54
UDF	19 489	1	8 224	1	2
Total valid	811 143	66		6	72

Source: The Namibian, 7 December 2009; www.ecn.na; www.electionwatch.org.na (accessed 14 December 2009)

Another feature of the political structure is the issue of party funding. The ruling party obviously has advantages in raising funds from a larger membership base and its own business holdings. It also benefits from benefactors who might hope to gain favourable access to government contracts and licences. In a small economy like Namibia's business tends to be linked to the state more tightly than in larger economies. Thus some some funding from business sources is not as readily available to the opposition parties. Again, widespread consulting and moderate policies do not leave sharp differences between business and government in terms of regulation, taxes or other key policies.

Some funding is available from foreign sources within the regulatory regime currently in place, but large donations must be declared from both foreign and domestic sources. Further funds are available from the public treasury. These public funds are available on the basis of the shares of the vote in the last national election, which disadvantage (but haven't prevented) new party formations. Table 4 lists estimates of recent amounts available to the various parties since 2000. The amounts are not fixed but are adjusted according to a formula each year by the Ministry of Finance depending on the availability of funds, which seems to be around 0.2 per cent of the state budget. The provision of public funding followed concerns in the early 1990s about the viability and survival of parties in the infant democracy. Both SWAPO and opposition politicians were concerned about their survival as an electoral force and negotiated a system that helped existing players but did not encourage new ones. Public funding began in 1997 but remains a bit obscure from both the government and political party sides. Despite provisions for auditing and reporting by parties no legislation or compliance has been forthcoming.[35]

Table 4: Public funding of political parties 2000--2011 (N$m)

Party	2000/1	2001/2	2002/3	2003/4	2004/5	2005/6	2010/2011*
CoD	1.25	1.4	1.8	1.9	1.6	1.0	.347
DTA-UDF coalition	1.57	1.8	2.3	2.4	2.0		-
MAG	0.08	0.1	0.1	0.1	0.1	0.2	-
SWAPO	9.6	10.8	13.8	14.7	12.2	11.7	18.75
RP						0.2	.347
DTA						0.9	.694
UDF						0.6	.694
NUDO						0.6	.694
RDP							27.7
APP							.347

Hunter 2005: 138 and original source cited there. *Authors' estimates for 2010/11.

Within the governmental structure, the most noticeable feature is executive dominance. As is generally true in recent decades, Namibians opted for an executive presidency; this not only strengthens the constitutional position of the office but provides the additional legitimacy of being directly elected by a majority of voters[36] to increase presidential authority within government. Nujoma combined institutional power with personal power across several layers. He was the founding president, one of the founders and the only president of SWAPO, as well as the leader of the independence process over four decades. As such he personally embodied the nation as no other could.[37] To some degree this elevated position has been institutionalised in the office. Disgruntled groups still march on State House for a personal audience with the president of the day, whether they are unemployed youth, former combatants or shebeen owners. The president can dominate within SWAPO's system of collective responsibility. Thus far such power has not been overused, which helps to maintain it.

In addition to presidential dominance, the executive dominates the parliament by virtue of the numbers of cabinet members serving simultaneously in parliament.[38] Since the cabinet is relatively large (compared, for example, to Botswana) and deputy ministers are included, there are few backbenchers and opposition members to constitute the parliamentary committees. Opposition members thus are fragmented and weakened in their committee work and outvoted by government in full session. With party discipline ensured by the parties' 'ownership' of the seats, executive dominance of parliament has been nearly complete, making separation of powers and checks and balances in some Montesquieu formulation meaningless.

For a time the upper chamber, the National Council, under its President Kandy Nehova, prided itself on being both more non-partisan and the only effective check on the executive in having sent back several pieces of important legislation for rethinking. Nehova was not returned to the regional party list due to factional infighting in SWAPO in 2004, and the National Council has since become nearly a one-party rubber stamp. Executive dominance is widely seen as a weakness in Namibia's democratic consolidation. Several remedies are possible: reducing the size of cabinet, including deputy ministers in the parliamentary committees, or even seeing opposition parties winning more seats.

The late former speaker of the National Assembly, Mose Tjitendero, remarked that at the beginning of the republic there was widespread agreement to unify power in the executive: 'Institutionally, the consensus around these needs and imperatives gave primacy to the executive – the president and his government.'[39] Although the SWAPO Politburo was able to curtail Nujoma's perceived ambitions for a fourth term, parliament has thus far been unable to reassert itself sufficiently to restore in a robust way the accountability of the executive. Fortunately, the executive has been restrained for the most part in its exercise of power.

The consolidation of democracy in Namibia requires, however, a more robust institutionalisation of restraint and accountability. A more robust parliament features, among other things, stronger opposition voices, more effective committee efforts and an improvement in quality of parliamentary debates.

An additional structural feature biased against opposition parties is Namibia's economic structure. In this Namibia is similar to Botswana and other small economies. Although the existing 40 000 public officials from 11 different ethnic administrations were guaranteed due process in their employment security (Article 141), government continues to be the country's largest employer, adding more than 40 000 new people to the public service since 1990. Through control over parastatals and other appointed positions, the ruling party operates a very effective spoils system of employment opportunities. Over the past five years or so the issue of reserving 'jobs for comrades' has been highlighted in speeches and media coverage, especially from the SWAPO Youth League leadership. Other African candidates seeking fresh opportunities reduce the bargaining power of education and skill in such employment settings. Educated professionals have limited private sector opportunities, since white youth and professionals must also compete almost exclusively outside government.

Although there is a Public Service Commission to screen for appropriate employment criteria and practices, there is also a constitutionally mandated affirmative action policy that is vigorously promoted. Job hopping in government positions is a common practice as previously exiled or disadvantaged Namibians seek first a pay cheque and then more lucrative opportunities. Opposition activists risk being closed out of such opportunities if they adopt a prominent position. Officials must relinquish positions to campaign for an opposition party, which again constitutes a livelihood risk. The 'culture of silence' has a firm material basis.

The spoils system is not limited to government employment. Firms seeking government contracts through the tender system may also be reluctant to be too visible in opposition politics. Fishing and other government- controlled licensing processes extend the reach of government employment influence. The recent emergence of black economic empowerment opportunities also constitutes an extension of economic influence into the private sector. Not only is the government the country's largest employer, but it is also the largest purchaser of goods and provider of services (bursaries, titles, licences, advertisements, etc), which provides it with multiple opportunities to reward loyal supporters and withhold opportunities from others. Businesses, international agencies and governments that wish to remain on government's good side can also be influenced or self-restrained. The demise of the DTA can in part be attributed to the reversal of its control over spoils. SWAPO has been very effective at using these and other opportunities – for example, manipulating traditional authority recognition to SWAPO's electoral benefit in Caprivi and Rehoboth, among others.

SWAPO also has become effective at using the opportunities at its disposal to retain and reward talent and loyalty, while restricting public and private space for opposition parties. These manipulations usually are not so visible or restrictive as to close all options; yet they are effective and reinforce the common perception that these powers are available and can be used. These perceptions strengthen the culture of silence and the culture of fear that many analysts perceive. Less civil features of the ruling party surfaced in 2009, though the political culture remains relatively open and tolerant but constrained.

Criticisms of opponents tend to be ad hominem and nasty, reminding potential opponents of the unexamined history of dungeons and the dark days of the past.[40] The party apparatus is diverse and large, but it can be assumed to be disciplined from the top. At times, though, it is unclear whether the Youth League or the SWAPO newspaper, Namibia Today, is expressing an independent view or the official view in some of the opinions that are expressed openly. More extreme views often find expression through these party vehicles.

SWAPO is also advantaged by its dominance of the government-owned media. National radio (the Namibia Broadcasting Corporation, NBC) reaches by far the largest audience with over 80 per cent coverage. NBC television also dominates the attentive public, especially in urban areas. Only in the print media is there competition. Although even the government-owned media is not monolithic, there is clear and demonstrable evidence of biased coverage especially over the longer period as opposed to the immediate election coverage. Content bias, as well as the intensity of coverage, reinforces the existing status quo. Opposition leaders frequently point to this bias but are often unable to use the airtime they are given effectively.

Civil society is also neutralised in part by the structural features of the current political arrangements. In the absence of a mass-based civil society presence, there is no independent mobilisation of voters. Most large civil society organisations are either affiliated to SWAPO or dominated by it. SWAPO also generally withholds participation by its members in other organisations, which limits their size and importance.

In the absence of a strong opposition party, other organisations are reluctant to affiliate too closely with any one party lest they alienate potential supporters. This is the case, for example, with the main labour alternatives to the SWAPO-affiliated National Union of Namibian Workers, which must attempt to maintain a non-party status. The churches, too, fear the wrath of SWAPO should they become too politically active in the opposition, and thus this most important and trusted societal component has a muted political presence, especially when compared to its role before Namibia became independent.

The final structural feature that gives SWAPO advantages over the opposition parties is incumbency and performance. SWAPO benefits from being in power in many of the same ways that any sitting government does.[41] These benefits multiply, however, when good fortune and good performance combine as they have for Namibia. At independence there was a flood of international goodwill in part due to the UN role and in part to the history of effective diplomacy by SWAPO during exile. Thus far the government of Namibia has been effective in maintaining favourable relations with diverse global partners ranging from Cuba and China to the United States and Europe. Windhoek is home to over 40 diplomatic missions and a dozen multilateral agencies – a large number for such a small country. Namibia has received one of the highest per capita development assistance levels in Africa during recent years.[42]

Namibia also has become a good, enthusiastic partner in dozens of international organisations, frequently playing host to meetings and always being timely in paying dues. This international effectiveness helps SWAPO to retain its international legitimacy.s

Namibia's economic growth has generally outperformed the SADC region and Africa as a whole since 1990. In the last few years Namibia's economy has been a bit sluggish compared to the region and Africa, but it has still seen positive real growth on a per capita basis. Namibia should benefit from the accelerated growth from neighbours South Africa and Angola, both of which are achieving record growth this decade. Continued problems in the fishing industry (biomass depletion and price weakness) and in textiles (the end of the multi-fibre agreement and weak Rand: US$ exchange rate) are largely seen as external factors that are not the government's doing.

The one exception in this rosy picture is employment, where both numbers of unemployed and the public salience of the issue disadvantage the government.[43] Employment has always been the most challenging problem on Namibia's short-term horizon and was chosen as the most important problem by 65 per cent of respondents in the 2006 Afrobarometer survey.[44] Comparable high levels were recorded in all Southern African Customs Union democracies, which were well above the African mean. Yet Namibia outperformed the 17 other countries in the 2008 survey in terms of how well the government was perceived to be creating jobs, with a 40 per cent favourable rating.[45]

The main domestic advantage of SWAPO's performance in government has been the high level of support and effectiveness of public policy in general and especially in contrast to the previous dispensation. The emphasis on education spending and primary health care (the two highest budget votes) indicates a broad-based public benefit to SWAPO policies. Indeed, the UN Economic Commission for Africa, among others, ranks Namibia among the top five African countries in a variety of measures (e.g., political freedom, policy effectiveness, corruption limitation). Although the public perceives much corruption, they experience very little in their own lives. Namibia usually ranks together with their regional neighbours, Botswana and South Africa, as the highest performers, while contrasting with Angola, Zambia and Zimbabwe among the worst, thus reinforcing the perception of governance effectiveness from both ends. With such consistently high scores on international indexes, it is hard for opposition parties to argue that they could perform better. Public perceptions of government effectiveness and trust are consistently very high while opposition parties receive little trust, as the Afrobarometer data in Table 5 suggests.

Table 5. Afrobarometer Namibian public perceptions survey results

Issue	2000	2002	2006	2008**	rank of 12
Macroeconomic conditions (% fairly/very good)	42	57	59	52	1st
Present living conditions (% fairly/very good)	42	40	43	37	3rd
Satisfaction with democracy (% fairly/very)	64	69	69	67	2nd
Trust in president (% somewhat/a lot)	73	76	80	81	5th 2008
Support for multiple parties (% agree/strongly agree many parties are needed for real choices)		62	57	59	3rd
Trust in opposition political parties (% somewhat/a lot)*			34	38	2nd 2008

Source: Bratton and Cho 2006: 7, 9, 19, 25, 21;* Keulder 2006: 28;** Little and Logan 2009, 20 countries compared.

Such historical and structural features as discussed above can account in large measure for the continued weakness of opposition parties as seen in the results of the 2009 elections (see Table 3) and in the 2004 contests (Table 6), despite some discontent within the governing party. Additional factors within the parties themselves and the general political processes at work in Namibia may give a deeper insight into the reasons for opposition weakness.

Table 6: Political party representation in the 2004 elections

Party	National Assembly	Regional council	Local authority
CoD	5	0	32 [2]
DTA	4	2 [2]	31 [16]
MAG	1	*	* [1]
NDMC	0	0	2
NUDO	3	3 [3]	9 [7]
RP [RDP]	1	0 [1]	7 45]
SWANU	0	1	*
SWAPO	55	96 [98]	168 [193]
UDF	3	5	25 [24]
Local associations	*	*	7 [& others 9 ?]
Total	72	107	281

Source: Le Beau and Dima, 2005: 21;
* Indicates party did not contest this level. Results for 2010 elections are indicated in brackets. www.ecn.na.

Opposition weakness – beyond structural explanations

In addition to the structural explanations outlined above, opposition politics in independent Namibia can also be explained with reference to more informal aspects. These turn mostly on party loyalty and a political culture that discourages party volatility and the shifting of loyalty and allegiance from one party to another. Also, the notion of a 'loyal opposition' and a bipartisan approach towards national development are not deeply embedded. For a public figure to change parties can be politically costly since much of politics can be informal and based on personal, intimate liaisons and social networks.

Another informal explanation that accounts partly for the weakness of the opposition has to do with the tendency to circulate elites, as opposed to renewing leadership. Many, if not most, of the opposition party leaders have been around for a while, others have migrated from one opposition party to the next. Electoral alliances on the whole have not been particularly productive. The WRP, for example, has had alliances with both the UDF and SWANU before renaming itself the Communist Party in 2009, while NUDO has moved out of and back into the DTA more than once. The RP was a constituent party of the DTA from 1977 and then left the fold in 2003 to reactivate the party.

Most of the opposition parties, perhaps largely due to the lack of fiscal resources and poor institutionalisation, do not engage in well-focused mobilisation and constituency outreach campaigns.[46] Parties have very thin structures and do precious little voter and civic education. In the 2004 National Assembly elections, for example, some of the opposition parties did not mobilise their supporters actively, while others did not produce policy manifestos. The print and electronic media does not profile the smaller opposition parties, so their ability to reach potential voters is inherently limited. Free election air time on NBC is allocated on the basis of the showing in the previous election, further restricting coverage. In 2009 bickering between the NBC management and some opposition parties resulted in the free air time being cancelled altogether. A cash-rich SWAPO and the biases of incumbency resulted in the ruling party receiving 70 to 90 per cent of party and election coverage in 2009.[47]

From the historical template presented above it is clear that ethnicity remains a factor in opposition politics for some parties. Few parties are truly trans-ethnic in their support, and because of this there is a widely held perception among the electorate that they are there to pursue sectional and personal interests. In the case of the smaller opposition parties with one or two representatives in parliament, this perception has been given credence. The leadership of such parties appear to the public to be in it for themselves, or alternatively they function as pressure groups rather than as political parties in the more general understanding of what parties should do in a democracy (see Table 7).

The findings of several Afrobarometer surveys in Namibia also show that political issues and ideology play a secondary role in the politics of the country. Personalities and party loyalty often count for more. These findings work against opposition politics, especially if one factors in the low levels of public trust in opposition parties as compared to trust in the president of the country.[48]

Table 7: Opposition leaders' views on opposition roles, 2005

Party	Roles and functions of an opposition party
CoD	• To control the executive • To support policies that are 'good for the country' and provide alternatives for government policies that are 'not good for the country'
DTA	• To criticise and provide alternatives to government policies where necessary
MAG	• To criticise and provide alternatives to government policies where necessary
NDMC	• To control the executive • To fight corruption
NUDO	• To inform the public about political platforms • To establish a 'Government of National Unity'
RP	• To consider themselves as an alternative government with an alternative policy • To contribute to the development of the country and its people
SWANU	• To criticise and provide alternatives to government policies where necessary
SWAPO	[No response given]

Source: Hunter 2005: 83

Conclusion

The analysis in this chapter has attempted to show that Namibia has developed a one-party dominant political system through a variety of historical, structural and informal processes. Despite effective constitutional and institutional provisions and practices of electoral democracy, the political opposition remains moribund as a vibrant political force. They remain stuck in the sand. Nonetheless, Namibia will continue to consolidate democratic practices that may create more favourable ground for a future that has a more competitive party-political environment. In the meantime Namibia's democracy depends primarily on the commitment of the ruling elite to maintain existing democratic practices and values.

ENDNOTES

1. Lindberg S 2006. 'The Surprising Significance of African Elections'. *Journal of Democracy*, 17(1), January.

2. The November 2009 elections for president and the National Assembly reproduced the earlier outcomes discussed in this chapter. Fewer voters turned out in the two-day process than in 2004, perhaps reflecting a relative lack of interest among younger voters, referred to as 'born frees' (to show they were born after independence). The counting of votes took a full week, provoking both suspicion and a legal challenge from the opposition. President Hifikepunye Pohamba was easily re-elected with 75 per cent of the votes. The SWAPO party claimed 54 seats (down one), while RDP (the new official opposition) gained eight seats, but did not cut deeply into the north-central SWAPO base. Three ethnically based parties – DTA, UDF and NUDO – gained two seats, and four others – RP, SWANU, APP and CoD – each acquired one. Five smaller parties trailed badly and may not survive. The elections received a generally positive response from domestic and international observer teams, but with some serious reservations.

3. After 1975 easy cross-border access for the majority Oshivambo-speaking population (estimated to be 50 per cent of the total population) facilitated escape from apartheid repression into exile in the newly independent Angola. This exodus solidified the dominance of Oshivambo forces within SWAPO, and the dominance of SWAPO in the then-called Ovamboland for the next 30 years. As will be discussed, such a solid constituency guarantees SWAPO a majority of the electorate. Other ethnic groups each only count for single digits in the total population and are hampered by residuals of the apartheid separation policies.

4. See Thornberry C 2005. A Nation is Born:
The Inside Story of Namibia's Independence. Windhoek: Gamsberg Macmillan, for a recent treatment.

5. Nujoma was able to engineer a change in the Constitution to exempt himself from the two-term limit on the grounds that he had been appointed to his first term by the Constituent Assembly, not elected by the people. The secrecy surrounding the troop commitments to the DRC also reinforced the impression among many that Nujoma was becoming an autocrat.

6. Chirawu TO 2003. 'Political parties and democracy in independent Namibia', in Salih, MMA (ed.), *African Political Parties Evolution, Institutionalisation and Governance*. London: Pluto Press, p153.

7   The editor of Namibia Today, the official voice of SWAPO Party of Namibia, launched a vitriolic attack against Ben Ulenga and the CoD. See for example: 'Pohamba fires Ben Ulenga', *Namibia Today*, 1, 9, Monday 15--Sunday 21 November 1999; See also 'What Uulenga told the enemy, *Namibia Today*, 1, 10, Monday 22--Sunday 28 November 1999; and 'Ulenga's folly to be exposed', *Namibia Today*, 1, 7, Monday 1--Sunday 7 November 1999.

8   The 1999 national election followed closely on an abortive secession uprising. Former DTA president Mishake Muyongo from the Caprivi was implicated and thus the DTA and other opposition voters sought a safer political home in the CoD at that time.

9   Hopwood G 2006. *Guide to Namibian Politics*, second edition. Windhoek: Namibia Institute for Democracy, p52.

10 CoD's Programme for a Better Namibia', 1999; see also 'CoD Political Declaration and Principles of the Congress of Democrats', 2000; also Congress of Democrats Constitution, 2001.

11 Du Pisani A 1986. SWA/Namibia: *The Politics of Continuity and Change*. Johannesburg: Jonathan Ball Publishers.

12 Interview 2006.

13 Du Pisani A, op. cit.

14 Hopwood G, *Guide to Namibian Politics*, op. cit., p56.

15 DTA of Namibia, *Manifesto*, 1999.

16 DTA of Namibia, *Election Manifesto*, 2004.

17 This re-emerged party survived a court challenge by the DTA over who could claim to be the rightful inheritors of the party's name and official status.

18 National Unity Democratic Organisation (NUDO), *Election Manifesto of the National Unity Democratic Organisation (NUDO)* 2004. Windhoek: NUDO, pp.5-6

19 Hopwood G, Guide to Namibian Politics, op. cit., p15.

20 United Democratic Front of Namibia (UDF), *Manifesto*. Windhoek: UDF of Namibia, 1999; UDF, *Manifesto*. Windhoek: UDF of Namibia, 2000.

21 CoD parliamentarian Tsudao Gurirab has repeatedly raised this issue in the National Assembly, while the counter question raised by government media is why so few whites attend such national events, despite the reconciliation policy of the government (*Namibian*, 22 June 2006, p1).

22 Although several parties have done this, the most interesting and exemplary case involved the Local Authority Council of Ongwediva (north-central Oshivambo-

speaking area), where the elected SWAPO councillors were removed from office between the election and the swearing-in ceremony – a matter of days. This action was one of many factional conflicts within SWAPO during the extended succession period. An urgent Supreme Court interdict sought by the dismissed candidates was turned down, reconfirming the absolute dominance of the central party authorities, even over the wishes of the voters. The court reconfirmed that the party 'owns' the seats. The issues too are almost entirely national even in local elections. Party ownership of seats weakens the potential negotiating position of backbenchers, while reinforcing cabinet dominance.

23 SWAPO leaders repeatedly choose not to hold truth and reconciliation hearings in part due to an uneven ability to access South African perpetrators and the blanket amnesty granted by the administrator general just before the 1989 elections. SWAPO has a long-standing unresolved confrontation with its own former followers, who were held in dungeons in Angola. (Leys C and Saul JS (eds). 1995. *Namibia's Liberation Struggle: The Two-Edged Sword.* London: James Currey; Groth S 1995. *Namibia: The Wall of Silence –The Dark Days of the Liberation Struggle.* Wupperthal: Peter Hammer Verlag.) The 2006 Afrobarometer asked the public what it thought about a truth commission in the wake of the discovery of 'mass graves' from the independence struggle and an ensuing controversy. The results show a slight majority (53 per cent) in favour with 60 per cent of the urban population supporting the idea. (Keulder C 2006. *Afrobarometer Survey Findings: Summary of Results, Survey in Namibia.* Cape Town: IDASA, p58.) SWAPO leaders remain adamant that these issues not be reopened, with the symbolic outburst after Dr Wouter Bassson's acquittal in South Africa being an exception.

24 The alternative was well understood to be violence and chaos similar to that in Angola or South Africa in the early 1990s.

25 Diescho J 1996. 'Government and opposition in post-independence Namibia: Perceptions and performance', Building Democracy. Windhoek: NID.

26 Ibid.

27 Keulder C, op. cit., pp23, 8, and 21. Afrobarometer Round 4 Summary 2009, Q46. www.ippr.org.na. SWAPO attacks on suspected RDP 'hibernators' in 2009 and 2010 may increase political fear, as may some early campaign violence in 2009.

28 Melber H (ed) 2003. *Re-examining Liberation in Namibia: Political Culture Since Independence.* Uppsala: Nordic Africa Institute.

29 Opposition parties seize any seemingly popular issues available, yet this often makes them seem opportunist and inconsistently favouring a hodgepodge

of ideas. Interviews for this chapter confirm that opposition parties lack a viable alternative to the ruling party.

30 Gyimah-Boadi E (ed.) 2004. Democratic Reform in Africa: *The Quality of Progress.* Boulder: Lynne Rienner Publishers.

31 It took more than ten years to attempt a codification of communal land policy, for example. Traditional authorities were brought into an official, paid advisry role and organisation, effectively co-opting them to government. The Traditional Authorities Act of the early 1990s attempted to limit leaders to one official political role in traditional or modern settings (e.g., parliament) but not both. Again this limits the potential popular appeal of opposition parties but also counteracts the apartheid experience and culture.

32 Office of the Prime Minister 2000. *Namibia: A Decade of Peace, Democracy and Prosperity 1990-2000.* Windhoek: OPM.

33 At independence such a system put a premium on the first choice preferences of voters who had long been denied any choice in their own governance. Such an election system enabled the Constituent Assembly the widest, most credible and legitimate outcome for negotiating a new political dispensation. Its continuation under present circumstances enables several 'splinter' parties some hope of success rather than forcing them to join larger coalitions of interest. Consequently, Namibia's national elections structurally encourage many small parties rather than grand opposition coalitions of those out of power.

34 At local authority level, elections were supposed to convert to a constituency-based approach. The first elections in 1992 were held on a party list system to avoid reinforcing the apartheid residential patterns with electoral constituencies. SWAPO actually favoured constituencies in the constitutional discussions. Since the first local elections, time and money to delineate new constituencies as well as the will to do so have been lacking. Local elections continue to be largely conducted on the basis of national party identities. A Tocquevillian local pluralism has failed to emerge thus far, although several local ratepayers' associations did contest and win a few seats. It is unclear what changes might emerge in a constituency system, but there is little urgency from above or below to change. Local authorities facing increased decentralisation have little popular trust compared to other institutions in Namibia, though voter turnout has been robust by African and other standards, with one exception in 1998.

35 Hopwood G 2005. 'Trapped in the past: The state of the opposition', in Hunter J (ed.), *Spot the Difference. Namibia's Political Parties Compared.* Windhoek: Namibia Institute for Democracy (NID) & Konrad-Adenauer-Stiftung, pp137-9. Some of the opposition parties challenging the court case in the 2008 National

Assembly election have refused to be sworn in until the case is resolved. They are not eligible for public funding until they start to serve their terms.

36 Namibia adopted a French-style dual executive of a president and prime minister. The president must be elected by a majority of voters, so a two-round system is in place, though not yet needed.

37 Discho J, op. cit.

38 Republic of Namibia 1995. *Agenda for Change: Consolidating Parliamentary Democracy in Namibia.* Windhoek: Office of the Speaker, p32; Bukurura SH 2002. *Essays on Constitutionalism and the Administration of Justice in Namibia 1990-2002.* Windhoek: Out of Africa Publishers, p80

39 Bukurura, SH, op. cit.

40 Leys and Saul, op. cit.

41 The use of government vehicles and phones as well as attention by the media are only typical examples.

42 World Bank 2003. African Development Indicators 2003. Washington, DC: The World Bank, p303; World Bank 2006. World Development Report 2006. Washington, DC: The World Bank, p299.

43 Bratton M and Cho W (compilers) 2006. 'Where is Africa going? Views from below. A compendium of trends in public opinion in 12 African countries, 1999-2006'. Working Paper No 60. Cape Town: IDASA; Sheefni P Humavinda J and Sherbourne R 2003. 'Less than 30,000 jobs in ten years? Employment trends in Namibia since 1991'. Institute for Public Policy Research Briefing Paper No 24. Windhoek: IPPR.

44 Bratton and Cho, op. cit., p29.

45 Q57c Summary of Results Afrobarometer Round 4, 2009. www.ippr.org.na. Comparative data for 2008 in Little Eric and Logan Carolyn, *The Quality of Democracy and Governance in Africa: New Results from the Afrobarometer Round 4.* Working Paper No 108, p21.

46 Kandetu VB 1999. 'Democracy in Namibia: Wind of change or withering breeze?', in O'Malley, P (ed.), Southern Africa: *The People's Voices: Perspectives on Democracy.* Cape Town: NDI, p107; Interviews with A du Pisani in Windhoek: Ben Amathila, SWAPO chief whip and MP, 7 July 2006; C Geertze, CoD secretary-general and MP, 6 July 2006; Nora Schimming-Chase, CoD deputy president and MP, 6 July 2006; J Viljoen, Monitor Action Group MP, 7 July 2006; and J de Waal, DTA chairman and MP, 7 July 2006.

47 For example, 'TV broadcasting coverage of the 2009 elections: Week 3', 24 November 2009. www.ippr.org.na.

48 Afrobarometer Survey summaries, 2003, 2004-5, 2006, 2008 are available at www.afrobarometer.org and www.ippr.org.na.

CHAPTER SEVEN
SOUTH AFRICA: OPPOSITION POLITICS POST APARTHEID
DIRK KOTZÉ

Introduction

Scholarly work on the political parties in opposition in South Africa since 1994 is limited. The exception is Roger Southall's edited issue of the journal, *Democratization* titled, *'Opposition and Democracy in South Africa'*.[1] Other prominent publications like Anthony Butler's *Contemporary South Africa*, RW Johnson's *South Africa's brave new world* or *Government and politics in the new South Africa*, edited by Albert Venter and Chris Landsberg, do not pay significant attention to opposition parties. Hermann Giliomee and Charles Simkins' *The awkward embrace* concentrates on single-party dominance, including the African National Congress (ANC), and therefore sets up the antithesis for opposition parties, though they do not receive primary attention.

Some publications are short political biographies of political parties and movements, notably the *Mail & Guardian's A-Z of South African politics* in 1994, 1999, 2004 and 2009.[2] Earlier publications include the one by Hennie Kotzé and Anneke Greyling[3] and Shelagh Gastrow's *Who's who in South African politics* (1985).

Before 1994, party politics followed much stronger ideological and separated lines and no publication exists that looked at it as an integrated phenomenon. DW Krüger[4] and Willem Kleynhans[5] concentrated on the white parties, while a host of authors – including Thomas Karis and Gwendolen M Carter in their series *From protest to challenge* – concentrated on the liberation movements.

The ANC's dominance in the party political arena has become the single most significant definitive factor for all other political parties. Several parties define their identity in relation to the ANC (notably the Pan Africanist Congress (PAC) that broke away from the ANC in 1958/59, followed by the Congress of the People (COPE) in 2008) and less by means of independent factors such as an interest-based constituency or societal philosophy. For the purpose of this chapter, the spectrum of opposition political parties should first be clarified.

Political parties in South Africa are required to register as a political party with the Independent Electoral Commission (IEC) before they can register for participation in any election. This immediately draws a distinction between loyal and disloyal opposition parties. Disloyal parties do not accept the current constitutional dispensation as legitimate and therefore refuse to participate in elections. The Herstigte Nasionale Party (HNP) and the Afrikaner Volksparty are two such examples. For the purpose of this chapter we shall concentrate only on the loyal opposition.

Of those parties registered with the IEC, about 80 per cent are only interested in municipal elections. It is a highly diverse group, ranging from taxpayers' and residents' associations to single-issue-based organisations. Our focus will be on the parties with representation in the national legislature in order to make the discussion manageable.

Social movements are another category of politically-relevant organisations. The best-known at the moment are the Treatment Action Campaign, the Anti-Privatisation Forum and the Poor People's Alliance, consisting of the Rural Network (KwaZulu-Natal), Landless People's Movement (Gauteng), Abahlali baseMjondolo and the Anti-Eviction Campaign (both Western Cape). They concentrate on specific issues, mobilise popular support for these issues and define themselves as part of civil society that does not participate in elections. They do not consider themselves as opposition parties and therefore they will also not be discussed here.

Before the focus moves to the opposition political parties, a general point about the opposition on the right wing is required, because it will not be discussed again. The main question is: What has happened to the conservatives who were in the past well-organised, who rejected the constitutional negotiations and transition in the 1990s, and who potentially posed a threat to the new South Africa.

This constituency was organised mainly in the Afrikaner-Volksfront that included the Conservative Party and the Afrikaner Weerstandsbeweging (AWB). They refused to participate in the 1994 general elections and insisted on a separate volkstaat. Participation in the election by the Freedom Front (led by Gen Constand Viljoen) created a loyal right wing and largely emasculated the disloyal right wing. Two other factors eroded their organisational strength, namely the Defence Force's decision to dissolve its rural commando network and the arrest of the Boeremag leadership on charges of conspiracy to stage a *coup d'état*. The death of the AWB's leader, Eugene Terre'Blanche, was the final step in the right wing's demise. Most of this constituency has withdrawn from active political participation and are engaged in other societal activities.

POLITICAL OPPOSITION AS A CONCEPT

Roger Southall[6] reminds us of the ground-breaking work done in 1965 with the formation of the academic journal *Government and Opposition*, which is still a leading scholarly journal, and the publication a year later of *Political opposition in Western democracies* by Robert A Dahl. Both emphasised the central place of opposition parties in any democracy. Dahl's work was an attempt to understand the conditions that would allow opposition parties to flourish, and the patterns that they would most likely assume.

Since the start of the 1960s, studies of opposition parties have not grown in proportion to the studies of governing political parties. Therefore, many opportunities exist to develop a better conceptual and analytical understanding of opposition political parties. In this chapter the approach is not a normative one of what the opposition ought to do to flourish, but an empirical approach focused on the current status of opposition parties in South Africa.

As a first step in analysing the South African opposition, it is necessary to identify the two main traditions (or political subcultures) amongst the opposition in South Africa. The first tradition is Westminster-oriented and can be related to Dahl's notion of party political contestation. The main premises in this tradition are, firstly, that constitutionalism requires checks-and-balances to prevent the possible abuse of state power. The opposition is one of the key instruments in this regard. The second premise is that political power corrupts and therefore regular rotation of the government is necessary. Multiparty elections are therefore a necessity so that the opposition can become the next government. Adam Przeworksi made the observation that a democracy is not yet consolidated until the government has lost an election and handed power to the new government. Whenever in doubt, we classify as democracies only those systems in which incumbent parties actually did lose elections.[7] This first tradition of opposition in South Africa maintains a sceptical view of the state and is ideologically suspicious of power. The former Democratic Party (DP) and the Democratic Alliance (DA), as well as the former New National Party (NNP) after 1996 represent this tradition. In this framework, the task of the opposition is therefore to be critical, act as a watchdog and try to win over supporters from the governing party. Tony Leon, leader of the DP/DA, personified this approach.

The second tradition concentrates on cooperation, consensus and unification. The opposition is expected to be constructive in their criticism and should engage the government in dialogue, instead of criticising it from a distance. This tradition is partly informed by the notion of former Tanzanian president Julius Nyerere and others in the 1960s that political opposition parties undermine the post-independence programme of state-building and national development. A one-party state, on the other hand, prevents political fragmentation and enables a national consensus to develop. Recently Uganda experimented with the alternative of a no-party movement approach. With the advent of the Economic Structural Adjustment Programmes, the international financial institutions have also insisted, as part of their package, on multiparty elections. A new emphasis on sound opposition and good governance therefore has emerged in several African states. A more recent variation on it is the African Union's African Peer Review Mechanism that also insists on sufficient space for political opposition.

Views about opposition in South Africa oscillate between the two traditions. The ANC refuses to call itself a political party and insists on being [treated as] a national liberation movement. It views itself as the custodian of a historical obligation to implement the National Democratic Revolution which is qualitatively more than a conventional party or government policy programme but a blueprint for fundamental societal transformation. It means that the ANC does not see itself functioning on the same level as other political parties, and therefore its view of political opposition is ambivalent. Cognitively, it accepts opposition as a necessary element of democracy, but the ANC finds it difficult to regard the opposition as legitimate representatives of broader society and reduces it to spokespersons of minority and sector interests. It creates an internal contradiction which captures the general predicament of the opposition in South Africa.

Two illustrations of this predicament are the roles played by the NNP and the Inkatha Freedom Party (IFP). Both parties participated in the Government of National Unity (GNU) in 1994. They assumed the role of partner in government and of constructive opposition. The DP under Tony Leon refused to participate and played the role of critical opposition. In 1996 the NNP withdrew from the GNU and also assumed the role of critical opposition. In the general election of 1999, the NNP's ambivalence about its identity (government or opposition) was punished by the voters and it lost almost half of its support to the DP. The IFP continued in a coalition government after 1999, but in 2004 changed its identity and joined the DA in the 'Coalition for Change', also as critical opposition. It also lost substantial support in the process.

Today it is quite difficult to reach an unqualified conclusion about which of these traditions was the dominant one amongst the opposition. Paradoxically, the internal leadership power struggle in the ANC in preparation for its 52nd national conference in Polokwane in 2007, played out in public, meant the end of any pretence of unity and consensus as the benchmark of party politics in South Africa. Not only did it affect internal ANC dynamics but it also served as a catalyst for sustained open and acrimonious contestation in other parties (notably in the Congress of the People – COPE – and the IFP) and a new political culture of dealing with internal matters in public or in court. Ironically under the leadership of Helen Zille the DA has toned down its role as critical opposition and since 2008 it has been positioned as a 'party of government'.

It is also noteworthy that over a period of time the generation of negotiators in the multiparty Convention for a Democratic South Africa and the concomitant culture of consensus-seeking and trust that they developed started to disappear. Those who retired from parliamentary politics included Valli Moosa, Mac Maharaj, Roelf Meyer, Leon Wessels, Colin Eglin, Zac de Beer and Constand Viljoen, while those who took public office in other spheres included Pravin Gordhan (South African Revenue Service), Dawie de Villiers (World Tourism Council) and Fanie van der Merwe (IEC). The group of negotiators is no longer the nucleus of parliamentarians whose mutual trust could bridge difficult situations.

The formation of COPE in 2008 has potentially far-reaching implications for the concept of political opposition in South Africa. COPE not only attracted about half of its seven per cent national support in 2009 from the ANC but almost its entire national leadership consists of former prominent ANC members. Thus, it is no longer possible for the ANC to delegitimise the opposition on the basis of race, as conservatives or as homeland collaborators. Many of COPE's leaders were prominent in the United Democratic Front or the Congress of South African Trade Unions (COSATU) before 1990. Hence, the ANC no longer has an exclusive monopoly on the liberation legacy. This reality has the potential to redefine government–opposition identities in future. The very fact that COPE claims custdianship of the Congress of the People held in 1955 to adopt the Freedom Charter – both icons in the ANC's history – and that in its formative stages in 2008 COPE challenged the ANC on who had the most authentic claim to the core values of the historical ANC is evidence of changing identities.

THE CONSTITUTIONAL-LEGAL FRAMEWORK OF PARTY POLITICS

The South African Constitution (1996) does not address the status of political parties directly. The political and organisational rights of individuals are entrenched in the Constitution, while the logic is that political parties will be affected as a collective articulation of individual rights.

The most entrenched aspect of the Constitution (requiring a 75 per cent majority) is Article 1, which determines the basic constitutional principles. It states that South Africa is 'one, sovereign democratic state' founded on a number of principles. One of them directly relevant for political parties is 'universal adult suffrage, a national common voters' roll, regular elections and a multi-party system of democratic government, to ensure accountability, responsiveness and openness'. Reference to a 'multiparty system' is the clearest entrenchment of political opposition parties and the responsibilities they must take.

This point of departure is further developed in the Constitution's Chapter 2 of fundamental rights. Political parties depend in the first instance on freedom of association. Thus, Article 18 states: 'Everyone has the right of freedom of association'. Article 19 concentrates on political rights. The first one emphasises political parties. (Again, it is noteworthy that these rights are ascribed to citizens and not 'everybody', as in some of the other clauses, and also not to political parties. They are therefore individual and not collective rights.) The first political right is that 'every citizen is free to make political choices, which includes the right –
- to form a political party;
- to participate in the activities of, or recruit members for, a political party; and
- to campaign for a political party or cause'.

Jörg Kemmerzell[8] identified an interesting aspect of the South African Constitution, namely that it does not provide for the banning of political parties, especially extremist or particularistic (racial or ethnic) parties. Many other African and European constitutions provide for such bannings. The only possibility in the South African Constitution is a limitation on these constitutional rights in accordance with Article 36. According to Kemmerzell, a limitation on freedom of association with the intention to ban a party will be legitimate only if the party resorts to massive violence and acts as a paramilitary organisation. A militant attitude without violent actions will not be sufficient for such a limitation.

Kemmerzell[9] identified three possible explanations for the absence of a mechanism in the Constitution for banning parties. The first was the beliefs of political actors that the negative legacy of party bannings during the apartheid period should not be repeated. Intolerance towards parties was seen as a threat to democratisation. Secondly, the nature of the transition in South Africa also contributed towards an anti-banning sentiment. The transition was characterised by inclusivity and a broad consensus amongst different participants. Banning would have been an antithesis of the transition spirit. Finally, political extremism and particularism (especially racism) were not considered as unmanageable threats to the emerging democracy.

The second group of political rights in Article 19 concentrates on elections. They are:

19 (2) 'Every citizen has the right to free, fair and regular elections for any legislative body established in terms of the Constitution,

19 (3) Every adult citizen has the right –
   (a) to vote in elections for any legislative body established in terms of the Constitution, and to do so in secret; and
   (b) to stand for public office and, if elected, to hold office.'

If one combines these rights with the freedom of association, it means that the right of opposition parties to participate in elections is entrenched. The Electoral Commission Act (51 of 1996) provides two qualifications to this right. According to Article 16 of the Act, the IEC may not register a party if the proposed name, abbreviated name or its party symbol –

i) 'resembles that of any other registered party, and therefore may deceive the voters, or

ii) contains anything which portrays the propagation or incitement of violence or hatred or which may cause serious offence to any section of the population on the grounds of race, gender, sex, ethnic, colour, sexual orientation, age, disability, religion, conscience, belief, culture or language'.

Refusal to register a party is not the same as banning it, because once a party complies with the registration criteria, it can be registered. While the IEC's decision implies an element of discretion, it is in accordance with a law of general application and therefore does not discriminate against a specific political movement.

The only direct reference to political parties in the Constitution is with regard to the composition of parliament's National Council of Provinces. Each province is represented by ten delegates: four special and six permanent delegates (based on the parties' proportional strengths). Article 61(2)(a) specifies that within 30 days after an election the provincial legislature must determine how many of each party's delegates are to be permanent and special delegates.

Though not referring to them directly, political parties that accept the Constitution's authority and principles enjoy constitutional protection on the basis of the rights granted to individual citizens. The Constitution provides for a level playing field in terms of legal rights to all parties, is not biased towards any political movement or majority party and does not load the scales against opposition parties. One malpractice for a constitution to avoid is to interfere in the political balance of power. Subordinate legislation – the Public Funding of Represented Political Parties Act (103 of 1997) – reflects this balance in the allocation of public funds by parliament on a proportional basis to the parties represented in the legislatures. Parties are therefore not treated equally but on the basis of their electoral performance.

Three Acts of parliament constitute the foundation of the party system in South Africa, namely, the Electoral Commission Act (51 of 1996) and the Public Funding of Represented Political Parties Act (103 of 1997) and the Electoral Act (73 of 1998). In the case of local government, other legislation is also relevant but will not be discussed here.

In addition to all the legislative arrangements for free and fair elections, the Electoral Act also established the Electoral Court at the same level as the High Courts. It has the jurisdiction to make judgements regarding prohibited conduct (Chapter 7, Part 1 of the Electoral Act) by a person or registered party that can include prohibiting them from using any public media, electoral advertising, holding any public meeting and similar sanctions. In a situation where judicial independence is in doubt, it can certainly be used against opposition parties. However, up to 2009 it had not happened and instead, the court's independence is a significant factor for the success of elections.

The court also has jurisdiction in all complaints about infringements of the Electoral Code of Conduct. Every registered party and every candidate must subscribe to the code before they are allowed to contest an election. The purpose of the code (Schedule 2 in the Electoral Act) is to promote conditions that are conducive to free and fair elections, including tolerance of democratic political activity, free political campaigning and open public debate. The code is arguably one of the strongest guarantees for opposition parties that their rights will be protected during elections.

The Electoral Commission Act is primarily concerned with the composition and functions of the IEC. Two of its functions that affect opposition parties directly are to compile and maintain a register of political parties, and to establish and maintain liaison and cooperation with parties. A party cannot participate in elections if it is not registered. Interesting is the Act's definition of a 'party' (Article 1(1)(vi): 'any registered party, and includes any organisation or movement of a political nature which publicly supports or opposes the policy, candidates or cause of any registered party, or which propagates non-participation in any election'.

This definition includes two negatives that have a direct impact on opposition parties: it includes organisations or movements that publicly oppose any registered party – therefore as a party of opposition. Secondly, it includes parties that propagate non-participation in an election. A registered (opposition) party can therefore not be prohibited or does not violate the Electoral Code of Conduct by campaigning against an election. It is an example of extending the liberal notion of freedom of expression (even if it constitutes an internal contradiction) to its extreme limits, but is another guarantee that freedom of political activity by opposition parties must be tolerated. So far, extra-parliamentary movements opposed to elections have not registered as political parties and therefore could not test this legislative tolerance.

A relatively unique function of the IEC is its task to establish party liaison committees. In this regard it observed that the commission 'keeps in close touch with all parties and fosters mutual cooperation through party liaison committees at the national, provincial and municipal levels. The involvement of political parties in the electoral process enhances transparency and credibility'.[10] These committees have made an important contribution towards encouraging proper communication amongst parties and with the IEC before and during elections, thereby preventing many electoral disputes. They enable opposition parties to raise matters that do not depend on their proportional weight in decision-making.

Public funding by parliament to all political parties represented in the national and provincial – but not local – legislatures is done on a proportional basis. Parties without public representatives – like the United Democratic Movement (UDM) before the 1999 elections and COPE before the 2009 general elections – do not receive any monies, and they experience it as a form of discrimination in the sense that it perpetuates the power position of parties already in a privileged position. Strictly speaking, public funding should not be used for electioneering and is terminated three weeks before election day. In practice, the funding period overlaps with the campaign period. For example, before the 2004 general elections the ANC planned an eight-week campaign period which means that the first five weeks were not excluded from the funding period. Article 5 in the Act determines that public money can be used for:
- development of the political will of the people;
- bringing political parties' influence to bear on the shaping of public opinion;
- inspiring and furthering of political education;
- promoting active participation by individual citizens in political life;
- exercising an influence on political trends, and
- ensuring continuous, vital links between the people and organs of state.[11]

The impact of these funds on opposition parties is quite substantial. In the financial year ended on 31 March 2009 a total of R88.335 million was allocated to all the parties. The ANC received R61.114 million while the opposition parties in total received R27.221 million: the DA R10.539 million; the IFP R5.403 million; the African Christian Democratic Party (ACDP) R2.177 million and the UDM R1.612 million.[12]

One of the most controversial aspects of funding that also involves opposition parties is public disclosure of their private funding sources. The Institute for Democracy in South Africa (IDASA) took the ANC, IFP, DA and other parties to the Cape High Court to insist on public disclosure of their funding sources. In the absence of any explicit legislative obligation, little progress was made in this regard.

The constitutional-legal framework does not affect the party system in either negative or positive terms, and creates a level playing field. Some small parties cannot meet all the registration criteria for elections; others experience the public funding formula as biased against them but no significant systemic discrimination – or even instances of manipulation such as gerrymandering – are present. The most debated issue is the electoral system of proportional representation based on inflexible party lists. The main point of criticism is its lack of direct representation and public accountability but it does favour smaller parties. In the next section the philosophical or ideological spectrum of opposition is discussed.

PARTY POLITICAL SPECTRUM

Political parties are usually categorised and placed on a spectrum between left and right. Norberto Bobbio struggled with this concept, because the 'two concepts "left" and "right" are relative, not absolute. They are not substantive or ontological concepts. They are not intrinsic qualities of the political universe, but situated in "political space". They represent a political topology'.[13] His conclusion was that the spectrum indicates a party's position on the political landscape in relation to its attitude towards tradition, emancipation, equality and egalitarianism.

The party political topography in South Africa is not characterised by denotations of left or right or left-of-centre. Parties do not define themselves in these terms, while parties in countries like Turkey use them as part of their self-definition. Therefore we should not try to impose them on the South African situation but rather structure the spectrum in other terms – in particular on the different notions about the nature of society and the preferred function of the state.

Starting with the nature of society, the first perspective sees South African society in individualistic or atomistic terms. It is closely associated with the liberal emphasis on individual freedom as the supreme value in society, which is mostly associated with first-generation human rights. It implies that individuals (or their families) must take responsibility for most aspects of their lives, and should not depend on public or state support. Individuals will fulfil their potential only by taking the initiative and will be rewarded in accordance with their performance. Private initiative (i.e. the free market) is therefore the main driver of development in society.

Justice and freedom in society are guaranteed by adhering to proper procedures, especially judicial procedures. If procedures are followed, the outcome will be just. The emphasis is therefore on administrative justice and the rules of natural justice, judicial independence, rule of law, separation of powers and constitutional supremacy.

In the South African oppositional arena this tradition is strong, starting with the DA and the former NNP. The economic – but not the social – dimension of it is also present in the IFP and the Freedom Front Plus (FF+).

The second perspective regarding the nature of society is a communitarian view or social democratic disposition. Society is seen in holistic terms (i.e. the whole is more than the sum total of its components). The individual depends on the community for self-realisation, and the supreme values are equity and equality (and not freedom) with the emphasis on social and not individual responsibility. In economic terms the private sector is viewed as too profit-driven, and therefore not suitable for socio-economic development. Partnerships between the private and public sectors, as well as state-owned enterprises, are considered as a more appropriate instrument for development. Justice is viewed more in a social context and less as a legal question. In this framework justice plays a restorative role that is more socially-dependent than procedural in nature. Justice has a role to play in social transformation and should therefore be more activist in orientation than in the first perspective, which is more positivist in its approach and primarily interpretive of legal principles.

In the South African context all the organisations in the liberation movement embraced this understanding of society. In the opposition arena it is still today associated with the PAC and the Azanian People's Organisation (AZAPO) and partly also with COPE and the ACDP.

A third, hybrid position regarding the nature of society combines a communitarian social perspective with a free-market economic orientation. The IFP depends primarily on a traditionalistic constituency for whom the liberal, atomistic notion of society is an anachronism. At the same time it supports a free-market economic strategy. This hybrid orientation enabled the IFP in 2004 to form an electoral alliance with the DA known as the 'Coalition for Change'. The FF+ is socially a more conservative party, embracing group rights – especially cultural rights – and is traditionally sceptical of liberal values. At the same time it favours a strong private sector, though the state also has a social responsibility. The latter view is strongly articulated by the trade union movement Solidarity, which is historically associated with the FF+.

The second indicator of the Party Political spectrum deals with parties' views about the function and purpose of the state. Opposition parties oscillate between two different views of the state: the state as either the product of a social contract that limits it to a minimum number of functions, or a public resource and an instrument for social transformation, i.e. a utilitarian view of the state.

The state as the product of a social contract is considered necessary, but subject to strict controls and public scrutiny. The state, according to this view, has to provide certain essential services, especially public security, but it should refrain from entering the domain of the private sector. The protagonists of this view assume that a government's natural inclination is to abuse state power. Thus, constitutionalism in a procedural sense is required as an antithesis. In addition to constitutional checks-and-balances, the best preventions of state abuse are regular rotation of government and decentralised government (or federalism).

The DA is the main protagonist of this state view, while the NNP also supported it in the latter stages of its existence. Some opposition parties, like the Independent Democrats (ID) and the UDM, also articulate variations of it, but it is not always clear whether they are informed by either a coherent state philosophy or pragmatic criticism of the ANC's dominance.

A variation of this first view is found in the IFP and FF+. The IFP argued for a federal dispensation in the constitutional negotiations mainly to prevent a central ANC government from exercising central control over the KwaZulu-Natal province. It is therefore motivated more by power relation considerations than by a state philosophy. The FF+, on the other hand, propagated a separate Afrikaner volkstaat either as an independent entity or as a federal sub-state. It is therefore motivated by a comprehensive state ideology or philosophy but not based on the liberal suspicion of state power in general.

The second general view of the state sees it in much more positive terms as a source of opportunities. The state is considered as a public resource, as an instrument for social transformation and not only as a promoter, but as an agent, of social welfare and development. (Land reform is therefore viewed as not only a form of restitution of historical discrimination but primarily as a means of addressing rural social transformation.) The state is in its own right a source of infinite wealth and therefore politics is about competing for, and protecting control of, the state and access to that wealth. Furthermore, the state is seen in maternalistic or paternalistic terms, as a benevolent provider of social welfare and social security. Therefore the state must create jobs, must build houses, and must provide health services – all of them are therefore not the individual's responsibility in the first instance. Black Economic Empowerment (BEE) is a variation within this view: the state must restructure the economy and create new opportunities for access to the economy in accordance with fundamental changes in the balance of power in society.

This notion of the state is in the first instance articulated by the ANC – except during the period when the Growth, Employment and Redistribution (GEAR) macro-economic policy was dominant. Since about 2004 they have embraced the concept of a 'developmental state'. Opposition parties like the PAC, AZAPO, the

Black People's Convention and some of the strands in COPE subscribe to this state view. It results in ongoing contestations about macro-economic strategies such as inflation-targeting between the trade union movement and government, about employment equity and BEE, or about land reform (such as the principle of 'willing buyer, willing seller' versus compensated expropriation). State-owned enterprises are also often the focus of attention of opposition parties, either as unacceptable extensions of the state and therefore resource opportunities precluded from the rest of society, or as centres of BEE.

BACKGROUND OF THE TWO MAIN OPPOSITION PARTIES

Democratic Alliance

The DA is currently the official opposition in parliament with its 16.66 per cent electoral support. Its immediate history commenced with the Progressive Party (PP), formed in 1959. Its historical roots are much older and are a combination of the 18th century 'Cape' liberalism, the Liberal Party and, notably, the writer Alan Paton, Gen Smuts' internationalism as well as Johannesburg's liberal and business tradition. Helen Suzman was the only MP of the PP for 13 years. In 1975 the PP merged with the Reform Party to form the Progressive Reform Party. Two years later it combined with members from the dissolved United Party to form the Progressive Federal Party (PFP).

According to Tom Lodge, the PFP's importance, especially under the leadership of Frederik van Zyl Slabbert, was in propagating constitutional reforms,[14] including the KwaZulu-Natal Indaba. In 1989 the PFP (led by Zac de Beer), the Independent Party (led by Denis Worrall) and the National Democratic Movement (led by Wynand Malan) formed the Democratic Party.[15] The initial triumvirate leadership was not successful and De Beer took sole control of it. He was succeeded by Tony Leon in 1994 after the DP's poor performance in the election.[16]

The DA was formed in 2000 as an integration of the NNP and the DP. The NNP leader, Marthinus van Schalkwyk, initiated talks for an alliance with the DP in preparation for the municipal elections in 2000. Because of the absence of floor-crossing arrangements at the time, it was impossible to establish a new party at the national and provincial levels. The new party could therefore officially function as the DA only at the local level until the general elections in 2004.[17] However, the NNP's participation in the DA came to an abrupt end soon after the municipal elections, whereafter it moved towards the ANC. In the meantime, floor-crossing legislation was approved and after the 2004 general elections the NNP joined the ANC. At the same time the DA established itself at the national level in cooperation with Louis Luyt's Federal Alliance.

Formation of the DA with the NNP was not without internal criticism. Tony Leon[18] recalls Suzman's attitude: 'Actually, Suzman, over the next months and years, became steadily less enthusiastic about the "odd bods" who joined us. She became an implacable opponent of the idea of the soon-to-be reality of the Democratic Alliance.'

At the end of 2006 a document drafted by the DA strategist, Ryan Coetzee, titled 'Becoming a party for all the people: A new approach to the DA', was internally circulated. According to Coetzee, the DA's challenge was to become attractive to South Africans of all races – at that stage the DA enjoyed about 1-2 per cent support among black Africans. In Coetzee's view constitutional democracy depends on an 'alternative political force that can offer South Africa a real prospect of a change in government'. The balance that the DA had to strike was: '... if the Democratic Alliance is going to be part of a political force that can challenge the ANC for power over time, then we will have to increase our support among black voters, while retaining the support we currently enjoy among minorities.'[19]

In 2008, after Helen Zille assumed the leadership of the party, the DA entered a new phase when it 'relaunched' itself at Constitution Hill in Johannesburg. Zille positioned the DA not as an opposition party but as a 'party of government' guided by the vision of an 'open opportunity society'.[20] A few days before the event Zille motivated it as follows:

"After the 2006 local government election, it started to become clear that the realignment of politics was beginning and the Democratic Alliance would play a key role in that process. The ANC's unravelling, which was just starting, together with the newly established multiparty coalition in Cape Town, indicated that there was a very real prospect of an electoral change of government in South Africa – through a coalition or otherwise – during the next ten years."[21]

In 2009 in the provincial general elections the DA took control of the Western Cape government with Zille as premier. Athol Trollip became the DA's national parliamentary leader. In Gauteng it remained the official opposition but lost its status as opposition in six other provinces to COPE. In KwaZulu-Natal it is in third position, after the ANC and the IFP.

Congress of the People (COPE)

At publication COPE is the second strongest opposition party in parliament. It was also the youngest opposition party, formed on 16 December 2008 in Bloemfontein. Its genesis was the demise of Thabo Mbeki's presidency when he was forced to resign by the ANC in September 2008, to be replaced by Kgalema Motlanthe as president. A number of ministers and deputy ministers (including Mosiuoa Lekota and Mluleki George) and the Gauteng premier (Mbhazima Shilowa) resigned in solidarity with him. Lekota and Shilowa (known as 'Shikota') took the lead and convened a National Convention on 1 November 2008 in Sandton.[22] The main rallying points were Zuma's personal lifestyle, his association with ANC Youth League president, Julius Malema, their accusation that the ANC was deviating from its core values as encapsulated in the Freedom Charter, and the alleged unethical conduct of the ANC leadership elected in 2007 in Polokwane and the threat it posed to the national Constitution.

Immediately after the Convention the new group intended to form a political party. Names suggesting a contestation with the ANC about who is the 'authentic' ANC were identified, such as the New ANC or the Congress of the People. Moral ownership of the Freedom Charter, the ANC's philosophical cornerstone adopted in 1955 at the Congress of the People, formed a central part of this contestation. Both in the National Convention Declaration and in the Preamble of COPE's constitution the Freedom Charter is activated: 'Determined to ensure that the freedom that our people won is defended and the values that are enshrined in the Freedom Charter and in the Constitution of the Republic of South Africa are deepened in our society'.[23]

Mcebisi Ndletyana attached a specific ideological interpretation to the formation of COPE:

"COPE represents a concession of defeat by the centre-right tendency within the liberation movement, which had been dominant within both the ruling alliance and government in the last ten years or so. In other words, COPE is a re-constitution of the centre-right component that was formerly dominant within the pre-Polokwane ANC, hoping to garner sufficient electoral support to continue its centre-right project either by returning to political office or giving it prominence both within the officialdom and in the public discourse in general."[24]

A year later it was unlikely that the same interpretation would be sustained. It was ostensibly based on the premise that former president Mbeki and his supporters would control COPE and that COSATU and the left would determine the direction of policy in the ANC. Neither of these scenarios materialised.

At its formation on 16 December 2008, an interim leadership was elected with Lekota as president. Cope was confronted with the task of being ready for the general elections within four months. Lekota decided not to be available for parliament and therefore Rev Mvume Dandala was identified as COPE's presidential nominee and parliamentary leader, and Shilowa as the party's chief whip. COPE was not properly prepared for the election and its campaign was not well-directed. Dandala[25] emphasised the fact that the campaign concentrated on values: 'We have recast the conversation on COPE's Agenda for Change and Hope through the prism of calling for a value-centred society in order to achieve that agenda'. COPE received slightly more than seven per cent support – the highest in the Northern Cape, followed by the Eastern Cape. It became the official opposition in six provinces.

Leadership struggles between Shilowa and Lekota since 2010 have continued to paralyse the party. The inaugural National Congress was planned for May 2010 but serious differences developed around accreditation of congress delegates.[26] The

Congress' National Committee presented a proposal to the Congress to convert it into a policy conference – but it was rejected.[27] At the same time Lekota was recalled as president but later reinstated by a court ruling. Dandala and one of the deputy presidents, Lynda Odendaal, resigned and deepened the leadership crisis. By December 2010 COPE was yet again unable to convene its first, elective, National Congress, due to factionalism within the party.

THE GENERAL ELECTION IN 2009 AND THE OPPOSITION

Different analyses of the 2009 election have been made – for example, by Southall and Daniel.[28] While many of them are a statistical analysis of election results, the election in 2009 was dominated by Zuma, the ANC's presidential candidate. More than two-thirds of the campaign period was preoccupied with his personal matters, especially the charges of corruption, fraud and other matters against him. It almost automatically set other party leaders up against him: Dandala (COPE) presented a moral voice from the church, Patricia de Lille (ID) as the campaigner against corruption (the Arms deal), Zille (DA) as the challenger of ANC favouritism and nepotism ('a closed, crony society'), and Bantu Holomisa (UDM) questioning continuous trust in the ANC. The focus was therefore on personal integrity, trust, good leadership and values.

The ANC, on the other hand, wanted to distinguish itself from the Mbeki era by its slogan 'Working together we can do more' and by its emphasis on five priority areas: job creation and economic development, crime prevention, education, health care, and food security and land reform.

The campaign was characterised by strategies focused on policy versus personality. It was not an election based on policy choices made by a 'rational voter'. Opposition parties that wanted to present alternative policy options were therefore at a loss in the election.

Another characteristic of the campaign was the difference in the points of departure in the parties' strategies. The DA's strategy was distinctly different from most of the others. Zille's tenure as executive mayor of Cape Town formed the core of its strategy. Her claims of successful government were the basis on which she made her call for a majority in the Western Cape. Similar successful spill-overs from the local to the provincial in other provinces would create, according to this strategy, a critical mass at the provincial level, which would project the DA in 2014 and 2019 to the national level, the DA's main focus was on the Western Cape. COPE, on the other hand, pursued a strategy starting at the national level and reaching down to the local level (in 2011). The ANC adopted a similar strategy, which meant that both had a more national distribution of their votes than the DA.

Voter turn-out

South African elections follow two patterns regarding voter participation: in national and provincial elections the turn-out has been between 76 per cent and 89 per cent, while local government election turn-outs have been between 48 per cent and 50 per cent. An increase in the number of voters registered on the voters' roll from 21 million to 23.1 million created the expectation of a higher voter turn-out in 2009. These figures are contested by researchers like Robert Mattes (Afrobarometer) but for the purpose of determining trends and not absolute figures the IEC's statistics can be used. A comparison of the percentages in the elections can be found below.

Voter participation in national elections

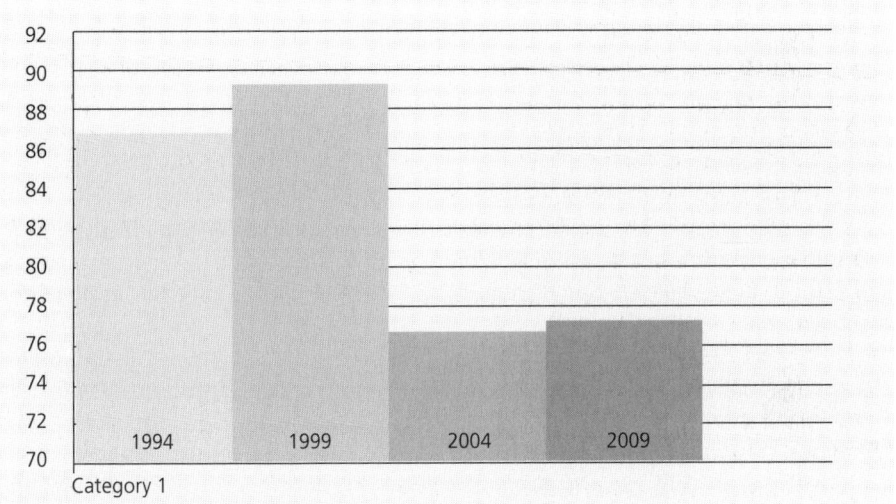

Source: Independent Electoral Commission

Immediately after the polling closed, the IEC predicted a turn-out of not less than 80 per cent. In the end the national percentage was only 0.67 per cent higher than in 2004, despite long queues at many polling stations and even an extension of voting at some of them. The explanation for the misperception of a much higher voter turn-out is the effect of Article 24A in the Electoral Act. It allows for registered voters to vote anywhere in the province in which they are registered. It means that logistical planning on the basis of the registered voters per polling station was not possible, and the designed distribution of voters to be about 3 000 per polling station did not materialise. The result was a concentration of voters at some stations, and very few voters at others.

DA Performance

The DP and, since 2004, the DA, results has been the most consistent opposition party in South African politics post-1994. It has been on an upward trajectory since 1994, as reflected in the following national election results:

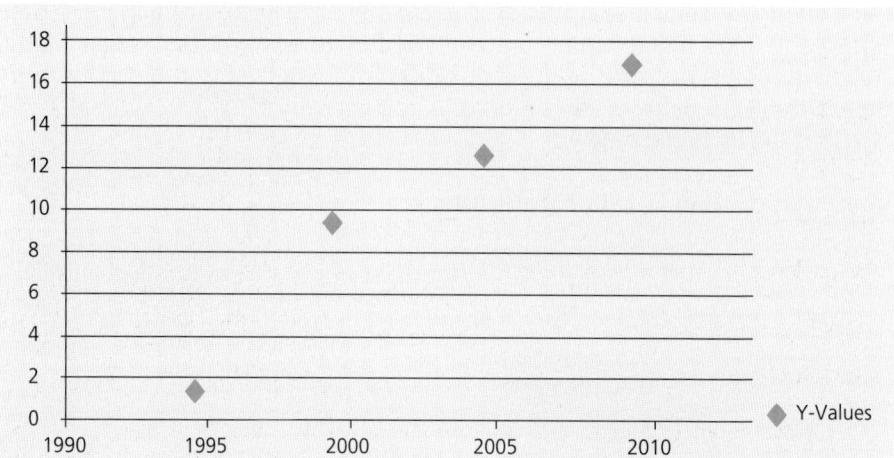

The results indicate that the DP made its breakthrough in 1999 by increasing its support by almost eight per cent (mainly from the NNP) and becoming the official opposition. Since 1999 it has increased by three to four per cent in each of the elections.

A characteristic of the DA's results is that they are concentrated in the Western Cape and Gauteng. In 2004 these two provinces constituted 59.26 per cent of the DA's total national votes. In 2009 it increased to 64.95 per cent of the total. If we consider the provinces individually, in 2004 Gauteng contributed 36.89 per cent and the Western Cape 22.37 per cent to the party's national total. In 2009 Gauteng's contribution declined to 31.37 per cent of the total and the Western Cape's increased to 33.57 per cent. All the indications are that the DA relies on the two provinces for its success, and that in 2009 it relied even more on the Western Cape.

One of the by-products of its emphasis on the Western Cape is that it lost its status as official opposition to COPE in the Eastern Cape, Free State, Northern Cape, Limpopo and North West. The IFP remained the official opposition in KwaZulu-Natal (KZN). The DA retained its opposition status only in Gauteng and Mpumalanga. However even if its exceptional performance in the Western Cape is excluded, in all the provinces, except in Limpopo and KZN, it increased its support. It is as follows (compared with the national average increase of 4.29 per cent):

DA gains and losses in 2009

Western Cape	+24.54%
North West	+2.78%
Free State	+2.73%
Eastern Cape	+2.65%
Gauteng	+1.53%
Northern Cape	+0.96%
Mpumalanga	+0.32%
Limpopo	-0.33%
KwaZulu-Natal	-0.85%

This table clearly demonstrates the dominance of the Western Cape in the DA's election strategy and results. The province where it also performed very well because of its intense competition with COPE was Gauteng. Many observers expected the DA in Gauteng to lose votes to COPE, which did not materialise.

In terms of the DA's declared strategy at the time of its 'relaunch' in December 2008, its next priority is to make gains at the local government level, and to extend its majority to other provinces in 2014. The question is, which province has the best potential for DA growth? Gauteng is the province with its second strongest support but the table indicates that its growth was very low (1.53 per cent). The province with the highest DA growth is the North West (2.78 per cent) but its base is very low. The only conclusion one can draw is that the DA has reached a glass ceiling. It will first have to make a dramatic breakthrough with local government elections, and thereafter it will have to systematically erode COPE support before it will be able to reach a new growth trajectory.

The provincial results in the Western Cape deserve special attention. It has already been indicated that the DA gained 24.54 per cent support. Where did it come from? The answer appears to be a mirror image of the coalition Zille formed to govern Cape Town: the losses suffered by the ID (3.29 per cent), UDM (1.14 per cent), ACDP (2.31 per cent), FF+ (0.81 per cent) and the IFP (0.1 per cent). The bulk of the gains came from the former NNP's support base in the 2004 election (9.44 per cent) and about seven per cent lost by the ANC (mainly the 'Coloured' portion of the ANC losses). What is left for the DA to gain in future elections are the ACDP's

1.47 per cent and the ID's 4.68 per cent. (Hence, inclusion of a member of the ID as an MEC in the Western Cape government is not a surprise.) The elusive constituency remains the black part of the population. COPE managed to capture most of those who deserted the ANC in 2009 in the Cape.

COPE Performance

The Congress of the People was formed just over four months before the April 2009 election. It is therefore understandable that it had a had little time to establish itself as a political party. Its history and performance in the local by-elections in December 2008 suggested that its main contention would be with the ANC. The expectation was that it would perform very well in the Eastern Cape. Opinion polls also suggested a good performance in Limpopo and the Free State.

COPE's results were lower than expected by most and could not reach the 10 per cent mark (7.42 per cent). The Eastern Cape was also not its main stronghold. In order to determine its main constituencies and where its support came from, the following table is presented. It includes COPE's overall percentages, its gains from the ANC, and the surplus gains from other parties.

COPE performance in the 2009 election

	Overall percentage	Gains from ANC	Surplus gains
Northern Cape	16.67%	8.00%	8.67% (NNP 2004), ID, ACDP, PAC)
Eastern Cape	13.67	10.45	3.22 (UDM, DA)
Free State	11.61	10.95	0.66 (UDM, PAC)
North West	8.33	8.33	
Gauteng	7.78	4.70	3.08 (UDM, ID, NNP 2004)
Western Cape	7.74	7.74	
Limpopo	7.53	4.84	2.69 (UDM, ACDP, DA)
Mpumalanga	2.91	0.79	2.12 (UDM, ID, ACDP, IFP)
KZN	1.29	1.29	

It is clear from the results that the core of COPE's support came from former ANC supporters. However, in the Northern Cape and Mpumalanga this was not the case, and COPE received more support from other party defections. It is also apparent that in six provinces it received support from a wider range other than former ANC supporters. The parties affected most by COPE were the UDM, ID and ACDP. In the Northern Cape and Gauteng it also received support from former NNP supporters.

The provinces in which COPE performed badly were KZN and Mpumalanga. These were also the provinces where the ANC performed very well. The two provinces appear to form a nexus in terms of voting behaviour. Given the fact that the Zuma/Mbeki divisions were duplicated in the ANC/COPE contestation, and the fact that KZN is Zuma's core constituency, it appears to have spilled over into Mpumalanga – hence, COPE's poor performance there.

The significance of the Northern Cape results is that they do not duplicate the Western Cape tendency. While in the Western Cape the DA captured the former NNP votes, in the Northern Cape they went to COPE. The same tendencies also affected the ID and ACDP losses. It means that the DA did not consolidate the 'Coloured' vote in the Northern Cape and only did well in the Western Cape. These results also deviate from the local government by-elections before the general election. COPE could not win a single seat in the by-elections while it made significant gains in the general election. This is another illustration that by-elections cannot be regarded as a credible barometer for general elections in South Africa.

Also significant of COPE's results was the fact that in four provinces its result were very close to the national average. The DA's results, on the other hand, were far from the national average, which meant that its median and average differed significantly. The closer they are, the more evenly distributed are a party's results and therefore its national presence. COPE is therefore the official opposition in all the provinces, except in KZN, the Western Cape, Gauteng and Mpumalanga.

Overall pattern

With the elections in 1999 and 2004 the ANC consolidated itself as a single-dominant party regime, with no opposition or minority party receiving more than ten per cent support, while it enjoyed a two-thirds majority. In 1994 three parties were prominent (ANC – 62 per cent, NNP – 20 per cent, IFP – ten per cent). That diversity disappeared after 1994.

The first impression of the 2009 results is they almost mirrored those 1994 election. Three parties were again prominent (ANC – 66 per cent, DA – 16.7 per cent, COPE – 7.5 per cent) and another one still important but gradually sliding away IFP (4.6 per cent). We can therefore typify it as a 3½-party system. All the other small parties together represented about five per cent support. It means that the minority parties are no longer fragmented; the opposition appears to be in a process of consolidation. John Daniel and Roger Southall[29] reached a similar conclusion.

It means also that the criticism that an electoral system of proportional representation encourages a proliferation of parties which can potentially paralyse formation of governments does not pose any threat to South Africa.

SUPER-OPPOSITION: DA ALLIANCES

The prospect of an alliance of opposition parties has always been seen as the only viable alternative to the dominance of the ANC. The sentiments expressed by almost all the minority parties at the National Convention on 1 November 2008 supported such a holistic approach, though it was not realistic for the April 2009 elections.

A limited tradition of alliance-formation already exists. In 2000 the NNP, Federal Alliance (FA) and Democratic Party formed the DA. In 2004 the DA and IFP formed the electoral 'Coalition for Change' and after the 2006 municipal elections the DA formed a governing coalition of seven parties in Cape Town.

An important impediment to party mergers is the fact that floor-crossing was abolished in 2008. It means that new parties can be formed only at the time of elections. As a result, an opposition alliance or super-opposition can be formed only within the following possible scenarios:

(1) A new, merged party is formed first at the local level and later extended to the national and provincial levels when their elections follow. This would be a repetition of the scenario in 2000 when the NNP, FA and DP formed the DA.
(2) An electoral alliance, and not a merger, is formed, based on inter-party cooperation in an election without competing candidates at municipal level.
(3) Post-election governing coalitions between parties who have reached a pre-election agreement. The 1999 agreement in the Western Cape between the NNP and DP is such an example.
(4) Post-election joint caucuses in areas where the ANC is in the majority.

In 2008 the suggestion of a super-opposition was mainly premised on COPE as the centre of such an alliance. The UDM leader, Bantu Holomisa, for example, presented the following view to the National Convention:

"We should encourage those who want to launch a new political party in the meanwhile to do so and to publish their platform. The second phase would be a bigger national convention after the elections – which is as inclusive as possible – where like-minded parties could meet as equals to discuss how we can build a strong new movement which would articulate the issues arising from this convention."[30]

After COPE's poor performance in the April 2009 elections the focus moved to the DA. According to the DA leader, 'the election results served to re-boost the prospects of coalition government'.[31] The reason was that the ID, UDM and ACDP had lost significant support to COPE and the DA. The ID was the first to actively consider a new path. The ACDP, on the other hand, took an official decision not to participate in alliance talks. The IFP never entered talks on the matter, while between the end of 2009 and the beginning of 2010, COPE also lost its motivation for such a process.

In addition to its power political ambitions, the DA has been motivated to form a super-opposition for two philosophical reasons: firstly, to develop a new value framework as a common basis for party politics. Zille articulated it at the DA's Federal Congress in July 2010 as: 'More and more South Africans want our politics to be an open contest of ideas and values, rather than a closed circle of conflict between race groups'.[32] Secondly, the alliance concept is meant to be the antithesis of identity politics. After the 2009 elections Zille made the following observation: 'Coalitions are an important way to go forward with [breaking through the barriers of identity politics]. We've achieved a lot with the coalition in Cape Town, and we've seen a very strong convergence between the parties that were in the coalition ... identity politics is still incredibly powerful, as it is anywhere in the world. Certainly coalitions help to take away many of the fears and misconceptions'.[33]

The alliance objective has produced only modest results so far. The DA and ID announced in August 2010 that they will merge at the 2011 and 2014 elections. The ID's contribution to the new entity is only 0.92 per cent and still declining. An analysis from the Council Scientific and Industrial Research (CSIR) in Pretoria[34] identified a trend that the ID was losing its main support to the DA in the 2009 elections. Its constituency is quite similar to the DA's, which means that it will slightly deepen the DA's support base but not widen it. Hence ID leader De Lille's observation that the merger is not about voter percentages but about 'building a political force that can hold the government accountable where it really counts – at the ballot box'.[35]

The demographic spread of the electorate in relation to the opposition's constituencies will be an important factor in determining the potential of any opposition. At present 19.3 per cent of all registered voters are in KZN, 23.56 per cent of the voters are in Gauteng and 13.19 per cent are in the Eastern Cape. This means that 56.05 per cent of all voters are registered in only three provinces. Any party with any hope of success must therefore have a substantial presence in those three provinces.

When the support bases of the parties mentioned in the context of a super-opposition are analysed, they are concentrated in the following provinces: DA (Western Cape and Gauteng), COPE (Eastern Cape and Northern Cape), UDM (Eastern Cape) and ID (Western Cape and Northern Cape). Collectively, they are therefore concentrated in the Western, Northern and Eastern Cape, with the DA also in Gauteng. None of them has a significant presence in KZN, while the situation in the Eastern Cape is better. Gauteng is their second weakest area.

CONCLUSION

Normalisation of opposition politics between 1990 and 1994 was one of the major transformations of South African society. Opposition parties are, however, confronted with the political weight of the ANC's historical legacy that makes 'normal' party politics still a distant objective. The 2009 general elections introduced some preliminary steps in enhancing the quality of opposition with a change in government occurring in the Western Cape. Several coalition governments at municipal level have been formed since 2006.

Opposition parties in South Africa are normally assessed in terms of how many parties exist, how strong they are and what are their prospects for defeating the ANC? Less attention is paid to the quality of opposition parties. The qualitative impact of the opposition on politics in South Africa should be more important than the quantity. The future of opposition in South Africa will partly depend on the qualitative improvement of political parties.

ENDNOTES

All the electoral statistics used in the analysis of the 2009 elections are based on the results provided by the Independent Electoral Commission (www.elections.org.za) and Independent Electoral Commission (2009a).

1. Southall, Roger 2001. 'Opposition in South Africa: Issues and problems' in *Special issue: Opposition and democracy*, Southall Roger (ed.). *Democratization* 8(1), Spring 2001.
2. Tabane, Rapule and Ludman, Barbara (eds.). 2009. *The Mail & Guardian A–Z of South African politics: The essential handbook 2009*. Auckland Park: Jacana.
3. Kotzé, Hennie and Greyling, Anneke 1991. *Political organizations in South Africa A–Z*. Cape Town: Tafelberg
4. Krüger, DW (ed). 1960. *South African parties and policies 1910–1960: A select source book*. Cape Town: Human & Rousseau.
5. Kleynhans, WA 1987. *South African general election manifestos 1910 – 1981*. Pretoria: University of South Africa
6. Southall, Roger, Op.cit, p4
7. Przeworksi, Adam et al. 2000. *Democracy and development: Political institutions and well-being in the world, 1950–1990*. Cambridge: Cambridge University Press, p16.
8. Kemmerzell, Jörg 2010. 'Why there is no party ban in the South African Constitution'. *Democratization* 17(4), pp687 and 693.
9. Ibid, p696
10. Independent Electoral Commission. 2009a. 'Elections 2009: to the future'. Information brochure. Pretoria: Electoral Commission, p26.

11 Kotzé, Dirk 2004. 'Public funding regulatory mechanisms to prevent the abuse of state resources' in Matlosa, Khabele (ed.). *The politics of state resources: Party funding in South Africa*. Johannesburg: Konrad-Adenauer-Stiftung, p92.
12 Independent Electoral Commission 2009b. 'Represented Political Parties' Fund: Annual report 2008/2009'. RP 248/2009. Pretoria: Electoral Commission, p10.
13 Bobbio, Norberto 1996. Left and Right: *The significance of a political distinction*. Cambridge: Polity Press, p56.
14 Lodge, Tom 2006. 'The future of South Africa's party system'. *Journal of Democracy* 17(3), p154.
15 Kotzé, Hennie and Greyling Anneke 1991. *Political organizations in South Africa A–Z*. Cape Town: Tafelberg, pp102-103.
16 Leon, Tony 2008. On the contrary: *Leading the opposition in a democratic South Africa*. Johannesburg and Cape Town: Jonathan Ball, pp244-245.
17 Ibid, Chapter 16.
18 Ibid, pp541-542.
19 Coetzee, Ryan. 2006. "Becoming a party for all the people: A new approach for the DA". (Internal document distributed by email and leaked to the media via ryancoetzeedocument@webmail.co.za, 28 November 2006), p2.
20 Zille, Helen 2008. Speech by Helen Zille, Leader of the Democratic Alliance. Constitution Hill. Johannesburg, 15 November 2008. Mime, pp1-2.
21 Zille, Helen 2008. 10 November 2008. Press statement: 'The re-launch of the Democratic Alliance'. Democratic Alliance homepage: www.da.org.za, accessed 2008/11/13.
22 Southall, Roger 2009. 'The Congress of the People: Challenges for South African democracy'. *Representation* 45(2), pp174-175.
23 COPE Constitution 2009, p1
24 Ndletyana, Mcebisi 2009. 'COPE – The beginning of the resolution of ideological contestation within the African National Congress'. Seminar paper presented at UNISA, 29 July 2009 Mimeo, p2.
25 Dandala, M 2009. 'Mr Mvume Dandala – Congress of the People (COPE)'. *The Thinker*, April 2009, p11.
26 COPE, 20 May 2010. The full letter of the General Secretary, document distributed by e-mail.

27 (COPE 2010. COPE branches reject leaders' deal, press statement distributed by e-mail info@congressofthepeople.org.za, 29 May 2010)
28 Southall, Roger and Daniel John (eds.) 2009. *Zunami!: The South African elections of 2009*. Auckland Park: Jacana and Konrad Adenauer Stiftung.
29 Southall, Roger and Daniel John (eds.) 2009. Zunami!: *The South African elections of 2009*. Auckland Park: Jacana and Konrad Adenauer Stiftung, p233.
30 Holomisa, Bantu 2008. 'South African democracy at a crossroad: Turning a new page'. UDM input at the National Convention: 1 November 2008, Sandton Convention Centre. Mimeo, pp8-9.
31 Zille, Helen 2009. 'The power of (more than) one'. Focus 54(2), p13.
32 *Business Day*, 24 July 2010 (DA not for minorities: Zille), www.businessday.co.za/articles/, accessed on 2010/07/27
33 Zille 2009. Op. cit p13.
34 Greben, Jan and Ittmann Hans 2010. 'Election night forecasting'. Electronic presentation at the ORSSA Pretoria Chapter, CSIR, 3 August 2010.
35 De Lille, Patricia 2010. Speech for the Democratic Alliance Federal Congress, 25 July 2010, ID homepage (www.id.org.za/newsroom/speeches/, accessed 2010/07/27).

CHAPTER EIGHT
SWAZILAND: OPPOSITION POLITICS WITHIN A FEUDAL SYSTEM
PETROS MAGAGULA AND ZWELIBANZI MASILELA

Introduction

Swaziland is the only country in the SADC region which is ruled by a monarch, wielding real political power and using traditional authority and institutions to this end. In Swaziland there are modern institutions of government running parallel to the traditional institutions. The king features in both institutions. Since independence the country has been characterised by this parallel rule. This dual system has hindered political developments that would have driven the country to become a fully-fledged modern democracy. Whilst the king features in both modern and traditional institutions, he ultimately relies on the latter to provide a bridle to the total transformation of the country into a modern democracy.

The opposition movements have been fighting to relegate the traditional institutions to a secondary role in the politics of the country. In response to their struggle for democracy, the opposition parties, and, indeed political parties intoto, were banned in 1973 and the independence constitution, which guaranteed freedom of political activity and association was repealed.[1] From 1973 "political activity" did not legally exist in Swaziland. It was only restored in 1978[2] when the Tinkhundla system of government was introduced.[3] But even in this instance political activity was only allowed in the Tinkhundla centres, parties continued to be banned. Hence there was no participation of political parties at the legislative and executive organs of government.

In February 2006, a new constitution came into force in the country. In spite of the formulation of the new constitution, it is not clear if political parties are allowed by law to operate in Swaziland.

The historical background is pivotal to the analysis presented in this chapter of the contribution of the opposition movement in Swaziland. Indeed, opposition parties have never had an opportunity to play a legislative role. From the time of independence up today parliaments in Swaziland have never had the benefit of learning from, or of being buttressed by, the contribution of the opposition parties.

However, the opposition movement has always existed in this country. The chapter later discusses the battle between the forces of traditionalism and nationalism that existed during the struggle for independence. This was the period when the king displayed his ingenuity in politics. King Sobhuza II continued to show his ability and that he was an astute politician even after independence, up to his death in 1982.

From 1973 the opposition movement was operating underground. They continued to operate underground until they, in defiance, operated openly in the 1990s. But this self-unbanning did not stop harassment from the armed forces – their meetings were interrupted, rallies were dispersed forcefully and some leaders were arrested and prosecuted in court.

All these activities of the state did not crush the opposition. They continued to press for changes and solicited the support of the international community. These efforts resulted in the "changes" that have been seen in the country, starting with the king's commissions (popularly known as Vuselas) of the early 1990s up to the promulgation of the present constitution.[4] The chapter later deals with the role played by the opposition – political parties, the main labour movements and NGOs – from 1968 up to 2009. Hence, part of this work elucidates the historical perspective of the political and constitutional developments in Swaziland.

The labour movement was particularly strong in the 1980's and 1990's. In the absence of political parties operating openly, the labour movement has tended to fill that gap in that they not only addressed bread and butter issues, but those of a political nature. For example labour movements have consistently called for the repeal of the 1973 King's proclamation and unbanning of political parties. The fact that the political parties have continued to be defiant in ther bid to operate openly has strengthened opposition forces. They have worked together with labour movements, NGOs and in some cases, the business community, to push the Swazi government to make some concessions viz the promulgation of the new constitution.

Nationalism, Traditionalism and the Road to Independence.

Nationalism and the call for self-determination in Swaziland were sparked off mainly by the events in Central, East and West Africa where African people had been engaged in the struggle for independence for several years by the late 1950's. Some of these colonies experienced the militant version of nationalism, for example the Gold Coast (Ghana), and others like Kenya took up armed struggles.. Due to the fear that Swaziland might experience either of these two versions, the European Advisory Council (EAC) petitioned in the late 1950's, the High Commissioner in South Africa, Mr. Liesching, to have it converted into a Legislative Council. The EAC fears were not unfounded seeing that in 1957 Mr. J.J. Nquku, one of the prominent and educated Swazi's had made an overseas tour of England, the USA and several European countries and came back full of ideas for 'democracy and progress' in Swaziland.

When the EAC petitioned the High Commissioner to have the EAC converted into a legislative council, the latter referred the matter back to the Resident Commissioners of Swaziland. This marked the beginning of constitutional talks which eventually led to the country being indipendent in 1968.

In the constitutional talks the main participants were (a) the Swazi Monarch and his traditional supporters, (b) the EAC, (c) the nationalist movements, viz the Swaziland Progressive Party (SPP) and their splinter group, the Ngwane National Liberatory Congress (NNLC) and (d) the Colonial Government.

The monarch had hoped that the British Government would hand over the powers to him. But his hopes were dashed when the British refused to do so. He eventually formed his movement called Imbokodvo National Movement (INM). Using this movement the monarch and his traditional supporters effectively participated in the constitutional talks.

The European Advisory Council (EAC) converted itself into the United Swaziland Association (USA). Under this organisation they participated in the constitutional talks. Threatened by radical nationalism of the modern political movements – the SPP and the NNLC – members of USA joined the traditional movement (the INM) and the USA itself was disbanded in 1965.

The SPP and the NNLC were the nationalist movements which drew support from educated Swazis and the working class. They participated effectively in the constitutional talks in the early 1960's. These nationalist movements also put pressure on the colonial government and employers to effect reforms that would benefit employees. They were eventually excluded from the constitutional talks after the 1964 elections which led to the inauguration of the First Legislative Council in Swaziland. They did not win any seats in that Legislative Council and the Colonial Office policy was that only parties represented in the Council should be involved in the discussions.

The next elections held before independence were in 1967. In these elections the INM won 80 per cent of the votes and the NNLC about 20 per cent but no seats in Parliament. So when Swaziland received Independence on September 6, 1968, there were no opposition parties in Parliament.

The Dynamics of Opposition Politics: Change and Continuity

The post-independence politics of Swaziland is characterised by parallelism, i.e. the existence of both the modern system of government and the traditional system. The repeal of the Independence Constitution in 1973 not only entrenched parallelism but also tilted the balance in favour of the traditional political institutions. This strengthening of traditional institutions alienated many educated Swazis from political participation.

Alienated Swazis initially displayed passive resistance to the domination of the political system by the traditional authority and institutions, but later participated in active resistance characterised by campaigns, demonstration, strikes, demands, petitions, legal actions, etc.

Parallel Rule since 1968

The Swazi Monarch and his supporters had mixed feelings about the Independence Constitution which curtailed the Monarch's powers. The Constitution gave every Swazi freedom of speech and political organisation. Hence at the time of Independence opposition parties existed albeit unrepresented in Parliament. The Constitution and the opposition parties were the traditionalists' great concern. King Sobhuza II did not like political parties at all. His INM was never referred to as a political party. Instead, it was depicted as a movement for the Swazi nation as a whole, a movement that signified the whole Swazi nation moving towards progress with their King who was a symbol of unity. According to the Swazi Monarch political parties were a source of disunity in many African countries. To emphasise the point that INM was not a political party, its candidates for both the 1967 and 1972 general elections were chosen by traditional regional committees (tinkhundla) and presented to the King for approval. They were then presented to the people in a huge national meeting at Lobamba Royal Kraal. Their campaign slogan was "We are from the Royal Kraal" (Siphuma Esibayeni saka Lobamba).

The Monarch used his office to campaign for INM. At the Incwala ceremony[5] in December 1971 he told the Swazi warriors to vote for INM and not to abstain or stay away from the forthcoming 1972 general elections. He warned that if they stayed away "... the nation would suffer for there are two ways of electing a person. In Western procedure you go to vote to elect a person. If you abstain from voting, thinking that by staying away you are not electing, you are in fact electing another by increasing his total against the one you really wanted in power.'[6]

Problems of parallel rule also manifested in having two bodies with legislative powers: the Swaziland Parliament and SNC. Theoretically the Parliament is supposed to leave issues pertaining to Swazi law and custom to the SNC. But in the twentieth century society it is difficult, if not impossible, to draw a line between modern issues and issues falling exclusively under Swazi law and custom. For example, in September 1979 a meeting of the SNC (which this time included adult females) was convened at Lobamba to discuss a wide spectrum of national issues, including the concept of dowry (lobolo), types of marriage suitable for Swazis and the wearing of trousers/jeans by women in the country.[7] On the last issue, the SNC decided it was unSwazi for women to wear trousers/jeans.

However, women continued to wear trousers/jeans. Thereupon Chief Mlimi Maziya (member of both Inner Council of SNC and Parliament) asked the Minister of Home Affairs, in Parliament, when he would enforce the law which barred women from wearing trousers. The issue was "rejected as unnecessary and demed as interference with the freedom of the individual"[8] by Prince Gabheni, who was supported by the Prime Minister and other MPs. This case illustrates the difficulty in identifying which issues were modern and which ones were traditional custom. The Home Affairs

Minister and the Prime Minister were defending and upholding a bourgeois right, i.e. the freedom of individuals to live their own lives, whereas according to the MP and SNC is was against Swazi law and custom for women to wear trousers. As a traditionalist, the MP viewed the adoption of 'foreign culture and practices' as the cause for the erosion of the Swazi way of life, amongst Swazi women. When Swaziland attained Independence in 1968, many traditionalists hoped that there would be a halt to this erosion of Swazi culture.

The potential conflict between these two systems was avoided by the power and skilful manoeuvre of Sobhuza. He had to assent to both SNC and Parliamentary Bills before they became law. In the case of the former the decision of the SNC (which includes the Advisory Council – Liqoqo) was taken to the Ngwenyama for assent. He would receive detailed explanation from Liqoqo about the SNC decision. If he agreed the decision became law. If he did not agree the matter would be referred back to the SNC for another debate until both the SNC and the Monarch reached consensus. Consensus was the backbone of decision-making in Swazi society. Decision by voting was unknown.

The Repeal of the Independence Constitution

The first elections of the post independence period were held in 1972. In this election the INM won 21 seats in Parliament. The remaining 3 seats were won by the NNLC. This was the first time that the opposition would be represented in the Swazi Parliament.

The monarch and the INM were not happy about the outcome of the elections, they detested the fact that there was growing support of the opposition. They challenged the validity of the election of Mr. T.B. Ngwenya, who was one of the elected NNLC members, on the ground that he was not a Swazi. The Court ruled that Ngwenya was indeed a Swazi.

However, the INM did not accept the court ruling in favour of Ngwenya. On April 12, 1973 Parliament met and resolved that the Constitution was unworkable. They resolved to surrender all the powers to rule the country to the monarch. On the same day (April 12, 1973) the monarch made a pronouncement to a large crowd that was gathered at Lobamba Royal Kraal. He said the Independence Constitution was being repealed and that he was assuming all legislative, executive and judicial powers. Political parties and all political activity were banned. Parliament was dissolved indefinitely and the monarch would rule the country together with his Council of Ministers.

A few months after the repeal of the Independence Constitution the Swazi Monarch issued a Gazette establishing the Royal Constitutional Commission "to inquire into fundamental principles of Swazi history and culture, as well as the modern principle of constitutional and international law with which they needed to be harmonised."

The Establishment of the Parliament of Swaziland Order, 1978

The implementation of a new political dispensation was reflected in the Establishment of the Parliament of Swaziland Order, 1978. This document introduced the Tinkhundla system of governance in the country. This system did not allow political parties to operate in the country. In other words, political activity continued to be banned in the country. The Monarch still had legislative, executive and judicial powers vested in him. In short, the King's Proclamation of 1973 was the effective instrument to govern Swaziland, while the Establishment of the Parliament of Swaziland Order, 1978, only provided the elections procedure based on the Tinkhundla constituencies.

After the report of the constitutional commission the 1978 constitution was promulgated and a new political dispensation came into being.. The repeal of the Independence Constitution had been a result of the Monarch's refusal to share power with modern government institutions and the fear by the traditionalists, including those in modern government, that they might lose their majority in Parliament sooner or later. It was logical therefore that the new Constitution would have no provisions which would require Sobhuza to share power and none that would allow opposition parties. In the following section it is argued that the new Constitution complied with the above logical expectations; that this Constitution caused political alienation amongst many Swazis; the Sobhuza's dominatin of Swazi politics, coupled with no political participation by the masses, resulted in a power vacuum after his death because there were no political structures which guaranteed continuity when the Lion (Ngwenyama) roared no more. In short the power struggles of the 1980's and the court prosecutions that ensued were struggles to fill the vacuum.

Problems of the New Political Dispensation

Problems of the new Constitution and the new political dispensation – the Tinkhundla system – are legion. However, this chapter will focus on the following: (a) the fact that the 1978 Constitution was not written has left many unanswered questions, (b) the non-existence of political parties coupled with the ban on political campaigning, (c) the open voting system in the election of the Electoral College, (d) lack of ballot papers in Tinkhundla elections, (e) the creation of the Regional Office and the Council, and (f) keeping the Electoral College for as long as the life span of the Parliament.

The gist of the problem with the unwritten constitution of Swaziland lies in the fact that there is no explanation on the relationship of the 3 main organs of government: the legislature, the executive and the judiciary. It is imperative to recall that on that historic afternoon of the 12th April 1973, when Sobhuza repealed the Independence

Constitution, he said "... I have assumed supreme power in the Kingdom of Swaziland and that all Legislative, Executive and Judicial power is vested in myself..."[9]

Another problem with the *Tinkhundla* system is the non- existence of political parties and the ban of political campaigning. As was previously mentioned the Swazi Monarch did not like political parties at all. He wanted the British Government to hand over the country to him. He loved to think of himself as the only one capable of coming to the rescue of Swaziland if the country was to escape the numerous political troubles being experienced by the newly independent African states in the north. Indeed on 12 April 1973 the Swazi Parliament called on Sobhuza to come to the "rescue" of Swaziland.

The *Tinkhundla* system was based on the philosophy that political parties which went around the country making promises to people were not genuine. They were there to get into power for the purpose of serving their own interests. Hence there was no resurrection of political parties in 1978, and there was a ban on campaigning – the philosophy being that the genuine leader would get the people's mandate without having to ask for votes or make any promises. One old Swazi saying goes: "To be entrusted with a position of great responsibility is tantamount to being killed" (Kubekwa Kubulawa). Therefore who, in their right senses, would go around campaigning to be killed?

The non-existence of political parties, coupled with no campaigning, generated criticism from the educated section of the population. The argument is that political organisations are a platform whereby people diagnose the problems of the country, advance and articulate their views and offer solutions.. Also it is from political organisations that individuals emerge as potential leaders. During the elections political parties and individuals address the people and the people are given an opportunity to make their decisions about the suitability of candidates. In the no political parties – no campaigning situation the electorate are not given a chance to choose their candidates. Instead, it is the chieftaincy and the Monarch that choose candidates. The people who criticise the *Tinkhundla* system are mostly those who hold Western views of a system of Government. They are former leaders and supporters of the banned NNLC, SPP, etc. Hence a few, including Dr. Ambrose P. Zwane (President of the NNLC), were detained after the announcement of the Tikhundla elections in 1978. It was obvious that chiefs would not choose people, as their representatives at *Tinkhundla*, who showed sympathy with opposition parties like NNLC or SPP. The doomed fate of the modern political parties, especially the NNLC, was sealed by the *Tinkhundla* electoral law which excluded any person who had been or was detained under the 60-day detention order as eligible for election.

More-over, the leaders of opposition parties were silenced with effect from 12 April 1973. The banning of political parties and "political" activity resulted in the official absence of opposition views. It resulted in lack of political education for the masses. There was no platform to criticise the Government's activities, or to point out their mistakes. If any opposition voiced their criticisms they were detained without trial. These conditions have resulted largely in the politics of silence and apathy in the country.

Political parties and campaigning for votes were not allowed under the system. Voting by queuing alienated many people, especially the educated, from participation in the Tinkhundla elections. Although the percentage of the electorate who participated in the 1987 elections was not given to the press, "The Times of Swaziland" (7 November 1987) pointed out that few people voted and that the Chief Electoral Officer admitted this fact. We should remember that there were no ballot papers to prove the authenticity of the figures which were released. This low turn out, even in rural areas where chiefs ordered their followers to go to the polls, was said to be due to lack of transport to the polling stations and flooded rivers. Be that as it may, the other fact is that the majority of rural illiterate people hardly understood the whole concept of voting. When political activity was still legal, political parties and campaigns acted as agents for politicisation and educating the masses. Since the closure of that chapter in 1973 it had been back to political ignorance in as far as modern politics is concerned. They were taken back to traditional politics, i.e. politics through the chieftaincy. Since Chiefs are born and not elected, it became difficult to comprehend the concept of elections. Therefore, the Chiefs had to order their followers to go to the polling stations. The people did not necessarily go out of their own volition. The contention is that many illiterate people who participate in the *Tinkhundla* elections do so blindly. The *Tinkhundla* system is responsible for the political bankruptcy of many Swazis.

Direct Elections Under the Tinkhundla System

The opposition political parties, civil society organisations, the labour movement and non-governmental organisations raised the concerns about the inadequacies of the *Tinkhundla* system. The outcry of these bodies also drew the attention of the international community. ILO, Amnesty International and SADC are some of the international organisations that raised the issue of governance in Swaziland. This added pressure on the Swazi authorities was due to the fact that the African continent was undergoing political change. There was a call for democracy, good governance and respect for human rights. Swaziland could not remain blind to what was happening in its surroundings.

Due to the pressures from the opposition from inside and outside of the country, the rulers of the country embarked on the process of "change". This process was orchestrated through what became a series of Commissions, popularly known as Vusela's. These Commissions travelled all over the *Tinkhundla* centres to hold meetings with the people to find out their views about the economic, political and social issues. The Commissions were doing consultative work, i.e. they were supposed to gather the people's views about the future economic, political and social policies of the country.

One of the first outcomes of these Commissions was an amendment in the electoral process in the *Tinkhundla*. Elections at an Inkhundla now produced a Member of Parliament (MP) instead of an Electoral College (which had been the practice as provided by the King's-Order-in-Council of 1978). The new version of the elections process was contained in the Establishment of the Parliament of Swaziland Order, 1992. From here onwards elections under the *Tinkhundla* system were direct, in the sense that MPs were elected at an *Tinkhundla* as their constituency. This is different from the past electoral process where an MP was elected by the Electoral College and could not associate himself with any particular Inkhundla or constituency.

Another major change in the electoral process was that voting since 1992, has been conducted in a secret ballot. In the past there was open voting as people openly walked through the gate where their candidate was physically seated. The counting was done as people walked through the gate.

The New Constitution of Swaziland

One of the products of the Commissions (Vuselas) was the new constitution of Swaziland. Due to the continuing pressures and demands of the opposition organisations and structures, the Swazi authorities set up a Constitutional Review Commission (CRC). The CRC was to get views from the citizens about the type of constitution that they would like to see in place in the country. The CRC was formed in 1996 and its chairman was Prince Mangaliso (it may be worth pointing out that all the Commissions and Committee – four in all – were chaired by princes). The CRC members were appointed by the Monarch and his committee.

This CRC was not accepted by the opposition organisations and bodies. Firstly, they argued that the political climate was not conducive to such an exercise. They wanted the removal of the 1973 Proclamation which banned political parties. In other words they wanted the unbanning of political parties before an exercise of this magnitude could he embarked upon. Secondly, they demanded that political parties, movements or organisations should choose their own representatives to the commissions if meaningful changes were to be realised. They did not agree with the method of constituting the commission. Third, they observed that a constitution review exercise could only be meaningful if the citizens have received civic (political) education prior to submitting their views. Such civic education can be properly done by a body that was not an interested party to the outcome of the whole process.

The Swazi authorities ignored the views of the opposition and went ahead with the exercise. Most of the opposition bodies boycotted the exercise. In fact some members of the opposition who had been appointed (by the Monarch and his committees) into the CRC withdrew – claiming that the process was a non starter as it was flawed from the onset. The CRC reported its findings in 2000. Amongst other things, they submitted that the majority of the Swazis wanted the *Tinkhundla* system of government, that they did not want political parties and that they wanted the King to have real political powers and not to be a figure-head.

Following this CRC report, the King and his committee's set up the Constitutional Drafting Committee (CDC) – led by Prince David – in 2001. The CDC produced the draft of the constitution in October 2004. The Constitution was promulgated by the Constitution of the Kingdom of Swaziland Act, 2005, and enacted in February 8, 2006.

Most of the opposition organisations did not accept the Constitution as a document that enshrines a democratic dispensation in the country. They pointed out that it had serious weaknesses. First and foremost, the Constitution spelt out that "The system of government for Swaziland is a democratic participatory, tinkhundla based system which emphasises devolution of state power from central government to *tinkhundla* areas and individual merit as a basis for election or appointment to public office".[10] This section suggests that the Tinkhundla system of governance is enshrined in the constitution. Under the Tinkhundla system there are no political parties. However, this Constitution contains a Bill of Rights where among other things the freedom of association is guaranteed. Section 125(1) of the Constitution reads "A person has a right to freedom of peaceful assembly and association". These two sections (i.e, 25 and 79) do not shed any light as to whether or not political parties can operate freely in Swaziland, it is not clear whether, political parties are free to contest national elections and, if they win, form a government. Hence the present Constitution of Swaziland is regarded as a controversial document. There are many provisions in the Constitution that are not acceptable to the opposition. Some of these points will be raised as we discuss the profile and dynamism and/ eclipse of the opposition.

The Profile of the Opposition

It is important to note that until February 8th, 2006, political parties remained banned. The Swaziland Constitution Act, 2005, states that Swaziland is a democratic kingdom. Swaziland subscribes to a "democratic, participatory *Tinkhundla*-based system". The Tinkhundla-based system of government is a unique democracy peculiar to the people of Swaziland. This system, it is argued, allows willing participation of citizens at grassroots level in decisions which affect them. In the referred to articles of the constitution, the principle of democracy is not defined.

The Constitution precluded the operation of plural political parties. In the Bill of Rights, the protection of the freedoms of expression, assembly and association are enshrined (sections 24 & 25). However Section 79 emphasises the continued operation of the *Tinkhundla* based political system whose fundamental feature is the election of people into parliament on individual merit.

Table: List of Post Independence Political Parties in Swaziland

Political Parties	Status	Estimated Membership
African United Democratic Party	Active	+/- 6 000
Inhlava Forum	Active – Not registered	Majority Members of Parliament (claimed)
Imbokodvo National Movement (INM)	Not Known – Suspected Active	Not available
Ngwane National Liberatory Congress (NNLC)	Active	Not available
People's United Democratic Movement (PUDEMO)	Active	+/- 20 000
Sive Siyinqaba – Sibahle Sinje Cultural Organization	Active – Registered as a cultural organization not Political Party	+/- 60 000
Swaziland National Front (SWANAFRO)	Active	Figures presented not conclusive.
Swaziland Progressive Party	Active	Figures presented not conclusive.
Swaziland Youth Congress (SWAYOCO) youth arm of PUDEMO	Active	Not available

Profile of the remaining active political parties:[11]

All political parties formed after 1973 are considered illegal and therefore are not registered.

African United Democratic Party (AUDP)

This is a new and unregistered party – it declared itself on October 2nd, 2005. It claims a membership of over six thousand members. The majority of members are middle class professionals. Propelling the AUDP into national headlines and public scrutiny is that it is the first organisation that has challenged the government in the courts thus testing the new constitution. The AUDP applied to be registered as a political party citing the relevant constitutional clauses using the Section 21 of the Companies Act of 1912 and the Protection of Names, Uniforms and Badges Act of 1969. The Companies Act has a very broad definition of what sort of entities can be legitimately registered by the Ministry of Justice and Constitutional Affairs as organisations The Register of Companies Clerk refused to register the party claiming the legislation is inadequate and/or does not include political parties as organisations that can be registered. The AUDP up to taday is challenging this matter in the courts.

The AUDP claims to be a liberal party with a centre left objectives. Whilst pluralist in view, in wants to create a welfare state where all national resources are "utilised to develop the Swazi nation." Its constitution sees the present status-quo as untenable and in need of change. It seeks to create a constitutional state however, the issue of the role of of the institution of the monarchy is left unaffected.

Inhlava Forum

This is a new organisation formed in April 2006 which proclaims itself as a democratic movement. It is led by a former Minister of Health and Social Welfare, who was allegedly fired by the Prime minister for challenging him in the courts after taking a decision to suspend the Minister from international state travel. Before being appointed Minister of Health and Social Welfare, the leader of the group was a very popular, and influential backbencher in parliament for two consecutive terms. He has returned to being an ordinary member of parliament after being fired from his ministerial position. In the 2008 elections he lost his seat and is no longer an MP.

Inhlava is neither registered nor has a constitution. Guiding Inhlava as a movement are its five objectives stated in its membership cards.. Inhlava illustrates schizophrenic behaviour by not defining itself as a party yet seeking to influence state decisions and competing for public office through the parliamentary elections. Its leader says they are a think-tank at the same time acting as secretariat to its members. The majority of the members of Inhlaava are members of Parliament. Because of its fluid definition, the leader of Inhlava argues that there is no need to register as a political party or any form of institution. This is until political parties are allowed to register or when members decide the form the organisation should adopt; or whichever comes first.

Ngwane National Liberatory Congress (NNLC) –

The NNLC went underground immediately after the 1973 decree with its leader, Dr. Ambrose Zwane, going into exile thereafter. Dr Zwane returned from exile in the 1980s under very strict conditions until he died in 1997. The NNLC used his death (funeral) to re-launch itself – ignoring its illegal status – by setting up an interim government and effecting a new constitution in November 1998. The NNLC is Pan-African in spirit.

The NNLC is the oldest active pre-independence political party. Theoretically, it is not the only remaining pre-independence political party as the Imbokodvo National Movement is suspected to be still active itself. However, there is no evidence that INM is active save to say that some politicians and people in influential state positions occasionally claimto be members of the INM in public forums. The NNLC after years of boycotting the country's electoral process, individuals within the NNLC including its President have in the last two elections participated. About two known members of the NNLC have been voted into office. The rational for going into parliament forwarded by the elected members was that they wanted to influence the constitutional process. However, some party members remain sceptical about: the political system as whole;) the approach of changing the system from within and the constitutional process, and now framework, of the country. Consequently these members did not participate and continue to argue for non-participation in the system.

The NNLC is the only party that was legally registered, or once enjoyed legal status, until the 1973 Proclamation to the Nation that banned political parties. The NNLC has gradually moved towards the centre left and present a more moderate position.

Peoples United Democratic Movement (PUDEMO)

The party was formed in 1983 during the upheavals caused by the interim Liqoqo regime (after the death of King Sobhuza II in August 1982). PUDEMO was formed with its main objective being to counter the Liqoqo interim regime. It fiercely protected the institution of the monarchy. The organisation is now calling for a constitutional monarchy with far less political power and involvement. The support of PUDEMO came mainly from the youth and labour force. PUDEMO is a socialist democratic party.

They perceive the status quo as undemocratic, discriminatory, nepotistic and oppressive. Whilst PUDEMO blames all atrocities on the Tinkundla system; the organisation makes no mention of the institution of the monarchy per se as a symbol of unity for all Swazis. They perceive this institution as a major obstacle, if not a challenge, but do not articulate how they would transform it in order to conform to the democratic ideals the organisation espouses.

PUDEMO, in its language, is more revolutionary and wants change sooner than the NNLC.

Sive Siyinqaba Sibahle Sinje

This is a relatively new organisation formed in 1996. It was ostensibly formed to counter the growing anti-monarchy sentiment allegedly propagated by the trade union movement. Sive Siyinqaba registered as a cultural organisation, but did not hide its political intentions in the event that party politics be legalised in Swaziland. The organisation has over the years shifted from being the shield of the status quo to being a quasi-political and uncompromising stronghold that is not afraid to comment on sensitive political developments. The support base of Sive Siyinqaba is wide, and includes members of the most conservative cadre in the traditional mainstream. The organisation provides a middle-right voice by appealing to the traditional sensibilities of most Swazis. It is conformist, geared to protecting the monarchy and all its institutions against the ridicule and contempt of some progressive elements. However, the politics of the organisation have shifted more recently to the centre, carefully criticizing the government and the monarchy in a conciliatory tone. The organisation believes that political parties can be accommodated in the Tinkhundla sysyem i.e. the people can be allowed to vite for political parties ithey so choose, while at the saem time those who want to vote for individuals according to the Tinkhundla sysyem may do so.

With the exception of the new Inhlava, all the organisations have well-written constitutions which define their aims and objectives, including the line of command from specialised constituencies such as the youth and women, to branch and regional structures and eventually to national executives and congress or conventions.

The combined membership of these organisations is estimated at about 140 000[12], about 10% of the national population. In the absence of political parties, organised civil society, primarily labour, has assumed some of the functions that would otherwise be the purview of political parties.

Civil Society in Swaziland

Democratic institutions, state institutions and political parties cannot be substituted by civil society; nonetheless civil society complements these institutions. In the event that one or the other institution, i.e. political parties, are ineffective, or in the extreme case do not legally exist as is the case in Swaziland; civil society organisations can exploit the vacuum by raising issues that would otherwise be the purview of political parties. Civil society is a collection of organisations, independent of the state and its machinery, which whilst continuously interacting with it, does not seek political power.

Non-governmental Organisations (NGOs)

The Swaziland Government National NGO Policy of 2004 (adopted in late 2005) defines non-governmental organisations as "...legally formed, autonomous organisations (locally or internationally affiliated) that are voluntary, not for profit, not self serving and whose primary motivation is to improve the well being of the people"[13]

The process of registration of NGOs as it stands today is quite complex.Civil society organisations in Swaziland are under the administrative ambit of the Ministry of Home Affairs; however they register with the Ministry of Justice and Constitutional Affairs. Registration is done through two statutes; Section 21 of the Companies Act of 1912 and then the Protection of Names, Uniforms and Badges Act of 1969. Both statutes are also used in the registration of private companies and or profit making institutions and herein lies the problem of regulation. If the registration statutes are the same for private companies and civil society organisations, it is difficult to legitimately administer these institutions as separate entities.

The Ministry expects all non-governmental organisations (including community based organisations, faith-based organisations etc.) to also register with the Co-ordination Assembly for Non-Governmental Organisations (CANGO). However, not all statutory registered NGOs at the Ministry of Justice and Constitutional Affairs continue to register with the Ministry of Home Affairs. Secondly, not all registered NGOs, after registering with the Ministry of Home Affairs, continue to join CANGO as members. CANGOs membership fluctuates depending on the payment of membership fees to the Assembly, for instance in 2000 (CANGO Annual Report 2000) CANGO had a total of 87 affiliates. In 2004-2005 CANGO had left 68 affiliates.

The Labour Movement

The activist history of organised labour in Swaziland can be traced as far back as pre-independence in the late 1960s. The marriage between opposition parties and labour unions effectively led to the constitutional crisis of 1973 when the opposition party won three seats in the first 1972 post independence national elections. The 1973 Proclamation to the Nation of April 1973 referred to in the introduction saw the first serious attempt at silencing civil society. The Proclamation was directed at the emerging opposition to the dominant conservative monarchical Imbokodvo National Movement, also referred to as the Kings Party. The lull in industrial labour activism was an unintended consequence of the banning of political parties (or freedom of association) that lasted until the mid 1980s when the Swaziland National Association of Teachers led by the present Deputy Prime Minister, Mr. Albert Shabangu, led the teachers through a historic industrial strike that shook the status quo. The consequent of the 1980's teachers strike was the subsequent targeting of union leaders for incorporation into government by the state – a common solution adopted by African heads of state to silence civil society and organised labour in particular.

Organised labour re-emerged very strongly again in the early 1990s reaching a climax towards the second half of the decade. The resurgence of organised labour was a result of four factors, namely;
- the weak leadership in the government and
- the conducive legal framework.
- politicisation of the labour movement.
- tensions within the labour movement and personality driven issues.

The combined consequence of all outlined above, and the length of the period in which these policies were strongly enforced, weakened the labour movement is evident today.

All industry and sectors – agriculture (e.g. sugar and pulp), manufacturing (e.g. textile) and commercial (e.g. banking, retail etc) – in Swaziland are unionised. However the most prominent labour unions and federations in Swaziland today are: the Swaziland Federation of Trade Unions (SFTU), Swaziland Federation of Labour (SFL),

Swaziland Manufacturing and Allied Workers Union (SMAWU), Swaziland National Association of Teachers (SNAT), Swaziland National Association of Civil Servants (SNACS) and Swaziland Nurses Association (SNA). The SFTU is the largest federation in the country with its membership from the agricultural and manufacturing industries. The SFL is the second federation in the country with its membership drawn from the commercial industry, specifically the banking sector.

The relationship between the trade unions and political parties was influenced largely by the fact that since 1973, political parties were banned. Trade unions picked up issues of a political nature to fill the vacuum that was created by the absence of political parties. When the political parties "unbanned" themselves in the 1990's it was natural that they would be allies with the trade union movement.

The Media

There are broadly two media types in Swaziland – Print media, and Electronic media which can be divided into Radio, Television and the Internet.

In the print media there are both state owned and privately owned print media houses, namely:

The Times of Swaziland.
The Times, as it is commonly referred, is privately owned. The Times is a daily circulation and it includes weekend papers; the Swazi News (Saturday) and the Times Sunday. The Times has become the most critical and arguably influential newspaper in the country. It enjoys the highest circulation[14] in the country.

The Swazi Observer
The Swazi Observer is a state owned daily and weekend newspaper (Weekend Observer – Saturday only). The Swazi Observer is funded through Tibiyo TakaNgwane. Tibiyo Takangwane is a royal business enterprise with massive investment in the country and equally immense income.

Other print publications
There are other print media that do not have as high circulation as the two above mentioned newspapers. These include the Nation Magazine – a periodical news magazine, the Voice – a fortnightly newspaper and a few others. The Nation Magazine is led by a young ferocious former Times Newspaper editor, Bheki Makhubu, who has made a significant effort to raise the profile of the magazine.

It is also worth noting that South African print newspapers also enjoy a significant circulation in the domestic market. These are the Sowetan Newspapers, the Mail and Guardian, the Sunday Times, The Star, and all usual Sunday newspapers.

Television
The electronic media can be divided into two groups radio and television:

Swaziland Broadcasting and Information Station (SBIS)
The SBIS is wholly state owned. The SBIS enjoys the largest coverage in the country thus is the most important and primary source of information for the majority Swazi population. The state has recognized this fact and has a very tight control on the content of SBIS. It is divided into two services; the siSwati service and the English service.

Swaziland Television Broadcasting Corporation (STBC), commonly referred to as Swazi TV
Swazi TV is also wholly state owned. It equally enjoys very stringent government control. The television station enjoyed a complete monopoly of this sort of media until late 1990s when another television station, Channel Swazi, was allowed. Swazi TV is one of the worst performing government public enterprise as it is consistently on the brink of closure due to insufficient funds. Because of the highly controlled content, the programming is focused on non-sensitive and therefore non-newsworthy material. The focus for the station lately is to present itself as an entertainment station.

Channel Swazi
This is a relatively new television station. The owner of the station is also an employee of the state television station – its direct competitor. The owner is also the senior reporter of royal events and trips and director of the Kings mobile television unit. Since inception, the station has become the royal defender and instrument for royal propaganda.

Internet Cafés
Internet cafés have mushroomed in the two capital cities and major towns without as much attention as expected from the state. Despite this, it remains an under-utilised medium. Indeed the internet has provided news information that the state is not pleased with. In 2003, the Sunday Times (RSA) reported an adulterous relationship of one of the king's wives. Before mid-morning that Sunday, the Sunday Times had been removed from the shelves. It was not banned completely from the country; however the removal of the newspaper from shelves illustrated the government's desire to limit access to certain information. However, the removal of the Sunday Times from the shelves did not prevent the accessing of the paper electronically.

Other Electronic Media
There are two other radio stations in Swaziland. These are the Voice of the

Church; an international Christian radio station that has a more or less specific target group. The other is a small community radio station in the Lubombo region of the country. This is a small station with an equally limited coverage. The success of this radio station – evident in the HIV/Aids content – has shown that community radio stations might have as much potential to influence public discourse as the radio does.

In terms of a legal framework, the media is tightly controlled by the Ministry of Public Service and Information. However, the media still has no media policy outlining the administration of such a sector e.g.code of conduct, registration of journalists etc. In the beginning of 2005, a proposed Media Council – a body representative of all concerned stakeholders was muted. This was going to be a Council formed after the media policy[15] had been established. It was to be formed by the end of 2005 with the financial support of the British High Commission. According to the Director of Swazi TV, the idea of the Council has suddenly disappeared from the media agenda. Therefore, in terms of a regulatory legal framework it would appear the media operates in an almost vacuum. However, there are pieces of legislation,[16] some dating the pre-independence period, which the media considers as restrictive and negatively impacting media freedom:
- The King's Proclamation to the Nation, 1973 – the Proclamation restricts coverage of political matters and therefore the content of media publications.
- Proclamation No.1 of 1981 – the Proclamation prohibits, through its vague terminology political comment, particularly criticism of the monarchy and its institutions.
- Proscribed Publications Act, 1968 – the Act empowers the minister of information to proscribe any publication arbitrarily on the reasons of public safety etc.
- Obscene Publications Act, 1927 – the major issue with this Act is that it does not adequately define what should be perceived as obscene or indecent thus opening it for subjective definition and abuse.
- Books and Newspapers Act, 1963 – the Act demands a prohibitive amount as bond from aspiring media owners whilst putting pressure to have publications in the siSwati. This exerts more pressure for publication in siSwati in that people who are more likely to establish a siSwati independent newspaper are Swazis who are not likely to have the amount as bond.

Other restrictive legislation includes:
- National Security Act, 1968
- Sedition and Subversive Activities Act, 1938
- Cinematography Act, 1968
- Emergency Powers Act, 1960
- Prevention of Corruption Order, 1993

In addition to the problems of the legal framework, the media has expressed serious reservations about its capacity. The media raised two significant challenges

that presently affect its efficiency:
- Inaccurate reporting by the media: this is a result of skills – investigative - short age within the fraternity.
- Lack of critical analysis of political, economic and social issues by the media

In the absence of legal political parties and a universally acceptable process of political engagement, organised civil society and the illegal political parties, have formed structures or alliances aimed at collectively putting pressure on the state and its institutions. Some such alliances have developed into permanent structures with a secretariat and offices. These include the Swaziland Coalition of Concerned Civic Organizations (SCCCO) and the National Constitutional Assembly (NCA). These alliances are not meant to be independent of their members, they have a specific and precise (short- or long-term) objective and do not substitute or compete with its membership.

The SCCCO enjoys a very broad membership which includes; business, labour, NGOs and other formations. It is a new alliance formed in about 2002. The SCCCO was formed at the height of political tensions and conflict in the country resulting from the state refusing to comply with judicial decisions primarily. Therefore one of the major objectives of the SCCCO was to put pressure on the government to bring about the respect of the rule of law and sustain the independence of the judiciary. The second objective of the SCCCO was to put pressure on government's fiscal management. The government had been, and still is, spending beyond the national means. One such intended spending that the SCCCO wanted stopped was the purchasing of the King's Private Jet costing close to half the national budget.

The National Constitutional Assembly (NCA) is also an alliance-based institution. It was formed mainly to challenge the constitutional making process and attempted at providing an alternative constitution. The NCA felt that the constitutional making process in the country was flawed in that it was centrally controlled, exclusive and therefore non-democratic. Their aim therefore was to create, on the one hand, a structure that would challenge this process in order to make the process more open, broadly inclusive and democratic. On the other hand, in the event the process failed, the NCA wanted to draft an alternate constitution using a process that is more inclusive, accommodating and popular based.

The Dynamism and Eclipse of the Opposition

From the foregoing it is clear that the opposition movement has been in existence since independence in September, 1968. There are a myriad of issues pertaining to opposition politics. But of major concern has been the domination of Swazi politics by the monarch, his committees and traditional institutions. The NNLC stated their policy, as early as the period of liberation struggle, that the monarch in Swaziland should wield very limited political powers. The NNLC wanted the Swazi

King to be a constitutional monarch. PUDEMO holds the same view, i.e the country should have a constitutional monarch.

There was a concern that the 1973 Proclamation (which had been in existence up to the formulation of the new constitution) created a dictatorship in the country. The proclamation vested all legislative, executive and judicial powers in the king. This gave the Swazi king absolute power to rule the country. This state of affairs was an antithesis of modern democracy. Therefore the political "changes" that have evolved under the *Tinkhundla* regimes have been labelled as meaningless. To the opposition these processes have been designed to deceive the citizens and the international community. In short, there were no substantive changes – the political systems in Swaziland remained undemocratic and continued to be a dictatorship.

This undemocratic rule in the country produced many problems which ranged from economic issues, to social and political issues. There is mismanagement of finances, corruption, lack of accountability, poor allocation of resources, inefficiency, lack of service delivery to the public, embezzlement of funds, lack of humanity on the part of the leaders, weak administrative institutions, no basic human rights, restriction of reporting by the media, failure to attract foreign investors.

These issues (and many more) have been raised by the opposition in their demands, campaigns, workshops and seminars. Some of the campaigns have been soliciting support from the international community. For example, SFTU has used the ILO platform to promote the protection of the rights of workers in the country. SFTU and PUDEMO have gone to the extent of calling for sanctions against Swaziland. SADC has also been mobilised to put pressure on Swaziland to force it to democratise.

It can be argued that the opposition believes that the contribution of the international community to the democratisation process in the country is essential, and probably indispensable. PUDEMO, NNLC, AUDP, CSC, SWANAFRO, SNAT and SFL subscribe to the idea that external pressure should be engaged to change the present political system in Swaziland.[17] PUDEMO has close relations with the ANC and COSATU in South Africa who have at times assited the opposition to blockade the country's border. Until recently SFTU enjoyed warm relations with COSATU.[18]

The media has also been active in pointing out the inadequacies of the political system in Swaziland. There have been reports about talks and presentations by people criticising the political system. Columnists have been afforded an opportunity to voice their opinions about the political situation in the country. This had been the case particularly with the print media. On 11 July, 2006, one columnist wrote an article titled "change Swazi polity to address our ills" where he was expressing his concerns about the continuing inefficiencies of the political system and the lack of care for the vulnerable citizens (he specifically referred to the HIV/AIDS pandemic in the country). The columnist went to the extent of appreciating the recent call by the Southern Africa Contact Group (formerly the Danish Anti-Apartheid Movement) to re-enforce sanctions on Swaziland.[19]

It could be argued that the opposition in the country derives its strength from both within and externally. The forces of change to the new democratic dispensation in Africa have acted as an impetus for the Swazis to take their own place and be counted. Internally, the oppressive policies and other government ills that have been mentioned above have driven many Swazis away from supporting the political systems. The political parties opposing the *Tinkhundla* system have gained support from a wide spectrum of social groups in the country. Some labour movements and NGO's are in alliance with these opposition parties in putting forward suggestions of real change in the country. They view the constitutional "changes" as nothing but continuity of the undemocratic and political dictatorial dispensation.

One of the organisations, Sive Siyinqaba was initially formed in 1995-96 to counter the power of the labour movement, particularly the SFTU, which, at this time, was probably at its peak (having organised strikes countrywide following their 27 demands).[20] Sive Siyinqaba, although designated as a cultural movement, commands the largest membership in the Parliament of Swaziland (although not voted for officially on the ticket of Sive Siyinqaba). In parliament the members of this organisation are articulate in debating issues and punching holes in the operations of the government.

A recent development in the politics of the country has been the formation of a new movement called Inhlava Forum. This movement was formed by the then Minister of Health and Social Welfare and was aimed at attracting MPs to educate them about politics so that they could become effective. The Minister has since been sacked and is now an ordinary M.P. (It is not clear why he was sacked because apart from forming the movement, he was being investigated for corruption and was contesting this investigation.)[21]

The NNLC and SWANAFRO are two political parties that have spelt out their objectives clearly that they are opposed to the Tinkhundla system. But the president of SWANAFRO was an MP (a Senator) in the previous government (1998-2003). He explained that he participated in the system in order to gain more insight into its intricacies.[22] The president of SWANAFRO likens the *Tinkhundla* system to apartheid in South Africa because he sees *Tinkhundla* as a political system which was crafted to reward a chosen few.[23] In the present parliament (2003-2008) the president of the NNLC and one executive member are Members of Parliament. According to the NNLC informant the policy of the party is not to participate in the political system. But individuals can join and participate, not on the ticket of the party.[24] It must be pointed out, though, that the NNLC MPs have not been vocal in Parliament in terms of challenging the policies of the government.

The opposition movement has played a crucial role in forcing some changes in the *Tinkhundla* system. They played a role in the promulgation of the new constitution which contained a Bill of Rights. The Bill of Rights may not be satisfactory, but it is an improvement on the past where there was none.

However, political movements have been faced with an uphill battle against the ruling authorities. Until the introduction of the February 2006 constitution, political parties were legally banned in Swaziland. Although these parties "unbanned" themselves in the mid 1990's, they did not operate freely. They were refused permission to hold meetings. As a result some of their meetings (e.g. PUDEMO and SNAT) have had to be held in South Africa. Their rallies have been dispersed by the armed forces of the country. This state sanction on the opposition movement has contributed to the forces that affect their dynamism and at the same time contributing to their eclipse.

Opposition movements have also been affected by the fact that they disagree in some fundamental issues, thus they hardly provide a united and coherent front to the present system. For instance, PUDEMO does not believe that participation within the Tinkhundla political structures will bring about fruitful results. On the other hand SWANAFRO believes that participation is the right thing to do.

PUDEMO and SFTU have a long history of alliance. However, recently there seems to be divisions. In April, 2006 PUDEMO called for the blockade of the Swaziland-South Africa border. COSATU participated in the blockade in solidarity with the struggle in Swaziland. SFTU and SNAT came out to state clearly that they were not party to this event. In fact tempers flared up where the labour movements (SFTU and SNAT) accused PUDEMO of using their organization for PUDEMO's own agenda. The SNAT President accused political parties for abusing unions. The reaction of PUDEMO was to the effect that the unions should not think that they have exclusive control over their membership because some of these members are also members of political parties. The columnist in one newspaper lamented the altercation among these organizations because in this he could deduce that "Divided extra-Parliamentary groups offer a weak alternative" to the present political system.[25] This weak opposition front is probably the reason for the birth of the Swaziland Coalition of Concerned Civic Organisations (SCCCO) in January 2003.

There is also disagreement within the movement itself. When the new look NNLC was revived there were those old stalwart members who did not feel that this was the same congress. There has been disagreement about whether or not to participate in the Tinkhundla political processes. When the reviews (Vusela) were started, there were debates within the NNLC as to whether they should participate in the process. There was disagreement about their member's participation in Parliament, albeit on an individual ticket.

There are disagreements within the labour movement. The birth of SFL in 1993 was as a result of differences between unions affiliated to SFTU at the time.[26] Recently there has been an altercation between Swaziland Nurses Association (SNA) and the Swaziland National Association of the Civil Servants (SNACS), on the one hand, and SFTU on the other. SNA and SNACS are affiliated to SFTU and the latter has suspended them SNA and SNACS challenge the leadership style at SFTU.

The present constitution has brought about new challenges to the opposition movements as they do not agree on its interpretation. For instance, PUDEMO's understanding is that the constitution does not allow political parties, while AUDP's interpretation is that the constitution allows political parties to exist alongside the Tinkhundla system. In fact, AUDP has applied for registration to be a legal entity in the country.

In order to be strong, organisations need funds. In Swaziland, most of the opposition movements lack funding. The political parties rely on membership and subscription fees and these are hardly able to sustain their activities. They do not have many members and yet they have work to do – to educate the masses on the subject of politics. Civic education is seriously handicapped by lack of funds, although credit can be given to PUDEMO as it holds more meetings and rallies than any other opposition political parties.

The labour movement's funding is slightly better than the political parties. Labour movements, as unions and federations have a steady source of income from subscriptions and membership fees from their members. Their members are employed, so there is a certain guarantee that monies will be paid regularly, unlike the political parties who have large followers who belong to the category of the unemployed.

The media's contribution to political change in the country is affected in two ways. First, some of the media houses are owned and controlled by the state. So there is very little, if any, latitude to be critical of the political system and state policies. Second, there are laws restricting the process of reporting in the country. SNAJ is not happy about the existence of these laws.[27] However, with the new constitution these restrictive laws need to be put into test using the courts. The constitution is the supreme law of the land, so any laws that are repugnant to its provisions should be put to test.

Conclusion

The repeal of the Independence Constitution gave more powers to the king and pushed opposition movements deeper into the dungeon. However, they continued to fight for a more equitable political dispensation. Both the opposition and the international community managed to put pressure on the Swazi government to bring about changes. The present constitutional dispensation is a result of these pressures. The opposition movement is not satisfied with these changes. They regard them as cosmetic. Hence they continue to challenge the present system.

Even though the traditional authority would love to maintain the status quo, change is inevitable in Swaziland. Swaziland cannot be an island in today's global village. The international community is determined to play their role to pressurise Swazi authorities to make meaningful transformation. This could come in the form of dialogue, isolation or sanctions. In the vacuum that has been created due to the fact that political parties are banned in Swaziland, civil society, the labour movement and the media have had to fill this vacuum. As recently as 2009 there have been attempts at strikes, blockades of the border and other such activities to force the government to change.

The opposition movement should continue to put pressure for substantive changes. But whilst they do that, they should put their house in order. It has been pointed out that they are divided on some major issues and this weakens their influence.. They need to come together a with the aim of forming an alliance.

When the opposition movement begins not to be transparent and accountable to their constituency, then they begin to lose touch with the people. They lose the support base. In fact the people begin to ask the question: is there a difference between the opposition and the government? If the answer is to the negative, then there is no reason to support the opposition. Therefore, the opposition has to practise the democratic principles that it preaches and demands from the ruling authorities in Swaziland. By practising what they preach they will then develop the culture of democracy, transparency, accountability and respect for human rights. They will also attract a support base which in turn may result in the improvement of their depleted financial resources (through subscriptions and membership fees). The international donor community may also be sympathetic to their cause.

To those opposition movements that are not tainted by the leadership crisis, we encourage them to continue being strong. In modern democratic societies opposition politics is indispensable. It provides checks to the ruling party. It can act as a bridle for an unruly horse.

ENDNOTES

1   His Majesty's Speech to a large crowd at Lobamba on the Historic Occasion in the afternoon of the 12th April 1973 (Swaziland National Archives).

2   Establishment of the Parliament of Swaziland Order, 1978

3   Tinkhundla – traditional meeting places for discussions, settlement of dispute or criminal cases. The tinkhundla political system entails that all political activity in the country is conducted at tinkhundla. In additions, elections are conducted at tinkhundla, which serve as consitutencies and MPs are elected at the tinkhundla.

4   The Constitution of the Kingdom of Swaziland Act, 2005.

5   Incwala: a ritual ceremony held every year in December to January to commemorate the end of year and to welcome the new crops of the season. It is also a

cleansing ritual for the iniquities of the year and symbolizes the rejuvenation of the Swazi nation through the Monarch.

6   Hilda Kuper op. cit
7   The Times of Swaziland, Monday, September 24, 1979.
8   Ibid.
9   Op. cit No.10 above
10 The Constitution of the Kingdom of Swaziland Act, 2005, Section 79
11 For detailed analysis see J.B. Mzizi – Political Movements and the Challenges for Democracy in Swaziland,. 2004
12 EISA: Consolidating Democracy in the SADC Region – 2005.
13 Ministry of Home Affairs 2004, National NGO Policy p.7
14 Circulation of 30 000 newspapers with readership of 150 000 people per day – Times Swaziland Managing Director Martin Dlamini, Septermber 06.
15 At the time of writing this document, a draft policy was being debated by Parliament, introduced by the Ministry of Public Service and Information
16 For a thorough discussion see Media Institute of Southern Africa – Undue Restrictions: Laws Impacting on Media Freedom in the SADC, 2004.
17 This information was gathered by the Research Assistant who interviewed leaders and senior employees of the political parties, the labour movements and the NGO, using the Annexure.
18 There seems to be developing a fall-out between SFTU and COSATU. It was reported in the Times of Swaziland, July 7, 2006, that COSATU was in Swaziland gathering information about the leadership of SFTU from its affiliates. Submissions by some affiliates were that the SFTU leadership was dictatorial. The newspaper continued to report that the SFTU leadership was "not happy with the fact finding mission of COSATU.
19 Times of Swaziland, July 11, 2006
20 Interview of one executive member of Sive Siyinqaba by the Research Assistant, in June 2006.
21 The Formation of this movement by the Minister is testimony to the fact that not only is the political system unstable, but also that the engine of the system (the government) is incoherent and has no lubricants.
22 Conversation between Mbho Shongwe (President of SWANAFRO) and P.Q. Magagula in May, 2006.

23 E-mail message to P.Q. Magagula by Mbho Shongwe on June 1, 2006 – Apartheid and Tinkhundla are brothers.
24 Interview of one executive member of the Youth League of the NNLC by the Research Assistant in July, 2006
25 Times of Swaziland, M ay 4, 2006
26 Interview of Secretary-General of SFL by the Research Assistant in June, 2006
27 Interview of the President of SNAJ by the Research Assistant in June, 2006

CHAPTER NINE
ZAMBIA: BETWEEN THE POLITICS OF OPPOSITION AND INCUMBENCY
JOTHAM C. MOMBA

Introduction

The amendment of Article 4 of the Zambian constitution in 1990 to allow for the formation of political parties other than the United National Independence Party (UNIP), which had ruled Zambia for 27 years, opened up the political space, not just for opposition political parties but for civil society as well. Indeed the very formation of the Movement for the Multi-Party Democracy (MMD) in 1990 and its victory in the 1991 elections were anchored on the campaign for the re-introduction of plural politics. The country was among the first on the continent to do away with the one-party system. Given this background, there were high expectations that the MMD as a ruling party would not, only be tolerant of the existence of political opposition, but would also establish a political atmosphere that would allow for a vibrant multiparty system in which the place of an equally vibrant and loyal opposition would be guaranteed.

As the name indicates, the MMD was formed initially as a coalition of civil society organisations (CSOs) to re-introduce a multiparty political system before it registered itself as a political party, which it did on 4 December 1990. Among some of the CSOs that constituted the MMD before its transformation into a political party were the Zambia Congress of Trade Unions (ZCTU), an umbrella organisation for all trade unions in Zambia; professional associations such as the Law Association of Zambia, the Press Association of Zambia and the University of Zambia Students Union.[1] The leader of the ZCTU, Frederick Chiluba, subsequently became the leader of the MMD and the president of the republic after the 1991 elections.

The emphasis on a strong party system in Zambia's democratisation process can be seen against the backdrop of the centrality of political parties in modern liberal democratic societies that have come to be closely associated with political parties and hence the party system.

The trajectory of opposition politics in Zambia

A number of political parties have emerged since 1990 and a number of political re-alignments have taken place. In the period immediately after the re-introduction of the multiparty system there were, however, only two major political parties that were serious contenders for political power. These were the MMD, the party that led the struggle against the one-party system, and UNIP, still in power. Since then, a number of political parties have emerged, some of which are products of the afore mentioned re-alignments.

There are currently more than 30 political parties in Zambia. This large number notwithstanding, there are only five major opposition political parties with a countrywide presence. These are the United Party for National Development (UPND), UNIP, the Patriot Front, Forum for Democracy and Development (FDD), and the Heritage Party.

United Party for National Development (UPND)

The UPND was founded in October 1998 and immediately thereafter formed an alliance with the National Party. The National Party was founded in 1992 following a split within the MMD in which nine MPs left the party, including five former cabinet ministers and two deputy ministers in the MMD government.

In the December 1998 local government elections, the UPND/National Party alliance won control of only one local authority, in North-Western Province where the candidates contested under the UPND ticket. But by the time of the 2001 elections, the UPND/National Party alliance was the biggest single political opposition bloc in Parliament, with a total of 11 MPs.

During the 2001 elections the party's presidential candidate, the late Anderson Mazoka, lost narrowly to the late president, Levy Mwanawasa: Mazoka won 26.7 per cent of the vote, compared to Mwanawasa's 28.3 per cent. The party won 49 parliamentary seats, becoming the largest opposition party in the National Assembly. In these elections the party won in four of the country's nine provinces (in Southern, Western, North-Western and Lusaka provinces) and lost narrowly in Central Province. The ruling MMD won in another four, while the former ruling party, UNIP, won in one province.

The party experienced a major split within its ranks as a result of differences over the succession to the presidency following the death of its founding president. The losing candidate in the race for the presidency of the party, who had been the acting president until the time of the elections, was unhappy with the outcome of the party elections. He resigned from the UPND and together with his supporters formed the National Liberal Party. They included the UNPD's former vice-president for political and economic affairs, Robert Sichinga and the party's former national chairman, Henry Mtonga. Several MPs and those who were elected members of the National Management Committee from the Western Province also resigned from the party to join the National Liberal Party.

The formation of the National Liberal Party greatly weakened the UNPD. At the time of the 2001 elections the support base of the UNPD was centred in the Western, Southern and North-Western provinces, with significant support in Lusaka and Central provinces. The Southern and Western provinces were the UNPD's strongest support base. However with the formation of the new party, the UPND lost the

Western Province, leaving the party with only one provincial stronghold, the Southern Province.

The UPND, together with UNIP and the FDD, formed an alliance called the United Democratic Alliance (UDA) in order to enhance their chances of winning elections that were held on 28 September 2006. The alliance elected the UPND leader, Hakainde Hichilema, as their candidate. Although the alliance had won a combined vote in the 2001 elections of more than 50 per cent, the UPND leader's performance as the alliance candidate in the 2006 elections was worse than that of his predecessor in the 2001 elections. He won only 25.32 per cent of the vote, placing third after the then incumbent president, with 42.98 per cent of the vote, and the leader of the Patriotic Front, with 29.37 per cent. Even the combined total of parliamentary seats that the three political parties in the alliance won in the 2006 elections was drastically reduced from those they had won in 2001. The alliance won a total of 26 seats in the 2006 elections, compared to 49 won by the UPND in the 2001 elections, 13 by the FDD and 12 by the UNIP, giving a combined total of 74 seats.

After the 2008 presidential by-elections the UPND formed an electoral pact with the Patriotic Front, in preparation for the 2011 elections. The party also seems to be regaining its support in the North-Western Province. It has won two by-elections from the MMD that followed the deaths of two sitting MPs. In the Solwezi Central Constituency, on 29 November 2009, the UPND candidate won 5 669 votes against the 4 457 won by the MMD candidate.[2] The seat had been held by a cabinet minister; and on 29 April the UPND won the seat which had been held by a deputy minister in the MMD government.[3]

United National Independence Party (UNIP)

The UNIP was formed on 24 October 1958, initially named the Zambia African National Congress, a breakaway party from the African National Congress, but subsequently acquired its present name. The party won the 1964 elections and was in power until 1991, when it lost the elections to the MMD. The UNIP boycotted the 1996 elections following its dispute over the management of elections and over the constitutional amendment that barred its leader, former Zambian president Kenneth Kaunda, from contesting the presidential elections.

In the 2001 elections, the UNIP came fourth in the popular vote in both the presidential and parliamentary elections, but had more parliamentary seats than the third-placed party. The UNIP won 13 seats, 12 from the Eastern Province and one from the Copperbelt Province. The party by then was part of the UDA alliance. However, after the collapse of the alliance the UNIP was left with only two MPs, one of whom died in 2007, and in the by-election that ensued the party lost the seat to the ruling MMD.[4] Currently the UNIP has only one MP. The party how ever, seems to be shifting towards some accommodation with the ruling MMD, however. Indicative of this is the appointment of the party's only MP to a senior cabinet position as minister of home affairs.

The party has experienced serious internal conflicts since its 1991 defeat, particularly over the question of leadership. Between 1991 and 2001 the party presidency changed four times. The first time was in 1992 when Kebby Musokotwane replaced the party's founding leader and former Zambian president Kenneth Kaunda. In 1996 Musokotwane was replaced by Kaunda when the latter decided to came back from retirement. The leadership changed again in 1998 when Kaunda was replaced by Francis Nkhoma, who was in turn removed and replaced by Kaunda's son, Tilyenji Kaunda. Each of these changes was preceded by serious internal skirmishes.[5]

Forum for Democracy and Development (FDD)

Also in the UDA alliance was the FDD, formed in 2001 following the aborted attempt by former president Chiluba to seek a third term of office as Zambian president. In the 2001 elections, the FDD's presidential candidate came in third, after the MMD and the UPND candidates. The party won 12 parliamentary seats, all of them from the Eastern and Lusaka provinces. As part of the UDA alliance which did not perform well in the 2006 elections, by the time the alliance collapsed, the FDD had only two MPs, the number it retains.

The Patriotic Front (PF)

The Patriotic Front was formed by Michael Sata when Chiluba was still the president of the country. Sata left the MMD when Mwanawasa was nominated as its presidential candidate in the 2001 elections. The party won only two seats in the 2001 elections and its presidential candidate came seventh with 3.35 per cent of the national vote. However, immediately after the 2001 elections the PF started its campaigns, organising rallies. A large number of people from the MMD and the FDD who were from the Northern Province and most of whom were Chiluba supporters and sympathised with the former president who was on trial for corruption, joined Sata's party.

The PF has therefore become a serious contender for power. In the 2006 elections, its party leader came second to the late Mwanawasa with 29.37 per cent of the valid votes cast against 42.98 per cent scored by the MMD candidate the UDA candidate came third with 25.32 per cent of the vote. Thus with 43 seats, compared to 26 that were won by the UDA alliance and 73 by the MMD, the PF overtook the UPND as the biggest opposition party in the National Assembly.

In the period after the elections the PF experienced a number of problems. Internal dissentions have led to some resignations with some MPs in particular defying party policies. For example a number of PF MPs defied the party over the National Constitutional Conference. The party was against participating in the deliberations of the National Constitutional Conference, but its 'rebel' MPs ignored the party position and joined the deliberations. Another incident was the expulsion of a former

Lusaka mayor and another councillor for participating in ceremonies welcoming the Chinese leader, defying instructions from the party leadership.

With the apparent reconciliation between the current president of the republic and Chiluba's acquittal on corruption charges, the former president has switched his support to the MMD and the current president. This further deepened dissention within the PF, with a number of MPs in particular siding with Chiluba against the party leader, even though they remain members of the party.

However, despite its internal problems, the party has retained most of the seats in the by-elections called to replace the defectors. The PF improved its performance in the 2008 presidential by-elections, where the PF leader obtained 38.13 per cent of the votes against 40.09 per cent for Rupiah Banda of the MMD, and 19.70 per cent for the UPND candidate. This represented an 8.76 per cent increase from its 2006 score of 29.37 per cent. It has also joined an alliance with the UPND to contest the 2011 elections with the possibility of the pact fielding one presidential candidate.

Heritage Party

The Heritage Party is another party with countrywide presence. It was formed, in the aftermath of Chiluba's attempt to run for a third term, by then MMD vice president, Brigadier General Godfrey Miyanda, who at the time was an ordinary cabinet minister. The party managed to win four seats in the 2001 elections – two in Central Province and two in Eastern Province. Miyanda came fifth in the 2001 presidential elections, receiving 7.96 per cent of the national vote. Two of his MPs subsequently crossed to the MMD where they re-contested their seats under the MMD, and one of them was appointed to a cabinet position. The party contested both the 2006 elections and the 2008 presidential by-elections with no success – the party did not win any seats in the 2006 elections, and in both elections, Miyanda as the party's presidential candidate received 0.76 per cent of the vote, much less than he achieved in the 2001 elections.

The National Democratic Forum (NDF)

Five other relatively smaller parties formed another alliance, the National Democratic Forum (NDF), to contest the 2006 elections. These are the Zambia Republican Party (ZRP), the Reform Party, the Party for Unity, Democracy and Development (PUDD), Zambia Democratic Conference (ZADECO) and the Zambia Direct Democracy Movement (ZDDM). The ZRP was founded some time before the 2001 elections out of a merger between the Republican Party, led by the former defence minister in the Chiluba government, and the Zambia Alliance for Progress. The latter, in turn, had been formed from a merger between the Zambia Democratic Congress and the National Lima Party with other relatively smaller parties. The Zambia Democratic Alliance had been established by two senior members of the MMD and had come second to the MMD during the 1996 elections. The ZRP had won only one seat during the 2001 elections and the party effectively split after its sole MP accepted a ministerial appointment, left the ZRP and was adopted as the MMD candidate in 2006 for the seat that she had held under the ZRP.

At the time of the formation of the NDF, the ZRP was led by Ben Mwila. The Reform Party was led by Reverend Nevers Mumba, the leader of the National Citizens Coalition which had participated in the 2001 elections. He suddenly dissolved his party in 2003 and was appointed vice president of the country, but was sacked within a year after he formed the Reform Party. ZADECO was founded just before the 2001 elections following a split within the ZRP in which Dean Mungomba decided to resuscitate his party, ZADECO. The other two parties in the alliance, PUDD and ZDMM, were then relatively new formations.

As in the case of the UDA alliance, the NDF alliance has not been able to hold together since the election of the leader of the ZRP as the leader of the alliance. Their problems began even before the elections, with the Reform Party leader disputing the election of Mwila as the leader of the NDF, and his party is effectively out of the alliance. It only managed to acquire one seat, won by the leader of the alliance, perhaps using his personal influence as a former cabinet minister in the Chiluba government.

Laws and regulations governing the formation and operation of political parties

A number of laws and regulations govern the operation of political parties in Zambia. The Societies Act governs the founding of political parties. The requirements for the formation of any society, which would include a political party, are that any group of ten persons can form a society and within 28 days of its formation or adoption, such a society should make an application to the Registrar of Societies for registration.

The Act provides for conditions under which a society can be denied registration. According to Article 8 of the Societies Act, the Registrar of Societies may refuse a society registration if it appears to him 'that such a society has among its objectives ... any unlawful purpose or ... any purposes prejudicial to or incompatible with the peace, welfare or good order in Zambia'. According to Article 9 of the Societies Act, a society can be denied registration for any of the following reasons:
- If it appears to the registrar that the terms of the constitution or rules of the society are in any way repugnant or inconsistent with the law;
- If the registrar is satisfied that the application does not comply with the provisions of the Societies Act;
- If the registrar is satisfied that the society does not exist;
- If it is identical with another existing society;
- If the society nearly resembles the name of another society, and in the opinion of

the registrar is likely to deceive the public or members of either society.[6]

Despite the existence of all these conditions under which a political party may not be registered, or may have its registration revoked, there has never been a case in which a political party was denied registration on account of any of the factors outlined in Articles 8 and 9 of the Societies Act. The most common causes of deregistration of political parties has been the failure to make annual returns, or returns whenever there is change of leadership.[7] In almost all such cases, though, the parties have been insignificant, barely existing in practice beyond the party leader.

Interviews with representatives of key CSOs that have concerned themselves with the issues of democracy and good governance reveal that there are generally no legal restrictions or regulatory impediments to forming political parties in Zambia. The existence of such a liberal atmosphere in this respect prompted the UPND vice president to suggest that in comparison to most other African countries, Zambia has moved significantly towards a thriving multiparty system. He pointed out that political activities have been deregulated and people can form political parties at any time. This view is shared by almost all the CSO leaders that were interviewed and was supported most emphatically by representatives of the state media organisations. However, the UPND vice president indicated that in terms of regulating the operations of political parties, there are still some restrictions against a functioning multiparty system, the most important of which is the existence of the Public Order Act. He also pointed to the bias of the public media against the opposition parties as another factor that has worked against a strong and thriving multiparty system in the country.[8]

The existence of the Public Order Act and its application by the police has been one important area of dissatisfaction noted by almost all opposition political parties and CSOs. Some of the provisions of the Electoral Code of Conduct that are considered discriminatory have also been regularly cited by leaders of opposition parties and CSOs as undermining the existence of a viable multiparty system in Zambia.

The Public Order Act, which governs the holding of public meetings by political parties, has been used adversely against opposition parties. Article 4 of the Act provides that any person who intends to convene a public meeting should give the police at least 'seven days [notice] of that person's intention to … convene such meeting' and Article 5 stipulates the conditions that may be imposed on the convening of such meeting, which include, among others, the date, time, place and duration of the public meeting, and the granting of adequate facilities for the recording of the proceedings of such a public meeting. Article 6 of the Act exempts the president, vice president, ministers, junior ministers, and the speaker and deputy speaker of the National Assembly from the provisions of the Act, as outlined in Articles 4 and 5. These officials, who in practice constitute the principal leadership of the ruling party of the day, can have a public meeting or organise a procession any time they want since the notice period does not apply to them.

The Public Order Act has been a source of major conflict between the government and the opposition and CSOs. All the observer groups and local monitoring groups have expressed dissatisfaction with the way the provisions of this Act have been applied by the police in all the elections that have been held. In a landmark ruling just before the 1996 elections in the case of Christine Mulundika and seven others versus the Attorney-General, the chief justice, sitting with two other Supreme Court judges, nullified sub-section 4 of Article 5(1), which compelled politicians other than senior government leaders to seek police permits to hold public meetings or processions. The Supreme Court declared the provisions of this sub-section invalid because they contravened the Constitution.[9]

Before 1996, political parties were required to get a permit in order to hold public rallies, but after 1996 they were only required to notify the police. However, in practice, notification has the same effect as permit requirement in terms of implementation by the police. As a result of the way the police have implemented the provisions of the Act, the Public Order Act has continued to affect adversely the right of opposition political parties to assemble.

As the late president of Transparency International Zambia (who was also dean of the School of Law at the University of Zambia) had pointed out, a major flaw of the Public Order Act is that the police 'broad and uncontrolled powers to stop meetings from taking place'.[10] There have been some occasions during election times when meetings of opposition parties have not been allowed to go ahead because the president would be addressing a meeting. For example, the Country Report on Human Rights of the United States State Department released by the Bureau of Labour in February 2001, reported that in July 2000 the UPND was denied a series of permits during the Sesheke by-election because 'several high- ranking government officials, including the president, would be in the area at the same time'.[11]

International election observer groups and local monitoring groups that have observed and monitored previous elections, including those of 2001, have mentioned that the Public Order Act has been used to disadvantage opposition political parties. For example, the European Union (EU) Observer Mission report noted that 'opposition parties have been denied permission for meetings, or have even had them cancelled, over periods of days, because the President "might be arriving"'.[12] According to a report by the Foundation for the Democratic Process (FODEP), 'while cadres and officials of the ruling party could hold public meetings, rallies and processions at any given time, those holding alternative views from those of the Government were denied the right to do so. In some cases meetings of the opposition parties were violently disrupted'.[13]

Yet another regulation which has been identified as working to the disadvantage of opposition political parties is the section of the Electoral (Conduct) Regulations (Statutory Instrument No 179 of 1996), commonly referred to as the Electoral Code of Conduct, which deals with the use of government transport and similar resources during elections. The Electoral Code of Conduct prohibits use of such government facilities during this time. However, the code exempts the president and vice president of the country from these restrictions. The ruling party has used this loophole to make extensive use of state resources.

Funding and its impact on the participation of opposition political parties

Despite the critical role that funding plays in meaningful competitive elections, access to campaign funding in Zambia is another area where the playing field is extremely uneven, to the disadvantage of opposition political parties. While the ruling party has used the advantage of incumbency to have unlimited access to state resources for campaign purposes, the opposition political parties have no access of any kind to state resources for campaign purposes.

On numerous occasions and in many forums it has been suggested that political parties participating in elections should receive some state funding in order to even the playing field. These attempts include a National Assembly resolution in 2004 that political parties participating in elections should receive state funding. But the executive has resisted all attempts to extend funding to political parties participating in elections. Thus, while there is a serious dearth of campaign funds for opposition parties, the ruling party has unlimited campaign resources due to its almost unlimited access to state resources. The latest attempt at addressing this issue was the decision by the National Constitutional Conference to provide for party funding in the draft Constitution which has yet to go through parliament.[14]

The abuse of state resources for campaign and political purposes by the ruling party has been extensively documented. For example in the Mwandi by-election in 2000, Coalition 2000 monitors recorded seven vehicles bearing government registration numbers in the campaign, while several other government vehicles had their number plates either fully or partially removed;[15] and in the September 2001 Isoka East by-election the UPND candidate filed an injunction against the use of government vehicles by government ministers.[16] In its critical report on the conduct of the 2001 elections, the EU observer group observed that "State resources have been openly used in support of the MMD, with, for instance, Government vehicles showing GRZ number plates noted in use in MMD campaigns ... The MMD has at times failed to maintain a distinction between government and the party"[17]

There has also been extensive use of other state resources for campaign proposes, contrary to the provisions of the Electoral Act. In the local government elections of 1998 the state made use of the Constituency Development Fund and the Food Relief Programme to their electoral advantage.[18] The issue of the use of public resources for campaign purposes by the ruling party was also raised in the 2006 elections[19] and the 2008 presidential by-elections. One local monitoring organisation, Transparency International Zambia, that monitored the 2008 elections made the following observation regarding the use of government resources for campaign purposes by the ruling party:

> "Our monitors noted... that a lot of government vehicles were being used to ferry cadres for the ruling party to attend their party campaigns. In one instance in Northern Province, the controller of government transport wrote to all government departments asking them to use their transport to ferry cadres to receive the then acting president."[20]

Private funding is one of the major sources of campaign funding for opposition political parties; however, even this is not very reliable and according to one opposition leader, not that forthcoming. The major problem that several opposition leaders identified is that a number of Zambian business enterprises depend on government contracts and at times on accessing donor money that is made available for some business projects. A large number of businessmen depend on remaining in the government's 'good books' in order to continue running their businesses profitably and are therefore not keen to be seen making donations to opposition political parties. When they do donate, they do so surreptitiously and only after they have made a much larger donation to the ruling party.

It was also alleged by a number of political and CSO leaders that many businessmen fear being victimised if it is known that they have made a donation to an opposition political party. The Zambia Revenue Authority is one arm of the state that, they alleged, is used by the state to harass businessmen who fall out of favour with the state, which would include giving financial support to an opposition party.

Thus even in the case of donations from the private sector, the ruling party gets the lion's share of this source of campaign funding. Whether voluntary, or through some arm twisting, the private sector has made very generous donations to the ruling party – the kind that is not offered to opposition political parties. It is difficult to establish the exact nature of these donations as they are done clandestinely. There are, however, several cases that have appeared in the press suggesting that some of these donations have been acquired through underhand methods. For example, it was revealed in 2003 that the MMD vice president secretly received K510 million ($106 250)[21] from Trans Sahara Trading, which he received as a donation to the MMD and which eventually led to his dismissal as vice president of the country.[22] The vice president himself revealed that a company owned by a Mr Paul Steele donated K100 million ($20 833) to the MMD in order to further his sale of maize to Zambia.[23] During the motion to impeach the president it was alleged that the Ministry of Finance made available K10 billion ($2.9 million) to Lendor Burton Construction Ltd for a government debt of which some money was donated by Lendor Burton to the MMD.[24]

The ruling party's exclusive access to state resources and its lion's share of resources from private businesses and other individuals has meant that the electoral competition is heavily unbalanced in favour of the MMD. Yet it has been pointed out that in a modern liberal democracy financing for election campaigns has become an integral part of the democratic process.

The role of the public and private media

The public print and electronic media have also been a critical factor in undermining opposition political parties and have become mere mouthpieces for the ruling party during the campaign periods. During the 2001 elections and previous elections, monitoring groups and foreign observer groups all made mention of the fact that the public media have shown open support for the ruling party. The EU observer group also commented negatively about the role of public media in providing fair coverage to all political parties. A FODEP report observed that the state media has continued to display bias towards the MMD contrary to provisions of the Electoral Code of Conduct. Among other provisions, the code provides that:
- All electronic media shall provide a fair and balanced reporting of the activities of all registered political parties;
- All media shall report news in an accurate manner and shall not make abusive editorial comments, and all media personnel shall conduct interviews with fairness; and
- All television and radio broadcasters shall allocate equal airtime to parties for their political broadcasts.[25]

Over the years, there has been growing doubt about the possible impartiality of the public media. A number of political leaders believe that the bias towards the ruling party is likely to continue. This was the position that was taken by the vice presidents of the two major political parties, the UPND and UNIP. For most of these leaders and leaders of non-governmental organisations (NGOs) that are concerned with the issue of democracy, this bias is evidenced in the make up of the management boards and chief editors who are appointed by the government through the minister of information and broadcasting.

In order to have some appreciation of the nature of the public media in Zambia, it is useful to understand that the public media has hardly changed from the way it operated during the one-party regime through to the transition to multipartyism. Under the Kaunda regime, specifically at the time of the 1991 elections, the government owned the only two daily papers, the *Times of Zambia* and the *Zambia Daily Mail*, as well as the entire electronic media, i.e. radio and television, which came under the Zambia National Broadcasting Corporation (ZNBC). There were only two weeklies that were not state-owned. These were the church-owned *National Mirror*, which was the most neutral, and the independent and heavily pro-MMD *Weekly Post*.

The government-owned print and electronic media were expected to reflect the position of the ruling party during the campaign period. Kaunda specifically ordered the *Times of Zambia, Zambia Daily Mail* and ZNBC to stop giving media coverage to MMD activities, and the latter was directed not to carry MMD advertisements. Despite these directives, the government-owned mass media carried articles favourable to the MMD as a result of the sympathy that the MMD enjoyed among the journalists. The MMD was unhappy with the position of the state-owned media vis-à-vis the opposition parties and Chiluba complained that democratic elections 'cannot take place without any open free and fair mass media'.[26]

The reluctance by the government-owned media, particularly the print media, to follow the presidential directives to the letter led to the sacking of the chief editors of the *Times of Zambia* and the *Zambia Daily Mail*.[27] The president's action against the chief editors of these two papers was not well received by the Press Association of Zambia. In turn, the association sought and was granted an injunction to restrain the new editors of the two daily papers, together with the director-general of the ZNBC, from performing their duties. The argument advanced was that the three were not formally qualified journalists.[28]

The effect of state ownership and control of the mass media was that despite the sympathy that most journalists had towards the MMD, as well as the intervention by the courts and observer groups, the mainstream mass media was heavily biased in favour of the ruling party and Kaunda. A content analysis of the news articles of television and Radio Zambia undertaken by the Z-Vote observer group shows the extent of this bias. Their content analysis of the 7pm television news bulletin and 1pm radio news bulletin – the main television and radio news bulletins of the day respectively – from 30 September to 27 October 1991 indicated heavy bias by the ZNBC towards UNIP.[29] Of 12 minutes 51 seconds, the MMD had a total of 47 seconds while other parties had 23 seconds.[30]

However, on coming to power the MMD maintained the status quo; the pattern of ownership remained unchanged. Pressure from local journalists, CSOs and concerned foreign organisations such as the Commonwealth of Journalists towards privatising the media has fallen on deaf ears. Subsequently the two major dailies and the ZNCB remain in the hands of the MMD government and the attitude of the press towards political parties is more or less as it was in 1991 – except the political parties have swapped positions.

A content analysis made by the Committee for Clean Campaign and FODEP during the 2001 elections showed heavy bias by the state-owned media towards the MMD: the state-owned media gave most coverage to the MMD, all of which was either positive or neutral, while most of the coverage given to the opposition parties was negative. Observer groups for the 2001 elections, notably the EU Observer mission, the Carter Center and the Southern African Development Community's (SADC) Parliamentary Observer Group, were critical of the role played by the public media during these elections.

In its report of the 2001 elections, the Carter Centre noted that state-owned television and newspapers gave extensive coverage to the ruling party during the campaign period. While coverage of the opposition parties was referred to as 'political adverts', the 'ruling party used news coverage as an opportunity to campaign'.[31] The SADC Parliamentary Observer Mission noted that coverage of election-related news by the state-owned media house was overwhelmingly favourable towards the ruling party, while the EU electoral observer mission reported that:

"Media monitoring carried out by the EU [Electoral Observer Mission] shows that the state-owned media, the Zambia National Broadcasting Corporation (ZNBC) - in both its television and radio transmissions - the Daily Mail, the Times, the Sunday Mail and Sunday Times, have heavily weighted in favour of the MMD; this culminated most vividly in the cancelling by the ZNBC of a long planned and carefully organised live debate on the eve of the poll with presidential candidates in order to transmit an hour long interview with President Chiluba which was an obvious campaign broadcast on behalf of the MMD."[32]

Although there seems to have been some improvement in the way the public media improved their coverage of political parties, most of the observer groups in the 2006 elections noted that they still displayed some bias towards the ruling party. The Commonwealth observer group made the following comment regarding the performance of the public media:

"The general impression was that there had been significant improvement in the performance of the media as compared to the 2001 elections. However there was still evidence of bias towards the ruling party by the government-controlled media, in terms of coverage of the campaign."[33]

These sentiments were also expressed by other international observers such as the EU observer group[34] and the EISA observation mission.[35] The cited Transparency International Report on the presidential elections expressed similar concerns regarding the violations of the provisions of the Electoral Code of Conduct as another area of concern during the 2008 presidential by-election.[36] Consequently one of the most regular criticisms levelled against the Electoral Commission of Zambia (ECZ) was its inability to enforce the Electoral Code of Conduct, in particular those provisions relating to public media coverage of political parties and the use of state resources by members of the ruling party.[37]

Given the negative role that the state-owned media had played in the previous elections due to the manner in which the boards of these bodies are constituted, all the party leaders and leaders of civic organisations that were interviewed for this chapter did not think that the attitude of the state-owned media towards the opposition would change in upcoming elections. However representatives of the public media have argued that they have in fact given the opposition fair coverage. The *Times of Zambia's* managing director stated that the public media has given coverage of the activities of opposition political parties such as their party conventions, while the deputy managing editor of the *Zambia Daily Mail* argued that even before the code of conduct was in place, the public media had demonstrated commitment to giving all political parties balanced coverage. He pointed out that opposition political parties are sometimes fond of issuing unsubstantiated and libellous attacks which the public media can only publish at the risk of being sued.

The private media has provided an alternative avenue for the dissemenation of the views and activities of opposition political parties. During the 2001 elections the private media gave overwhelming support to opposition political parties, as was noted by the SADC Parliamentary observer group. Some of the civil society leaders interviewed stated, however, that at times private newspapers such as *The Post* have not been objective in their coverage of the ruling party. In a meeting held with the newspaper's managing director and representatives of political parties, several complaints were raised against *The Post*, one of which was that the newspaper sometimes tended to be personal in its coverage of news and at times used unacceptable language in its news reports of political leaders.

The private media has been generally viewed as anti-government largely because of its alternative coverage given to opposition parties. As such, it has suffered constant harassment and intimidation from the state. During the 2001 elections, for example, a private radio station in the Copperbelt Province was physically attacked by MMD cadres and the police did little to protect them. Radio Phoenix was closed during the campaign period, while Radio Maria and Trinity Broadcasting Network were threatened with closure by the state. The latter was specifically ordered to confine itself to religious matters in accordance with the terms of the licence issued to it. The at times openly hostile stances adopted by *The Post* have also been used as justification for adoption of this negative attitude towards the private media.

Role played by state institutions

The role of the state institutions has been another source of dissatisfaction among opposition political parties. Several monitoring groups were of the view that state structures have not played a neutral role in party politics, particularly during election times. The police, intelligence and district administrators have been particularly targeted for criticism. The police service has been criticised for using its wide powers selectively under the Public Order Act to the disadvantage of opposition parties.

Local monitoring group reports made reference to the presence of officers from the Office of the President at some polling stations during the 2001 elections. One opposition party leader explained that so many myths surround the manner in which intelligence officers work that their mere presence at a polling station is likely to intimidate voters. Hence, in the run-up to the 2006 elections, the director of elections assured all stakeholders that although he did not believe that the officers of the Office of the President would participate in rigging elections, they would not be allowed to be involved in the elections, as their participation makes people uneasy.[38] During the petition trial against the election of then-president Mwanawasa, it emerged that the director general of intelligence was playing a critical role in raising campaign funds for Mwanawasa's campaign efforts.[39]

Furthermore, local monitoring groups and the international observer group monitoring the 2001 elections reported that district commissioners, who are civil servants, were not neutral and were actively campaigning for the ruling party during the elections. The Zambia Revenue Authority has at times been used to harass opponents of the ruling party, particularly those who defect to the opposition, and as previously mentioned, some opposition political party leaders stated that business people are generally afraid to make donations to opposition parties because they fear being victimised by the Zambia Revenue Authority. By the very nature of the activity, it is not easy to establish any concrete evidence of this. However, several allegations have been made and these institutions have been forced on a number of occasions to deny that the ruling party uses them to blackmail political opponents. For example, it was alleged that a Heritage Party MP who voted with the MMD during the 2001 election of the speaker, contrary to the official position of his party, may have been blackmailed by the Zambia Revenue Authority to take that position.[40]

The management of elections by the ECZ has been fairly competent and impartial, although over time issues have been raised concerning the impartiality of the elections office. During the 2001 elections, the EU observer mission hinted at possible collusion between the ECZ and the ruling party to the disadvantage of opposition parties. For the 2006 elections, the ECZ raised the nomination fee for presidential candidates from K500 000 to K20 000 000, and for parliamentary candidates from K40 000 to K500 000. The nomination fees for city, municipal and district councils were put at K100 000, K75 000 and K50 000 respectively.[41] Some opposition parties protested against this move,[42] saying it disadvantaged the opposition, further depleting their already meagre campaign funds.

Internal factors affecting the strength of opposition political parties

Among some of these problems are those related to intra-party conflicts largely over leadership positions, inability to retain membership, the quality of leadership, problems of poor party funding, the 'big man' syndrome and its negative impact on intra-party democracy, and a lack of intra-party democracy in general.

The problems of internal divisions over leadership positions within the party, factionalism and lack of party discipline seem to be endemic among political parties. Several factors can be advanced to account for this.

An explanation that was commonly given by CSO leaders is what one can call 'an appetite for positions', particularly for party presidency positions. This, together with the problems of ethnicity and regionalism, was advanced as one of the reasons why attempts to form alliances among opposition political parties have failed.

There is therefore a general feeling that opposition parties are not only inadequately prepared for elections but are so fragmented that they are unable to offer a serious alternative to the MMD. For example, the programme officer of the Anti-Voter Apathy project, an NGO involved in political education campaigns, noted that while the ruling party had already announced its candidates for the 2006 elections and put its campaign structure in place, opposition parties were 'still quarrelling'. One opposition leader that was interviewed, however, hinted at the possibility of infiltration by state agents masquerading as party members as another possible cause of internal instability among opposition political parties.

Yet another serious problem that faces opposition political parties is an inability to maintain steady membership and in some cases even quality leadership below the level of party president. There are several factors that may account for this. The first has to do with the inability of opposition political parties to provide a distinct policy or even ideology as a pull for party membership. The opposition political parties have at times found it difficult to justify their existence in view of the fact that their policy positions are not distinct from those of the ruling party. This factor has been pointed out by a number of political observers and diplomats in the country. Thus there are no strong factors which would motivate an individual to join one party instead of another. Instead, the motivations to join political parties tend to be highly self-serving; individuals are just looking for political parties that have the best chance of winning elections and in which they are likely to be appointed to some lucrative position.

Indeed most party and NGO leaders interviewed thought that defections to the ruling party were a major factor weakening opposition political parties and that these defections were motivated purely by self-interest. Since the 2001 elections the UPND has lost five MPs to the ruling party, including the party's general secretary, deputy national secretary and deputy national chairman, who were subsequently re-elected on the MMD ticket. The FDD has also lost a number of MPs: one was appointed a cabinet minister and three others were appointed as deputy ministers. The same fate has faced UNIP and the Heritage Party. The latter lost two of its MPs who were appointed to the cabinet.

Owing to the level of poverty in Zambia, most opposition party leaders believe that in the main, people who join political parties or defect do so with the hope that the party they join will form a government and once that happens they will be given jobs and other handouts for ordinary 'party cadres'. As a former UPND vice president put it, it requires a great deal of resilience to be in opposition for five years when one has the option to reap all the benefits of being a member of the ruling party. He pointed out that the UPND had managed to sustain high quality because most people who have remained loyal to the party are financially independent.

But the biggest problem affecting the strength of opposition political parties is one that has already been mentioned, namely the lack of any finances to fund party activities. Since many political parties do not have adequate sources of funding most of their activities are funded by the people who come to lead such political parties, resulting in the 'big man' syndrome in most political parties in the country. This was one of the major problems that faced the UPND, and earlier, the Zambia Democratic Congress of Ben Mwila. It has adversely affected internal democracy in the country; the problem was graphically revealed in the succession crisis that faced the UPND after the death of its leader. In addition, most of the party leadership work on a part-time basis as the parties cannot afford full-time salaries. Consequently party workers tended not to put in as much effort as they could, had they been paid.

Another important weakness of opposition political parties is a lack of intra-party democracy. As mentioned, most of the political parties have not had conventions to elect their leaders. Shortly before the 2006 elections, only three political parties – the FDD, MMD and UPND – held national conventions to elect new leaders. Lack of intra-party democracy also tends to discourage people from within and outside the country to give financial assistance to a party that is perceived to adhere to undemocratic principles.

Conclusion

It has been argued in this chapter that while formal rules for the formation of political parties in Zambia are liberal and the right of assembly is relatively permissive, on balance, the political atmosphere is not conducive to the existence of vibrant opposition parties, which in turn is a necessary element of a multiparty system. The role played by public institutions against opposition parties, the negative role played by the state media and the poor funding environment for opposition parties, together with the inadequacies of the private media, have all combined to make it difficult for opposition political parties to compete effectively and fairly during election periods.

The political atmosphere that exists in a country can, to a very large degree, determine the nature of the opposition. French politician Michel Debre identified three forms of opposition. First there is pragmatic opposition, opposing the policies of the government of the day. This opposition is characterised by the nature of opposition parties in Anglo-Saxon Commonwealth countries. The second type of opposition is the opposition that is opposed to the regime, and this is the kind of opposition that characterised the opposition to the state and its rules and institutions, such as that which existed in the Third and Fourth French Republics. The third kind is revolutionary opposition; this is the opposition that is directed against the social order. For Debre, the only opposition that is acceptable is that which recognises the legitimacy of the institutions of the regime and acts for the purpose of replacing the government, one that accepts the 'peaceful alteration of government'.[43]

In order to achieve any meaningful co-existence, therefore, the opposition parties also have a responsibility to accept the right of the majority opinion to govern as legitimate and in the process accept the role of a responsible loyal opposition. This, however, is only possible if there is a large measure of consensus that the political system allows for the opposition party to have an opportunity to also form the government in some future date and does not condemn the opposition parties to perpetual opposition. It is this kind of political environment that can make opposition political parties play the role of a responsible and loyal opposition.

It is here, therefore, that free and fair elections at every level become critical for the co-existence of political parties in the first sense that Debre describes. The absence of such an environment forces the opposition to lose faith in the system and hence to operate as an opposition in Debre's second and third senses – one that aims to destroy the regime. Thus rotation of the party in power is healthy prerequisite for liberal democracy.

ENDNOTES

1 See Momba JC 2004. 'Civil Society and the Struggle for Human Rights and Democracy in Zambia', in Zeleza, Tiyambe and McConnaughay, Philip J (eds). *Human Rights, the Rule of Law, and Development in Africa*. Philadelphia: University of Pennsylvania Press, p218.

2 http://maravi.blgospot.com/2009/11/upnd-pf-pact-scoop-solwezi-central.html

3 http://www.zambianwatchdog.com/2010/04/30/upndf-pact-grabs-mufumbwe

4 http://www.zambian-economist.com/2008/10/rolling-election-results-update-3.html

5 For a detailed discussion of the serious internal conflict that had existed in the party see Momba JC 2002. 'Political transition and the crises of an African nationalist party: The case of UNIP', in Salih M (ed), *African Political Parties: Evolution, Institutionalisation and Governance*. CITY: Pluto Publishers.

6 Government of the Republic of Zambia. The Societies Act CAP. 119 of the Laws of Zambia, Article 8.

7 Ibid.

8 Interview with the then-UPND vice-president for political and economic affairs.

9 *Times of Zambia* 11 January 1996.

10 Chanda AW. 'Public Order Act', p8. ZAMLII lecture series, available at http://zamlii.ac.zm/lecture-series.html.

11 Bureau of Labour 2001. *Country Report on Human Rights*, February.
12 EU Election Observation Mission. *Second Interim Statement on the 2001 Zambian Elections*, p2.
13 Chanda A 2002. 'Interim Statement on 27 December 2001 tripartite elections'. FODEP press briefing, 3 January 2002.
14 'Initial Report of the National Constitutional Conference' at http://www.znbc.co.zm/documents/The_Initial_Report_of_the_National_Constitutional_Conference_June_2010.pdf
15 Coalition 2001. 'Monitoring Report on the Mwandi Parliamentary By-election', 14 November 2000.
16 Coalition 2001. 'Monitoring Report on the Isoka East Parliamentary By-election', 7 September 2001, p4.
17 EU Election Observation Mission, op. cit., p2.
18 FODEP, Zambia's 1998 Local Government Elections Report. Lusaka: Multimedia, 1999, pp79-81.
19 Commonwealth Secretariat 2006. *Zambia Presidential, National Assembly and Local Government Elections 18 September 2006 – Report of the Commonwealth Observer Group*. At http://aceproject.org./ero en/regions/africa/ZM/zambia-final-report-general-elections-commonwealth.
20 Final TIZ Presidential Elections Statement – 2008. At http://www.tizambia.org.zm/documents/Final%20TIZ%20Presidential%20Elections%20Statement-%202008.pdf, p4
21 The exchange rate in January 2001 was K3 350 to US$1.
22 *The Post*, 2 June 2003.
23 See *The Post*, 3 June 2003. For grounds for the impeachment of the president, see *The Post*, 8 August 2003.
24 *The Post*, 8 August 2003.
25 Government of the Republic of Zambia, Electoral (Conduct) Regulations (Statutory Instrument No.179 of 1996).
26 *Times of Zambia*, 11 July 1991.
27 *Zambia Daily Mail*, 18 December 1990.
28 *Times of Zambia*, 8 October 1991.
29 National Democratic Institute for International Affairs, *The 31 October 1991 National Elections in Zambia*. Available at http://www.ndi.org/ndi/library/192_zm_oct31_91_nat.txt.

30 Ibid.
31 Carter Centre. 'Carter Center Observation Assessment of the 2001 Zambian Pre-election Period, 13 December 2001'. Available at http://www.cartercenter.org/documents/298.dpf.
32 EU Election Observation Mission, op. cit.
33 Commonwealth Secretariat 2006. *Zambia Presidential, National Assembly and Local Government Elections 28 September, 2006 – Report of the Commonwealth Observer Group*. At http://aceproject.org/ero-en/regions/africa/ZM/zambia-final-report-general-elections-commonwealth
34 European Union Election Observation Mission Zambia 2006. Final Report, Lusaka, Novembeer, 2008: pp22-23. At http://www.delzmb.ec.europa.eu/en/EU%20EOM%20-%20Final%20Report.pdf
35 Electoral Institute for Sustainability of Democracy in Africa 2006. Interim Statement EISA Regional Observation Mission to the Zambian 2006 Tripartite Elections, 28 September 2006: p6. At http://www.eisa.org.za/WEP/zam2006is6.htm
36 Final TIZ Presidential Elections Statement 20089: p5. At http://www.tizambia.org.zm/dmdocuments/Final%20TIZ%20Presidential%20Elections%20Statement%20 2008.pdf
37 Government of the Republic of Zambia. The Electoral (Conduct) Regulations (Statutory Instrument No 179 of 1996) (The Code of Conduct)
38 *Zambia Daily Mail*, 29 July 2006.
39 This is the evidence on the role played by the Director General of Intelligence in the Office of the President, given by Michael Sata, who is the current president of the Patriotic Front. He had served as a cabinet minister in the Chiluba government and had also served as the MMD's national secretary right up to the time he left the party in 2001. His evidence was reproduced by The Post, November 13 2002. Other newspapers, the *Zambia Daily Mail* and the *Times of Zambia*, reproduced bits of this evidence but their accounts were not as detailed as was the coverage in *The Post*.
40 See The Post, 7 February 2002.
41 See press release by ZEC chairperson available at http://www.elections.org.zm/press_releases/nominations. See also the announcements by the ZEC chairman reported in *Zambia Daily Mail*, 20 July 2006.
42 See The Saturday Post, 22 July 2006. The Heritage Party presidential candidate described the decision as unjustified and undemocratic. See also *Zambia Daily Mail*, 28 July 2006.
43 Le Monde, 2 December 1962.

CHAPTER TEN
ZIMBABWE: OPPOSING AN AUTHORITARIAN SYSTEM - THE CASE OF THE MDC
JOHN MAKUMBE

Introduction

The Lancaster House Constitution, also known as the Constitution of Zimbabwe, under which Zimbabwe attained national independence, clearly envisaged a multiparty political system in the former British colony.[1] That document also made provision for Zimbabweans to be free to form and join political parties and other organisations of their choice. Since the attainment of national independence in 1980, there have been numerous political parties, although some of them have tended to be small and ineffective in terms of their performance at the polls.

The purpose of this chapter is to identify and discuss a selection of Zimbabwe's major opposition political parties since 1980. The main focus will, however, be on the Movement for Democratic Change (MDC), which is the largest opposition political party in Zimbabwe, in spite of its 12 October 2005 split. At the time of writing, there are two MDC formations, one led by the founding president, Morgan Tsvangirai (MDC-T), and the other led by Arthur Mutambara (MDC-M). This chapter proceeds from the basic premise that the strengths and weaknesses of opposition political parties is the function of both the national Constitution and the manner in which the incumbent ruling political party manipulates that basic law.

Opposition political parties, prior to the advent of the MDC, always struggled to effectively scrutinise and criticise government policies and practices. They lacked the platform, resources and even the skills to undertake this crucial function of effective and democratic governance. As a result, the ruling Zimbabwe African National Union – Patriot Front (ZANU-PF) made some of the worst ever socio-economic and political policies without any real fear of opposition criticism. For example, ZANU-PF awarded more than 50 000 former liberation fighters rewards amounting to ZW$50 000 each in 1998 from unbudgeted funds, and this subsequently led to the collapse of the Zimbabwe dollar. Furthermore, the opposition parties lacked the capacity to mobilise public opposition and resistance to even the most glaring blunders that the Mugabe regime proposed and implemented. The opposition political parties' performance in the role of watchdog was generally very poor prior to 1999. As such, there was limited restraint, transparency and accountability in governance by the ruling ZANU-PF.

The Movement for Democratic Change (MDC)

Formation and initial composition

Formed in 1999, the MDC emerged as the most serious challenge to the ZANU-PF regime of Robert Mugabe.[2] Largely labour-based and drawing most of its personnel and ideas from civil society under the National Constitutional Assembly (NCA), the MDC, is however, supported by numerous professionals, intellectuals, business enterprises and farmers.[3] According to Masipula Sithole, the MDC '... has widespread support, relying heavily on the organisational infrastructure of the powerful Zimbabwe Congress of Trade Unions (ZCTU) which Tsvangirai also led as its Secretary General'.[4]

The MDC was highly instrumental in the rejection of the government-sponsored draft Constitution in a referendum in February 2000. This marked ZANU-PF's first major defeat at the polls since Zimbabwe's national independence in 1980. The popular support that the MDC received in virtually all urban areas of Zimbabwe put such a scare into the ruling ZANU-PF party that the former liberation movement had to resort to violent farm invasions and gross human rights violations in order to 'win' the parliamentary elections of 2000 and the presidential elections of 2002.[5]

The MDC posed an especially serious threat to the regime because MDC ranks included not only workers, but [also] large numbers of students, professionals, whites, and business people. It was as if everyone opposed to Mugabe's continued tenure had joined the MDC. Most impressive was the support that the MDC was able to mobilise in all the major cities. It was also tenacious and committed to using all legal means at its disposal in order to pursue its fight for peaceful change.[6] Perhaps one of the MDC's critical attributes was that it clearly emerged as a viable alternative to the ruling ZANU-PF party, unlike its smaller predecessors. Eleven years after its formation, the MDC still commands popular support in virtually all the major population centres around Zimbabwe, including in some rural areas. The MDC, as a young and inexperienced political party, grossly underestimated the capacity of ZANU-PF to manipulate the electoral system to its advantage. The visibly overwhelming popular support that the MDC was enjoying in the run up to the presidential election fooled that party into assuming that it would win the contest by a large margin. ZANU-PF has been notorious for rigging elections since 1985.[7]

This level of political naivety has been one of the major obstacles to the success of opposition political parties in ousting the Mugabe regime from power. Indeed, it is this author's view that the majority of Zimbabwe's opposition political party leaders need a thorough grounding in the 'politics of incumbency'. The situation becomes even more imperative when the incumbent ruling political party has dictatorial and authoritarian leanings such as ZANU-PF. A dictator is not readily amenable to removal from political office through democratic means. This is certainly a lesson that opposition political parties in Zimbabwe are still learning, albeit slowly.

The composition of the MDC was thus legitimately national in outlook. The party was, indeed, like an omnibus onto which everyone who desired to participate in Mugabe's departure from State House jumped on board. This was both a strength and a weakness for the fledgling party, as shall be argued later.

It is therefore accurate to note that there were no serious ethnic, racial or even class differences among the majority of the people who initially joined and supported the MDC. Equally significant, however, is that there was no general agreement on the best method of removing Mugabe from power. It was this lack of a consensual approach that eventually led to the infamous MDC split in October 2005.

MDC's political programme

Like most political programmes of opposition parties the world over, the MDC's programme sets out to improve significantly on whatever is perceived to be the ruling party's mistakes in governance. The MDC's economic policy is outlined under the label 'Restart', claiming that the Zimbabwe economy has collapsed to the extent that it would have to be restarted by a future MDC government. An internal MDC document that discusses the political programme states that everything that could possibly go wrong in Zimbabwe has gone wrong. "We live in a hyper-inflationary environment where normalcy is impossible to sustain. The situation is so bad that only extraordinary steps must be taken at the collapse of the dictatorship and the attendant crisis of expectation, to avert the state from receding into some form of spontaneous anarchy, if not total collapse."[8]

To this end, the MDC's economic policy seeks to '... restore, stabilise and grow the economy ...' in line with the party's values of social justice and solidarity. The policy recognises the rampant corruption within the current regime, and proposes a reconstruction and transformation programme targeted at specific developmental initiatives such as fiscal, monetary, exchange rate and trade policies. Contrary to ZANU-PF's disregard for property rights, the MDC's economic policy proposes to respect private property rights '... in order to reclaim our previous position as an investment destination'.[9]

The proposed plan of action envisaged has as its basis the need to accept the reality on the ground and to move out of the denial stage by taking the following steps:
- restore political legitimacy as a forerunner to building local and international confidence in Zimbabwe as a member of the family of nations;
- recognise the immense challenges ... huge humanitarian emergencies, the death of the power sector, lack of fuels, food insecurity, collapse of the transport and communications industry, social service backlogs in the health sector, education and welfare, and a bloated [and] inefficient bureaucracy;
- negotiate bridging support to address ... immediate humanitarian emergecies and to save [lives];

- restore agriculture to enable the sector to realise its [economic] and food security obligations;
- [restore and] respect the rule of law, private property rights ... adopt international business practices in line with the demands of the global investment community.[10]

The policy document further proposes to create an enabling environment for the recovery of the private sector by fighting against corruption, providing basic security for both local and international investors. This will in turn reduce unemployment and poverty among the people of Zimbabwe. The civil service will be restructured by ensuring that public resources are more efficiently utilised for the benefit of the generality of the citizenry. These are all noble ideals, but are to be expected from every serious opposition political party. The MDC political programme covers numerous other aspects of democracy, governance and human development. In theory, the overall thrust of the political programme is sound and very ambitious, given the devastation that has been visited upon Zimbabwe by the Mugabe regime.

With reference to the vexing land issue, the MDC's political programme is emphatic that land redistribution is necessary as it was the unfinished business of the liberation struggle. It bemoans, however, the manner in which ZANU-PF has gone about violently undertaking land reform since the year 2000. The programme rightly points out some of the dire consequences of the ZANU-PF strategy of land reform. "There is no activity in former commercial farms, ranches, and agro-processing units because of what happened during the past six years. Our nation has no food. Beef and milk are unaffordable. Agro-industry has collapsed and exports have dried up. A chaotic land redistribution exercise failed to address agrarian reform in a meaningful way. The result is clear to all: food shortages, the collapse of the economy, flight of capital, and a nation on its knees."[11]

To remedy this situation, the MDC political programme proposes to set up an independent land commission '... vested with the powers and authority to fulfil its role of formulating, planning and co-ordinating an all-inclusive and well-crafted resettlement programme ...'.[12] The setting up of the proposed land commission will be preceded by a land audit aimed at establishing who owns what land, and to what use the land is being put. The primary goal will be to re-establish commercial farming in Zimbabwe while also transforming communal farmland into commercially viable entities that qualify for incentives and the attraction of investment through the awarding of title.

Party structure

According to the MDC's constitution, there are ten organs of the party, each with its specific composition and responsibilities. The Congress is the supreme organ of the party, which meets once every five years. Its functions include those of formulating the policies and principles of the party, supervising the implementation of policies, principles and programmes, electing members of the National Council, and approving audited financial statements, among several other functions. The latest MDC Congress was held in Harare in March 2006 and the next one will be held during 2011.

Political structure of the MDC

Congress (Held every five years)

National Conference (Members drawn from party structures as per constitution)

National Council (Members drawn from party structures as per constitution)

National Executive Committee (Members drawn from party structures as per constitution)

National Standing Committee (Members drawn from National Executive Committee)

Provincial Executive (12 provinces)

District Executive (120 districts/constituencies)

Ward committees (Approximately 1,900)

Branch committees (Unknown number)

Ordinary membership (Approximately 2 million)

The National Conference constitutes the MDC's second highest party organ. It meets annually in between congresses but does not meet in the year when Congress will be convened. The primary purpose of the National Conference is to receive reports prepared by the party secretaries, and to review and update policies. It also reviews the progress of the implementation of the party's programmes in between congresses and fills any vacancies arising in the National Council. All these functions need to be performed without conflicting with the powers and functions of Congress.

The National Council is the MDC's main policy-implementing organ, and it has the authority to lead the party and execute its aims and objectives. The National Council primarily implements the decisions and resolutions of the Congress. It issues instructions and directives to, as well as receives reports from, the National Executive Committee – the equivalent of a shadow cabinet. The National Council supervises and directs the work of both the women's and youth assemblies. It is also the custodian of all the MDC's property. It has the power to suspend or dissolve a provincial executive committee, and to call and conduct elections within four months of such action where necessary. The National Council is mandated to rectify or reverse any decisions of the National Executive Committee.[13]

The National Executive Committee of the MDC is responsible for exercising all the functions of the National Council in between meetings of the latter, '... provided that the National Executive Committee shall have no power to make any decision in conflict with a standing decision of the National Council'.[14] It is the administrative and implementing authority of the MDC and meets at least once every two months. The National Standing Committee is responsible for the day-to-day running of the party's affairs and its membership is drawn from the National Executive Committee. The Standing Committee is, however, not allowed to make any executive or policy decisions. Both the National Conference and the National Standing Committee were recently created as part of the measures undertaken by the MDC following the factionalism that led to the split within that party.

The 12 October Crisis

Given the seriously uneven political playing field created by ZANU-PF in its own favour, opposition political parties have faced an uphill task whenever they have participated in elections. After the alleged rigging of the election results of both the 2000 and the 2002 elections by the Mugabe regime, the MDC engaged in serious debate regarding whether or not to participate in the 2005 parliamentary elections. In the end, and after announcing to the general public that it would not participate, the MDC leadership later decided to participate, much to the confusion of the electorate. An internal report of the MDC states that the MDC participated in the March 2005 election reluctantly "because we knew that the electoral terrain would never produce a free and fair expression of the people's political choice. The electoral process and the result vindicated us."[15]

One of the results of the parliamentary elections of 2005 was that the MDC's representation in the legislature was reduced from 56 to 41. Soon after these elections, ZANU-PF pushed through parliament the notorious Constitutional Amendment No 17, and since it had the numbers the amendment was passed despite the MDC's spirited fight against it. This new provision in the Constitution of Zimbabwe, among other things, facilitated the resuscitation of the previously abolished upper chamber of the legislature. The Senate was raised from the dead for no apparent redeeming purpose in terms of democracy and good governance.

The MDC was again confronted with the question of whether or not to participate in the meaningless senatorial elections. It was clear to the majority of Zimbabweans that for the MDC to participate would be tantamount to further strengthening the hand of ZANU-PF while weakening its own. There had been ample evidence of the futility of participating in ZANU-PF managed elections since 2000. In its report to Congress, the Tsvangirai-led faction of the MDC admits to this reality. The MDC had demonstrated in June 2000, March 2002, March 2005, and during countless parliamentary by-elections that free and fair elections are impossible until an electoral framework fashioned along the lines of the RESTORE document are in place. The question was what value would participation in the senate elections add to people's struggle for democracy, good governance, the rule of law, and economic recovery.[16]

Thus on the one hand the Tsvangirai faction was of the view that further participation in elections under the current electoral framework would be a negation of the basic cause of the masses of the people of Zimbabwe. The Arthur Mutambara faction, on the other hand, felt that since Constitutional Amendment No 17 had been passed by parliament, the MDC had an obligation to participate in the senatorial elections. The differences between the two factions came to a head on 12 October 2005 during a National Council meeting to decide on the matter. When a vote was taken, the result was that the Mutambara faction had won by 33 votes to 31. As president of the MDC, Morgan Tsvangirai insisted that the MDC would not participate in the senatorial elections, effectively forcing the faction that had won the vote to split from the rest of the party.

During the following months, the two MDC factions engaged in vicious attacks against each other, much to the amusement of the ruling ZANU-PF. The Mutambara faction moved offices from Harare to Bulawayo from where some of their senior officials came. The MDC headquarters in Harare remained the national base of the Tsvangirai-led faction. The split was unfortunate in that, firstly, it seriously weakened the MDC and diverted its energies from fighting against Zimbabwe's major liability – ZANU-PF and Mugabe's continued tenure of office. The second unfortunate development was that the split divided and confused the majority of the MDC supporters at a time when the Mugabe regime was actively churning out additional repressive legislation against the people of Zimbabwe. Perhaps the third consequence of the split was that it effectively exacerbated political apathy and despondency among the people of Zimbabwe.

The fourth development was the apparent emergence of the ugly-headed monster of African politics - ethnicity. The majority of the senior officials who had gone with the Mutambara faction were Ndebeles, while the majority of the Shona senior MDC officials remained with Tsvangirai. This was unfortunate since the issue of ethnicity had not been a significant factor in the politics of the MDC since its formation. What is even more interesting to note is that white senior members of the MDC also split in half, with some of them supporting Mutambara and others supporting Tsvangirai.

After a short while it became clear, however, that the majority of the grassroots had remained faithful to Morgan Tsvangirai and had not supported the Mutambara faction of the MDC. Indeed, when the two factions held separate congresses, only 3 000 delegates showed up for the Mutambara faction, compared to a massive 15 000 who attended the Tsvangirai faction's congress. It therefore would appear that whereas the Mutambara faction had won the battle, they had actually lost the war.

Reports from interviews with Tsvangirai, have indicated that efforts are being undertaken to end the conflict within the opposition party. There are serious attempts being made to re-unite the two factions into one MDC. A code of conduct has already been signed to the effect that the two factions shall not attack one another in public. Tsvangirai further indicated that should these efforts fail to reunite the party, then it would be necessary to formalise separate identities and accept that the two factions become two separate political parties.[17]

Tsvangirai stated that the split within the MDC was inevitable because there had not been any consensus regarding the method of removing Mugabe and ZANU-PF from power. He noted that the Mutambara faction had essentially been influenced to pursue a parochial agenda by both ZANU-PF and former South African president Thabo Mbeki, charged by the Southern African Development Community (SADC) to mediate between ZANU-PF and the MDC. Mutambara realises now that his political career is likely to be frustrated if he does not redirect himself and his faction into mainstream opposition politics in Zimbabwe.

A representative of the Mutambara faction, who declined to be named, indicated that reunification efforts are indeed in progress, and that the Mutambara faction realises that even though they were 'right' in all their actions they had basically lost grassroots support, which largely stayed with Tsvangirai.[18] Reunification efforts have, however, failed to bear any fruit, and the two MDC formations
participated in the 2008 elections as separate entities. The MDC-M has, however, suffered numerous defections from its rank and file as some of its members have returned to the MDC-T.

The opposition's lack of resources

Perhaps the most inhibiting weakness of Zimbabwean opposition political parties is the lack of financial resources. As is common with most incumbent African ruling parties, ZANU-PF is notorious for helping itself to all kinds of public resources, but opposition political parties do not have such access to the same resources. The Political Parties (Finance) Act makes provision for the public funding of all registered political parties that have representation in the legislature. Parties that are not represented in parliament do not qualify to receive these funds. The result of this arrangement is that only political parties that are large enough to command a meaningful proportion of the electorate receive this benefit.

Recently, however, the Mugabe regime has made amendments to the act, and these changes prohibit political parties from receiving funds from 'foreign sources' – including from Zimbabweans who are in the diaspora. The irony of the matter is that ZANU-PF has often received large sums of money from foreign sources, especially at election times. This recent amendment is clearly aimed at ensuring that the MDC does not receive financial support from the more than three million Zimbabweans who have left the country in the past few years. The majority of these people are suspected of being hostile to ZANU-PF and sympathetic to opposition political parties.

The MDC's Tsvangirai, however, pointed out that his party does not receive much financial support from Zimbabweans in the diaspora. He stated that most of the funding that the MDC receives comes from membership subscriptions. Indeed, in 2005 the state funds disbursed under the Political Parties (Finance) Act were made available only to the Mutambara faction of the MDC. The Tsvangirai faction did not receive any of that money. This was obviously a deliberate attempt by ZANU-PF to weaken the Tsvangirai faction, which they find more undesirable, while strengthening the one they prefer to accept, namely the Mutambara faction of the MDC.

The Mugabe government has been critical of any foreign donor agencies suspected of supporting financially both civil society and opposition political parties. Some elements within the ZANU-PF government have castigated donor agencies for interfering in the internal matters of their host country.[19] Virtually all election results since the advent of national independence in 1980 indicate very poor performance by opposition political parties. We argue here that one of the major factors for this is the lack of financial and other necessary resources. Table 1 indicates the dismal performance of opposition political parties during the 1990 parliamentary elections.

Table 1: Results of the 1990 parliamentary elections in Zimbabwe

Party	Valid votes	% of Valid votes	Seats won
ZANU-PF	1 690 071	81	117
ZUM	369 031	18	2
ZANU-Ndonga	19 448	1	1
UANC	9 667	1	0
NDU	498	0	0
Independents (7)	9 478	5	0
Total	2 098 193	100	120

Source: Sithole, M & Makumbe, J, 'Elections in Zimbabwe: The ZANU-PF hegemony and its incipient decline,' African Journal of Political Science, 2, 1, 1997, pp.122-139.

The situation reflected in Table 1 was repeated in the 1995 election, as is reflected in Table 2. ZANU-PF even managed to hold on to the 117 parliamentary seats that it had won in the 1990 elections.

Table 2: Results of the 1995 parliamentary elections in Zimbabwe

Party	Valid votes	% of Valid votes	Seats won
ZANU-PF	1 126 822	76	117
ZANU-Ndonga	93 546	6	2
Forum Party	88 223	6	0
Zimbabwe Aristocrats	147	0	0
Independents (29)	62 025	4	1
Total	1 370 676	100	120

Source: Compiled from results published in The Herald, 11 April 1995.

This situation was dramatically transformed after the formation of the MDC, as was noted earlier. The MDC's performance in elections has been unprecedented in Zimbabwe's opposition politics since 1980. We note, however, that the MDC's performance in the 2000 elections has since declined. as is demonstrated by the results of the March 2005 parliamentary elections (Table 3). One reason is the confusion the MDC sowed among the electorate by prevaricating on whether or not to participate in the 2005 elections. There is also the possibility that the ruling ZANU-PF had further improved on its capacity to manipulate election results, or that it had suddenly become popular once again with the electorate. Smaller political parties, however, showed no sign of making any significant gains against the two major political parties, ZANU-PF and the MDC.

Table 3: Results of the 2005 parliamentary elections in Zimbabwe

Provinces	ZANU-PF votes	ZANU-PF seats	MDC votes	MDC seats	Other seats
Bulawayo	22 611	0	85 454	7	0
Harare	112 143	1	234 138	17	0
Manicaland	191 577	13	146 538	2	0
Mash East	243 398	13	85 600	0	0
Mash central	229 525	10	43 092	0	0
Mash West	200 699	12	77 942	1	0
Masvingo	211 435	13	99 044	1	0
Mat North	58 727	1	85 883	5	1
Mat South	70 805	3	70 033	4	0
Midlands	228 887	12	139 386	4	0
Total	1 569 807	78	1 067 11	41	1

Source: Zimbabwe Electoral Commission, 2005; Herald, 4 April 2005.

The situation changed dramatically in 2008 when the so-called harmonised elections were held. The run-up to the 29 March 2008 elections was fairly peaceful and all political parties were able to campaign without the fear of violence. The political playing field was fairly even and opposition political parties were allowed to flight their election campaign advertisements both on radio, television and in the print media. The MDC-T won a total of 99 House of Assembly seats, while ZANU-PF won 97 seats. The MDC-M managed only 10 seats. At the Senate level, the MDC-T won 24 seats while the MDC-M obtained six to ZANU-PF's 30 seats. At the presidential level, the MDC-T leader, Morgan Tsvangirai, won the majority of the votes as the results in Table 4 indicate. These results were delayed by at least five weeks, and there were numerous allegations that the Zimbabwe Electoral Commission (ZEC) was manipulating the figures during this time to ensure that the margin between Tsvangirai and Mugabe was respectably narrow.

Table 4: Presidential Poll Results 29 March 2008

Candidate:	Number of votes:	Actual percentage:
Makoni, Herbert Stanley Simba	207 470	8.3%
Mugabe, Robert Gabriel	1 079,730	43.2%
Towungana, Langton	14 503	0.6%
Tsvangirai, Morgan	1 195 562	47.9%
Spoiled ballots	39 975	
Total votes cast	2 537 240	
Percentage poll		42.7%

Source: Zimbabwe Election Support Network (ZESN) report, August 2008.

Since none of the presidential candidates was able to attain the stipulated 50 per cent plus one vote to be declared the winner, a run-off had to be conducted between Tsvangirai and Mugabe. The run-up to the run-off became very violent, with the ZANU-PF militia, war veterans and the military unleashing such beatings, torture, rape and murders as had not been experienced in Zimbabwe since the 1982 to 1987 Gukurahundi (dissident) war, waged by the Mugabe government against Joshua Nkomo's supporters in the Matabeleland provinces. The MDC-T claims that no fewer than 200 of its supporters were murdered during this period. One week before the run-off election was to be held, Tsvangirai withdrew from the race, alleging that the level of violence was so high and so severe that it was not possible to hold a free and fair election. Mugabe insisted that the election should proceed, and when the results were announced, he claimed to have won by two million votes. There was not a single country in the world that recognised this sham election. This led to the negotiations that eventually resulted in the forging of the fragile government of national unity (GNU).

Other opposition weaknesses

One of the major weaknesses of opposition political parties prior to the formation of the MDC was a lack of political excitement among opposition leaders.[20] This was exacerbated by the lack of oratory skills that some of them have displayed. This problem was most acutely demonstrated by the leadership of the now defunct Forum Party, whose president, the late Justice Enoch Dumbutshena, was such a gentleman that one could easily sleep right through his campaign speech. It must be stated, however, that the youthful MDC speakers have since changed this and now give senior ZANU-PF MPs a torrid time even in the legislature. This in turn gets the public politically excited and ready to vote in support of the MDC.

The lack of adequate and effective grassroots organisation constitutes another opposition weakness. Thus, whereas ZANU-PF has been actively engaging the rural masses, most opposition parties have been hesitant to venture into the countryside to organise and mobilise the rural folk for political support. Rural areas are not easy to access, especially for opposition political parties in Zimbabwe where ZANU-PF has declared some of these to be 'no-go' areas. Numerous supporters of opposition political parties have lost their lives and property to ZANU-PF hoodlums in the past. But the rural areas of Zimbabwe are populated by some of the poorest of the poor, and can be effectively organised and mobilised to give opposition political parties much needed political support.

A third possible weakness of Zimbabwe's opposition parties is the leaders 'unwillingness to unite and form some type of common front to confront the ruling ZANU-PF party. There have been several futile attempts at unity,but none of them have really been successful to date. It would appear that the major problem has been selfishness on the part of most of the leaders of opposition parties. One of Zimbabwe's most courageous politicians, Margaret Dongo aptly put it, "There is no culture of power sharing where the best from each party comes into the new party in a different role. They go to these meetings with preconceived ideas of maintaining the positions they occupy in their parties, even the party name."[21]

As was earlier noted the MDC was largely an alliance, '... a conglomeration of different social interests'.[22] Sachikonye argues that the removal of Mugabe from power was too narrow a focus and therefore a weakness for the MDC.[23] The split in the MDC, which has been discussed previously, is testimony to this weakness.

Further, the fact that the MDC received most of its funding from businesses and white commercial farmers exposed it to severe ZANU-PF critcism as a puppet of the West. To this day, one of Robert Mugabe's favourite insults against the MDC is that it is sponsored by Great Britain and the United States. Hence Mugabe's refrain: 'Zimbabwe will never be colonised again.' Although both the United Kingdom and the United States have denied ever funding the MDC, the allegation had done considerable damage to the image of this party, both internally within Zimbabwe, and externally.

Another weakness of opposition political parties in Zimbabwe is their penchant for close relations with opposition political parties in other southern African states. For example, the MDC forged close links with South Africa's Democratic Party (DP) and Mozambique's Renamo, much to the chagrin of the ruling parties of both these countries.[24] It is generally argued that this natural development has cost the MDC considerable sympathy and the moral support of South Africa's powerful African National Congress (ANC). Sachikonye writes, "At the same time, it needs to be pointed out that with the possible exception of the ruling party (the Botswana Democratic Party) in Botswana, the ruling parties in most countries in the region were not initially friendly towards the MDC."[25] The MDC has recently reduced its overt support for both the DP and Renamo in a tactical move aimed at regaining more substantial support from both Frelimo and the ANC.

Failure to transform a broad movement like the MDC into a viable and cohesive political party is probably one of the key weaknesses of opposition political parties in Zimbabwe. Thus, while we have argued that the MDC split was largely due to the lack of a consensus on the methodology of removing a dictator from power, we further note that there is a close relationship between the methodology and the special interests of the various groups in the MDC.

The current debate within both factions of the MDC centres on the question of values, with each faction accusing the other of reneging on the observance of the party's original values.[26] The extent to which common ground can be identified and attained will determine whether or not the two factions can be reunited. It is therefore logical to argue that the split of the MDC constitutes part and parcel of that struggle. Available evidence would tend to support the claim made by the leadership of the Tsvangirai faction of the MDC that the only values, and therefore interests, which matter are those of the majority of the people of Zimbabwe. The Mutambara faction claims to adhere to the values of democracy, good governance and the people's representation.[27] Indeed, that faction alleges that Tsvangirai betrayed the struggle by rejecting the results of the voting in the National Council on 12 October 2005. They argue that Tsvangirai's action was tantamount to a departure from the foundation values of the MDC.[28] Tsvangirai denies this as he points out that the values of the MDC must always be those of the people, and not those of the elite.

Views of opposition MPs

All the MPs that were interviewed for this study are members of the opposition MDC. When asked about the major achievements of their party since they entered the legislature most of them indicated that their party had survived and performed well in a harsh and hostile political environment. They claimed that it was a major feat to win as many as 57 seats in parliament against ZANU-PF. Most of them alleged that they struggle to reach their constituents because of the obstacles they face through such draconian laws as the Public Order and Security Act (POSA), which, inter alia, requires that persons that wish to hold political meetings must first inform the police. For some reason, the police have interpreted this to imply that they can actually refuse to give clearance, in which case the meeting will be deemed illegal. They also pointed out that sometimes they do hold political rallies without obtaining police clearance and that this results in their arrest and imprisonment. The majority of MPs indicated that they consider this to be a small price to pay in order to gain access to and interact with their supporters. As one MP put it: 'Freedom is not free; there is a price to pay and we are willing to pay it.'[29]

Practically all the respondents in this category bemoaned the lack of access to the public electronic media, which results in their being virtually unknown to most Zimbabweans. One respondent sarcastically stated that the only times that the general public sees him on television is after he has been arrested for defying such laws as POSA and the Access to Information and Protection of Privacy Act (AIPPA). We asked the respondents why they do not seem to be able to undertake any meaningful development activities in their constituencies. Virtually all of them indicated that their party lacks the requisite resources for the execution of development projects. They blamed the Political Parties (Finance) Act, which prohibits political parties from receiving financial resources from outside Zimbabwe, and from foreign-based Zimbabweans.

The respondents were highly critical of the current Constitution of Zimbabwe and the Electoral Act as variously amended. They argued that both the foundation law and the Electoral Act are designed in such a manner as to create a political playing field in which only ZANU-PF can win elections. They also pointed out that existing legislation enables the ruling party to steal election results and get away with it. They referred to several petitions that had been placed before the courts, and the verdicts that nullified certain election results. Sadly, because the affected ZANU-PF MPs appealed the judgements, they continued as MPs while the Supreme Court deliberately delayed the hearing of the appeals until after the expiry of the life of the parliament concerned. To the question, "What have been the achievements of your party to date?", respondents indicated these to be:

- facilitating the people's participation in governance;
- insisting on the restoration of the rule of law in Zimbabwe;

- raising the people's awareness of the essence of democracy;
- exposing ZANU-PF's intolerance of dissent and diversity of views;
- insisting on government observation of human rights;
- encouraging public debate on constitutional matters;
- insisting on democracy and good governance; and
- exposing some of the acts of corruption within ZANU-PF.[30]

All the respondents were of the view that most of the achievements of their party would not have been realised if the MDC had not been represented in the legislature. They further argued that, in a small way, their party is making its contribution to meaningful political development in Zimbabwe. They admitted, however, that in the 11 years since the MDC's formation its achievements should have been a lot better than they currently are.

In relation to the MDC's failures over the first seven years of its existence, the respondents indicated that the party had still to win the majority of seats in the legislature. The party had also not been adequately effective in influencing the policy-making process since ZANU-PF still manages to pass any laws that it wants passed. This is largely a function of a highly partisan Constitution, which enables the president to appoint 30 MPs into the lower house, and at least eight into the upper house, the Senate. Mugabe has always appointed persons that will vote with his own party into these seats.

The respondents also agreed that they had not succeeded in stopping the rot and decay that is prevalent in the ruling ZANU-PF. They argued that under the current circumstances they are powerless to ensure that corruption peddlers are arrested, prosecuted and sentenced. Virtually all the respondents indicated that the resources available to their party are inadequate for the party to fully implement its mandate. They were, however, proud that the bulk of the funds that the MDC uses comes from its own members.

We asked the respondents what they perceive as the MDC's contribution to the nation through its continued participation in the legislature. The respondents indicated that the MDC had:

- managed to bring back democratic space which had long died in Zimbabwe;
- advocated for people's rights to participate in politics;
- given a new dimension to Zimbabwean politics through its participation in parliament, which had remained a de facto one-party state legislature;
- won 57 seats and several mayoral positions;
- changed the political playing field;
- managed to lobby SADC that the principles guiding democratic elections be encouraged;
- shaped a new Zimbabwe society based on key values of tolerance and freedom; and
- put Zimbabwe in the international spotlight.[31]

Virtually all the respondents from the two MDC factions regretted the 12 October split, but they also indicated that the experience would be a learning exercise. They vowed that there should not be a repeat of the differences that caused the split and claimed that there was no real animosity between the two factions since they continue to work together amicably in the legislature. Respondents from both factions also indicated that they suspect that both central intelligence and ZANU-PF spies may have infiltrated them. Both factions are currently re-vetting their members with the hope of resolving the issue. Tsvangirai admitted that his party had not done a good job of vetting new members since its formation. This is, being rectified now to prevent a recurrence of the events leading to the embarrassing split.[32]

Respondents indicated that after the 12 October 2005 split, there are now no serious tensions within the MDC. There is now a genuine desire to forge ahead and return Zimbabwe to a democratic path. They fully understand the need for unity in diversity, and will guard their democratic values against those that would wish to dilute them for short-term gain and benefit. They totally reject the suggestion that ethnic differences may have contributed to the October split, but argue that the MDC is both multi-ethnic and multiracial in its composition. They also claim that regionalism does not play any meaningful part in the MDC's operations and decision-making processes. Furthermore, the party's leadership comprises 33 per cent women, which is consistent with the SADC principles and guidelines for democratic elections.

Several respondents were emphatic that the MDC has done very well in its performance, given the vicious and brutal treatment it faces from Mugabe's ZANU-PF. In its 'Roll of Honour', the MDC lists some 146 named individuals who have lost their lives to ZANU-PF political violence between 2000 and 2004. The Zimbabwe Human Rights NGO Forum reports that the highest per cent of victims of ZANU-PF and state violence since 2000 has been directed at the MDC and its supporters (see Table 4).

Table 4: Political affiliation of victims of ZANU-PF and state violence since 2000

Unknown (farm workers, civilians, etc.)	52.8%
MDC (people at rallies, MDC officials)	37.8%
Other political parties (UP, ZUD, etc.)	4.8%
Police	0.8%
ZANU-PF (war vets, farm invaders, officials and Z-PF youth)	3.8%

Source: Amani Trust, Harare, 2000.

The following important observations need to be made in relation to Table 4. First, most of the victims in the 'Unknown' category are likely to be MDC supporters. Numerous white commercial farmers openly supported the MDC from the day of its formation in 1999. The violence that accompanied the farm invasions was deliberately targeted at both the white commercial farm owners and their workers. This makes the cumulative percentage of the violence against the MDC exceed the 90 per cent mark. It is only fair that the MDC's performance as an opposition political party be assessed with this kind of information in mind.

Views of civil society

Practically all of the respondents in this category claimed that although they are non-partisan, they find themselves relating more closely to opposition political parties than to ZANU-PF. They indicated that in the main they are opposed to the manner in which the Mugabe regime is running (or ruining) the country. Civil society organisations (CSOs) tend to agree with opposition political parties in relation to the need for a new, democratic constitution, as well as the need for the observance of human rights, justice and good governance. Most of the respondents commended opposition political parties for having the courage to challenge ZANU-PF and for being instrumental in exposing some of the evils that are perpetrated by Mugabe's political party. They further attributed some of the failures of opposition political parties to the extremely hostile legal and political environment in Zimbabwe.

A few of the civic respondents were of the view that opposition political parties could have performed better than they were currently doing. For example, they could have walked out of parliament when the Mugabe regime carried out Operation Murambatsvina, which resulted in the demolition of hundreds of so-called illegal structures and the destruction of flea markets. It is estimated that more than 700 000 people were displaced as a result of this operation. Opposition political parties represented in parliament could also have walked out in protest at the passing of Constitutional Amendment No 17, but they did not do so. One respondent strongly argued that the MDC had missed numerous golden opportunities to embarrass Mugabe and his ZANU-PF. It became clear that the level of political polarisation currently existing in Zimbabwe effectively forces civil society straight into the political arena and on the same side as opposition political parties.

Non-partisan opposition

One of the outcomes of the stranglehold on power by the ZANU-PF government has been the generation of various forms of non-partisan opposition groups. Basically, these are formal organisations or associations that have expressed their opposition to the manner in which Zimbabwe is governed under Mugabe and his party. This section will briefly discuss a selection of these groups, which are generally viewed by the Mugabe government as sympathetic to the cause of opposition political parties, including the MDC.

The churches

The most prominent para-church organisation that is well known for its criticism of the Mugabe regime is the Christian Alliance (CA). Formed in 2006, the CA comprises church leaders from across the spectrum of Christian churches in Zimbabwe. Soon after its formation, the CA convened a public meeting at which all political parties and civic organisations were invited to become members of the activist organisation. Virtually all serious opposition political parties agreed to become members of the CA, and this infuriated the Mugabe regime, which proceeded to arrest and detain some of the top CA leaders. Charges against these leaders were subsequently dropped before they had been taken to court.

The CA has openly stated that it is opposed to the manner in which the Mugabe regime is running the country. It cites especially the lack of a democratic constitution, the breakdown of the rule of law, corruption, and the escalation of the cost of living for the majority of Zimbabweans as their main grievances. Exceedingly popular with the masses, the CA in late 2006 launched public protests by way of whistling and hooting for five minutes every Wednesday afternoon. It is proposed to eventually escalate such protests to the level of work boycotts and street demonstrations.

In an attempt to thwart the efforts of the CA, the Mugabe government pursued the 'divide and rule' principle by inviting a carefully selected group of church leaders to a four-hour lunch with the president. A few months after the infamous lunch, the pro-state clergy launched what they call the National Vision Document. There aim was to distribute this document among Zimbabweans and gather feedback to be utilised in the finalisation of a national vision for Zimbabwe. Attempts to merge the two church groups have so far not yielded any fruit.

Zimbabwe Congress of Trade Unions (ZCTU)

Created by the ruling ZANU-PF party during the heyday of socialism soon after the attainment of national independence, the ZCTU is the largest and most powerful labour umbrella body in Zimbabwe. Growing socio-economic hardships and political disenchantment with the Mugabe regime forced the ZCTU to become critical of ZANU-PF's economic policies in the late 1990s. The formation of the mainly labour-based MDC in 1999 effectively made the ZCTU adopt an anti ZANU-PF perspective in the interests of the workers. Although the ZCTU has claimed to be non-partisan, the fact that the majority of its members are also members of the opposition MDC has left the Mugabe regime with no choice but to allege that the labour body is an appendage of the MDC. The fact that the founding president of the MDC is the ZCTU's former secretary general has further served to confirm the regime's allegations.

The ZCTU has consistently opposed the Mugabe government, which it accuses of mismanaging the national economy. Work boycotts and street demonstrations have been organised by the ZCTU with varying degrees of success. The ZCTU has been an active campaigner against the dictatorial regime at both the national and regional levels. It boasts a close relationship with the Congress of South African Trade Unions, which is in an alliance with the ruling ANC in South Africa. Recent attempts by the ZCTU to conduct street demonstrations against the Mugabe regime have been met with vicious acts of police brutality, imprisonment and trials of the ZCTU leadership.

Consistent with its pursuit of the principle of divide and rule, the Mugabe regime has created what is generally viewed as a pro-state labour body, the Zimbabwe Federation of Trade Unions (ZFTU). The ZFTU is shunned by the majority of Zimbabwean workers who view it as the labour wing of ZANU-PF. The creation of the ZFTU thus only served to make the ZCTU more popular with most of the workers in Zimbabwe. At the time of publication, the ZFTU has not yet been able to organise any meaningful collective job action by the few labour unions affiliated to it.

Civil society

The Zimbabwe government generally views mainstream civil society as patently hostile to the ruling party and therefore aligned with opposition political parties. For its part, civil society in this country has grown to be critical of government policies, the majority of which are considered to be inimical to national development, democracy, good governance and the upholding of human rights. Indeed, there are numerous reports prepared by civic bodies that lambaste the Mugabe government for corruption, economic mismanagement and human rights violations. For some time now, civil society in Zimbabwe has been agitating for a home-grown democratic constitution, transparency in elections, and Mugabe's speedy departure from the presidential office. For example, various groups of civic bodies filed official complaints with the African Union's (AU) Human and People's Rights Commission in 2004 alleging gross violations of human rights by the Mugabe regime. To date, the toothless commission has not been able to get the AU General Assembly to hear the matter and make a decision.

Because they are generally very small, though numerous, CSOs and non-governmental organisations in Zimbabwe have found it necessary to form coalitions and strategic alliances in order to confront the ZANU-PF on behalf of the citizenry. The coalitions and alliances have scored numerous successes against the government, and they act as effective watchdogs which closely scrutinise government actions as well as inform the public about some of the acts of maladministration that are committed by the Mugabe regime. To this extent, the ZANU-PF regime regards these civic bodies as constituting part of the opposition.

Opposition media

The media has borne the brunt of state restrictions and even brutality in Zimbabwe since the year 2000. One of the results has been the closing down of such newspapers as the *Daily News*, the *Daily News on Sunday* and the *Tribune*. Through the promulgation of the notorious Access to Information and Protection of Privacy Act (AIPPA), the Zimbabwe government has severely restricted the publication of what it regards as information that reflects the ruling party, Mugabe, or the ZANU-PF government in a bad light. Several journalists have been arrested, tortured and prosecuted under the AIPPA for publishing stories that the regime has labelled as falsehoods. The few remaining independent newspapers such as the *Zimbabwe Independent* and the *Standard* are constantly threatened with closure should they violate any of the provisions of the AIPPA. The third non-state paper, the *Mirror*, can hardly be regarded as an independent paper since it was infiltrated and then taken over by the Central Intelligence Organisation in 2005.

Unlike the state-owned and controlled media which publish stories that overflow with 'praise and worship' for the ZANU-PF government, independent newspapers are highly critical of practically everything that the beleaguered regime does. It is for this reason that independent newspapers are labelled opposition papers by the Mugabe regime. It must be emphasised, however, that independent newspapers in Zimbabwe do publish stories that would otherwise not see the light of day in state-owned papers. Over the years, the Mugabe regime has demonstrated its desperate fear of and hostility towards freedom of information among the citizens of this country. To cater for the several millions of Zimbabweans living outside the country, all these newspapers are now available online for those who have access to the internet.

Restrictive media legislation in Zimbabwe has resulted in the creation of several news websites that focus on developments in that country. At least ten such websites have so far been established, the most notable being *zimonline.com*, *newzimbabwe.com*, *zwnews.com* and *zimbabwesituation.com*. All of these are operated from outside Zimbabwe, while such sites as *kubatana.net*, *sokwanele.com* and a few others are operated from Zimbabwe. The ZANU-PF government is currently drafting legislation to enable it to monitor (and obviously curtail) these cyberspace entities in a desperate bid to keep 'undesirable' information away from Zimbabweans.

Finally, there are currently three major independent radio stations that beam their programmes into Zimbabwe from overseas and from neighbouring countries. These are the *Voice of America's Studio Seven*, *Short Wave Radio Africa*, which broadcasts from London, and the *Voice of the People* from South Africa. The Broadcasting Services Act imposes prohibitive fees for the procurement of a broadcasting licence. Although this act allows non-state actors to participate in the electronic media in Zimbabwe, to date no private broadcasting house has been licensed to operate in this country. The three externally based radio stations tend to be very popular with the information-starved Zimbabweans, and costly Chinese-made equipment has been installed by the Mugabe regime to jam some of these broadcasts. The dictatorial regime is also desperately confiscating solar-powered (and wind-up) radios that are being freely distributed to Zimbabweans in remote parts of the country.

Conclusion

The crisis that Zimbabwe is currently experiencing is clearly a leadership crisis. Mugabe and ZANU-PF have so desperately devised all manner of ways and means of holding onto power that they have had to subvert even some of the laws that they formulated and implemented. They have taken a directly opposite position to what they originally claimed was their liberation war objective – that is, equality, liberty, justice, democracy and good governance. The people of Zimbabwe are now at a crossroad between rejecting their erstwhile liberators turned 'oppressors', and embracing an opposition political party that has the courage to confront ZANU-PF. As this chapter has demonstrated, the opposition political parties in Zimbabwe still have much work to do to improve on their performance. The odds against opposition political parties in Zimbabwe are, indeed, enormous, but they are not insurmountable.

ENDNOTES

1 Government of Zimbabwe (GoZ), Constitution of Zimbabwe, Section 21(1).

2 Sithole M 2003. 'In Search of a Viable Democratic Alternative in Zimbabwe: A Study of Opposition Political Parties Since Independence'. Unpublished departmental monograph, p30.

3 Makumbe J 2002. 'Zimbabwe's hijacked election'. *Journal of Democracy* 13(4), October, pp87-101.

4 Sithole M, *op. cit.*

5 See Makumbe J 2003. 'The stolen presidential election', in Lee MC and Collard K (eds), *Unfinished Business: The Land Crisis in Southern Africa*. Pretoria: Africa Institute of South Africa, p225.

6 Makumbe J, 'Zimbabwe's hijacked election', *op. cit*, p90.

7 Makumbe J, 'The stolen presidential election', op. cit., p226.

8 MDC 2006. 'Programme Summaries'. Harare, March, p1.

9 Ibid.

10 Ibid, pp1-2.

11 Ibid, p3.

12 Ibid.

13 MDC Constitution, as amended at the Second Congress 19 March 2006.
14 Ibid., p12.
15 MDC 2006. National Council Report to the National Congress, 18-19 March, p14.
16 Ibid, p15.
17 Interview with MDC president Morgan Tsvangirai.
18 Interview with MDC MP.
19 Makumbe J and Compagnon D 2000. *Behind the Smokescreen: The Politics of Zimbabwe's 1995 General Elections*. Harare: University of Zimbabwe Publications, p10.
20 Ibid.
21 Sithole M, op. cit., p22.
22 Sachikonye L 2003. 'Between authoritarianism and democracy: Politics in Zimbabwe since 1990', in Lee MC & K Collard (eds), op. cit., p112.
23 Ibid.
24 Ibid, pp112-113.
25 Ibid.
26 Interview with an opposition MP.
27 Ibid.
28 Ibid.
29 Ibid.
30 Interview with several opposition MPs.
31 Ibid.
32 Interview with MDC president, Morgan Tsvangirai.

BIBLIOGRAPHY

Chapter 1
CONCEPTUAL OVERVIEW OF OPPOSITION POLITICAL PARTIES IN SOUTHERN AFRICA
Hussein Solomon

Amnesty International 2010. Amnesty International 2010: *The State of the World's Human Rights.* www.thereport.amnesty.org/en/download. [accessed 31 May 2010]

Githongo John 2010. 'Fear and Loathing in Nairobi'. *Foreign Affairs*, 89(4), July/August.

Heywood Andrew 2002. *Politics*. London: Palgrave Macmillan..

Rotberg Robert 2010. "Mugabe Uber Alles: The Tyranny of Unity in Zimbabwe'. *Foreign Affairs*, 89(4), July/August.

Sadie Yolanda 2001. 'Political Parties and Interest Groups', in Venter Albert (ed) *Government and Politics in the new South Africa.* Pretoria: Van Schaik Publishers.

Chapter 2
BOTSWANA: OPPOSITION POLITICS WITHIN A FRAYING DOMINANT PARTY SYSTEM
Balefi Tsie

Acemoglu D, Johnson S and Robinson JA 2003. 'An African Success Story: Botswana' in Rodrik D (ed), in *In Search of Prosperity: Analytical Narratives on Economic Growth.* Princeton, NJ: Princeton University Press.

Ake C 1995. "The Democratization of Disempowerment in Africa", in Hippler, J (ed). *The Democratization of Disempowerment.* London: Pluto Press.

Ball A and Peters BG 2000. *Modern Politics and Government, sixth edition.* London: Macmillan.

Bauer G and Taylor SD 2005. *Politics in Southern Africa: State and Society in Transition.* Boulder: Lynne Rienner.

Beetham D 1994. 'Conditions for Democratic Consolidation'. *Review of African Political Economy*, No 60.

Du Tuit P 1995. *State Building and Democracy in Southern Africa: Botswana, Zimbabwe and South Africa.* Washington, D.C: US Institute of Peace.

Elklit J and Reynolds L 2002. 'The Impact of Election Administration on the Legitimacy of Emerging Democracies.' *Commonwealth and Comparative Politics* 40(2).

Fatton R 1990. 'Liberal Democracy in Africa'. *Political Science Quarterly* 103(3).

Harvey C and Lewis S 1990. *Policy Choice and Development Performance in Botswana.*

Houndsmills: Macmillan.

Leith C 2005. *Why Botswana Prospered.* Montreal and Kingston: Queen's University Press.

Lekorwe MH 2005. 'The Organization of Political Parties', in Maundeni Z (ed). *40 Years of Democracy in Botswana.* Gaborone: Mmegi Publishing House.

Lodge T, Kadima D. and Pottie D 2005. *A Compendium of Elections in Southern Africa.* Johannesburg: EISA.

Lotshwao K 2010. 'The Weakness of the Opposition in Botswana: A Justification for More Internal Democracy in the Dominant Botswana Democratic Party (BDP)'. Unpublished. Memeo.

Maipose G 2008. 'Policy and Institutional Dynamics of Sustained Development in Botswana'. Working Paper No 35, Commission on Growth and Development, World Bank. Washington DC: World Bank.

Masire QKJ 2006. *Very Brave or Very Foolish: Memoirs of an African Democrat* (edited by Stephen R Lewis). Basingstoke: Palgrave Macmillan.

Matlosa K 2005. *Political Parties and Democratization in SADC: The Weakest Link.* Johannesburg: EISA.

Mkandawire T 1998.'Crisis Management and the Making of Choiceless Democracies in Africa', in Joseph R. *State, Conflict and Democracy in Africa.* Boulder: Lynne Rienner.

Molomo M. 2000a. 'In Search of an Alternative Electoral System for Botswana'. Pula: Botswana Journal of African Studies 14(1).

___ 2000b. 'Understanding Government and Opposition Parties in Botswana'. *Commonwealth and Comparative Politics* 38(1).

___ 2003. 'Political Parties and Democratic Governance in Botswana' in Salih, Mohamed MA (ed). *African Political Parties.* London. Pluto Press.

Munger E 1965. Botswana: *Pan-African Outpost or Bantu Homeland.* Oxford: Oxford University Press.

Nengwekhulu H 1979. 'Some Findings on the Origins of Political Parties in Botswana'. *Pula: Botswana Journal of African Studies* 1(2).

Neocosmos M 2002. 'The Politics of National Elections in Botswana, Lesotho and Swaziland' in Cowen M and Laakso L (eds). *Multiparty Elections in Africa.* London: James Curry.

Osei-Hwedie B 2001. 'The Political Opposition in Botswana: The Politics of Factionalism and Fragmentation'. *Transformation* No 45.

Parson J 1984. Botswana: *Liberal Democracy and the Labor Reserve in Southern Africa*. Boulder: Westview.

___. 1993. 'Liberal Democracy, Liberal State and the 1989 General Elections in Botswana' in Stedman S (ed). *Botswana: The Political Economy of Democratic Development*. Boulder: Lynne Rienner.

Picard L 1985. 'From Bechuanaland to Botswana: An Overview' in Picard L (ed). *The Evolution of Modern Botswana*. London: Rex Collins.

___ 1987. *The Politics of Development in Botswana*: A Model for Success? Boulder: Lynne Rienner.

Ramsay J and Parsons N 1998. 'The Emergence of Political Parties in Botswana' in Edge W and Lekorwe M (eds). Botswana: *Politics and Society*. Pretoria: Van Schaik Publishers.

Raphaeli N et al 1984. 'Public Sector Management in Botswana: Lessons of Pragmatism'. Staff Working Paper No 709. World Bank, Washington, DC: World Bank.

Sadie Y 2006. 'Political Parties, Interest Groups and Social Movements' in Venter A and Landsberg C (eds). *Government and Politics in the New South Africa*. Pretoria: Van Schaik Publishers.

Samatar AI 1999. *An African Miracle: State and Class Leadership and Colonial Legacy in Botswana's Development*. Portsmouth, NH: Heinemann.

___ 2002. 'Botswana: Comprehending the Exceptional' in Samatar AI and Samatar AI (eds). *The African State: Reconsiderations*. Portsmouth, NH: Heinemann.

Sebudubudu D and Osei-Hwedie B 2010. 'In Permanent Opposition: Botswana's Other Parties'. *South African Journal of International Affairs* 17(1).

Selolwane O 2007. 'Statecraft in Botswana: Renegotiating Development, Legitimacy and Authority' in Agbese PO and Kieh GK (eds). *Reconstituting the State in Africa*. London: Palgrave Macmillan.

Somolekae G 2005. *Political Parties in Botswana*. Johannesburg: EISA.

Shugart SM and Wattenberg MP 2001. *Mixed Member Electoral Systems*. Oxford: Oxford University Press.

Tsie B 1996. 'The Political Context of Botswana's Development Performance'. *Journal of Southern African Studies* 22(4).

UNECA 2008. *The Progress of Good Governance in Botswana*. Gaborone: BIDPA.

UNDP 1997. 'Botswana Human Development Report: Challenges for Sustainable Human Development'. Gaborone: TA Publications.

DOCUMENTS
BCP Manifesto 2009. A Nation at the Cross Roads: Which Way Now; Democracy and Prosperity or Dictatorship and Economic Collapse. Gaborone.

NEWSPAPER ARTICLES
Pilane S 2009. 'Would Lt Gen Ian Khama Please Stand Down and Make Way for Mr Ian Khama' in Sunday Standard, 1 June 2009.

Chapter 3
LESOTHO; POLITICAL PARTIES IN A FRAYING POLITY
Francis K Makoa

Afrol News. 'Lesotho economy stagnating'. Available at http.//www.afrol.com/articles/36263 [accessed 28 July 2010]

Bardill, JE and Cobbe, JH 1985. *Lesotho: Dilemmas of Dependence in Southern Africa.* Colorado: Westview Press.

CBL Economic Review. January 2009. 'The Global Economic Downturn: Economic Implications for Lesotho'.

Ferguson, J 1990. *The Anti-politic Machine: 'Development', Depoliticisation, and Bureaucratic Power in Lesotho. Cambridge*: Cambridge University Press.

Gill, SJ 1993. *A Short History of Lesotho: From the Late Stone Age until the 1993 Elections.* Morija: Morija Archives and Museum.

Green T and Chikwana, AB 2006.'Changing attitudes towards democracy in Lesotho'. *Afrobarometer Bulletin,* Lesotho, 22 May.

Machobane,LBBJ 1990. *Government and Change in Lesotho, 1800--1966: A study of Political Institutions.* Houndsmill: Macmillan Lesotho.

Makoa, FK 2004.'Electoral reform and political stability in Lesotho', *African Journal of Conflict Resolution,* 4(2).

___2005.'Conflict resolution and peace building through electoral and parliamentary reforms: A note on Lesotho's mixed-member parliament', *Lesotho Law Journal,* 15(1).

___2005. 'Strengthening parliamentary democracy in Southern Africa : Lesotho country report'. *South African Journal of International Affairs,* 12(1).

Matlosa, K 2008. 'General Election in Lesotho: Managing the Post-Election Conflict' in J*ournal of African Elections, Special Issue: Elections and Democracy in Lesotho,* 7(1), June.
Public Eye. 30 June 2006. 10(26)

Ramsamy, P 2001. 'SADC: The way forward', in Clapham C, Mills G, Morner AM and Sidiropoulos, E (eds). *Reginald Integration in Southern Africa: Comparative Perspectives.* Johannesburg: SAIIA.

Rural Poverty Portal.'Rural poverty in Lesotho'.http://www.ruralpovertyportal.org/web/guest/country/hometags/lesotho [accessed 31 August 2010]

Thabane, M 2002. 'Aspects of colonial economy and society', in Pule NW and Thabane, M (eds) *Essays on Aspects of the Political Economy of Lesotho 1500--2000.* Department of History, National University of Lesotho.

Thakalekoala, T 2005. 'Food shortage, assistance needed' in *Mopheme/The Survivour.* 26 July-1 August.

'The Kingdom of Lesotho Economy, Economic Overview'. 2005. Available at http://www.lesotho.gov.ls//sseconomy.

Van den Bosch, Servaas 2010.''The Story Underneath: Southern Africa Unexpected Low Custom Revenue Causes Budget Shortfalls'.Windhoek: Inter Press Service, March 17. Available athttp://www.ipsnews.net/print.asp?idnews=50700 [accessed 24 June 2010]

World Fact Book 2006. Available at https://www.cia.gov/cia/publications/factbook/geos/it.html#Econ [accessed 7 August 2006].

Documents
Constitution of Lesotho, section 16.
National Assembly Election Order, 1992, section 35.
Societies Act No 20 of 1966.

Chapter 4
MAURITIUS: BEYOND ELITE COMPACTS AND INCESTUOUS POLITICS
Sheila Bunwaree

Bibi JC 2006. 'The Best Loser System – Rights of Citizens and the Ethno Religious Logic'. Paper presented at the Institute of Social Development and Peace conference on 'Electoral Reform – Moving towards an Inclusive Democracy'. Port Louis, Mauritius, 17-18 February.

Bowman LW 1991. *Mauritius, Democracy and Development in the Indian Ocean.* Boulder: Westview Press.

Bunwaree S 1994. *Mauritian Education in a Global Economy.* Rose-Hill, Mauritius: Editions de l'Ocean Indien.

___. 2005. 'The ballot box and social policy in Mauritius'. Paper presented for the social policy and democratisation project of UNRISD, Geneva.

____. 2006a. 'Elections, gender and governance in Mauritius'. Journal of Elections 5(1).

____. 2006b. 'The Role of Civil Society in the APRM Process'. Paper presented at the Banjul meeting on the APRM, June 2006.

____. and Kasenally R 2005. *Political Parties and Democracy in Mauritius.* Johannesburg: EISA.

____. and Yoon M 2006. 'Women and the Mauritian Legislature: A grave democratic deficit". *Journal of Contemporary African Studies* 24(2).

Carroll B and Carroll T 1999. 'The consolidation of democracy'. *Democratization* 6(1).

____ 1999. 'Civil networks, legitimacy and the policy process'. *Democratization* 12(1).

Dahl R 1971. Polyarchy: *Participation and Opposition.* New Haven: Yale University Press.

Darga LA 2005. *Strengthening Parliamentary Democracy in SADC Countries: Mauritius country report.* Johannesburg: SAIIA.

Haddenius A and Uggla F 1996. 'Making civil society work, promoting democratic development: What states and donors can do'. *World Development* 24(10).

Kadima D and Kasenally R 2005. 'The formation, collapse and revival of political party coalitions in Mauritius', in Kadima D (ed.). *The Politics of Party Coalitions in Africa.* Johannesburg: EISA.

Keane J 1998. *Democracy and Civil Society.* London: Verso.

Lallah R 2006. 'The Best Loser System – Transformation of Democratic Political Votes into Communal Ones'. Paper presented at the Institute of Social Development and Peace conference on 'Electoral Reform – Moving towards an Inclusive Democracy'. Port Louis, Mauritius, 17-18 February.

Lehembre B 1984. *L'ile Maurice.* Paris: Karthala.

Mannick AR 1979. *The Development of a Plural Society.* Nottingham: Russell Press Ltd.

Mathur H 1991. *Parliament in Mauritius.* Rose-Hill, Mauritius: Edtions de l'Ocean Indien.

Miles WFS 1999. 'The Mauritius enigma'. *Journal of Democracy* 10(2) April.

Mohamed Y 2006. 'The Best Loser System – Protecting Minority Rights'. Paper presented at the Institute of Social Development and Peace conference on 'Electoral Reform – Moving towards an Inclusive Democracy'. Port Louis, Mauritius, 17-18 February.

Reynolds A and Reilly B 1997. The International IDEA Handbook of Electoral Systems Design. Stockholm: International IDEA.

UNECA Expert Panel Study on Governance in Mauritius 2003. UNECA: Addis Ababa.

Van Walle N 2002. 'Elections without democracy: Africa's range of regimes'. *Journal of Democracy* 13(2).

DOCUMENTS

Constitution of Mauritius, Section 5(3). Port-Louis, Mauritius.

Cuttaree J 1982. Extracts from Council Debates. No 16 of 1982.

Ramgoolam S 1973. Extracts from Council Debates. No 18 of 1973

Sachs et al 2001/01. 'Report of the Commission on Constitutional and Electoral Reform'. Prime Minister's Office, Port Louis, Mauritius. Available at http://www.gov.mu

Chapter 5
FROM CIVIL WAR TO LOYAL OPPOSITION:
FiveJoão C.G. Pereira, Sandra Manuel and Carlos Shenga

Barany Z 2002. 'Ethnic mobilisation without prerequisites: The East European gypsies'. *World Politics* 54.

Bratton M et al 1994. 'Neo-patrimonial regimes and political transition in Africa'. *World Politics* 46.

Cahen, M 1998. 'Dhlakama e maningue nice: An atypical former guerrilla in Mozambique electoral campaign'. *Transformation*, 35.

___. 2002. *Les Bandits: Un historeie au Mozambique*, 1994. Portugal: Fundacao Colouste Gulbenkian.

Carbone G 2003. 'Emerging Pluralist Politics in Mozambique: The FRELIMO-RENAMO Party System'. Crise States programme Working Paper no 23. London School of Economics/Development Research Centre.

___. 2003. 'Developing Multi-Party Politics: Stability and Change in Ghana and Mozambique'. Crise States programme Working Paper no 36. London School of Economic School/Development Research Centre.

Chabal P et al 1999. *African Works: Disorder as Political Instrument*. Oxford: James Currey.

De Brito L 1996. *Political Actors in the PALOPs Countries*. Maputo: UEM-Texto de Apoio.

___. 1996. 'Voting behaviour in Mozambique's first multiparty elections', in Mazula B (ed), *Mozambique: Elections, Democracy, and Development*. Maputo: Elo Grafico

___. et al 2003. *Moçambique: 2003-Avaliação do potencial de conflito*. Maputo: CEA.

Geffray, C 1991. *A causa das armas em Moçambique: Antropologia de guerra contemporanea em Moçambique*. Porto: Edições Afrontamento.

___. et al 1986. 'Sobre a guerra na provincia de Nampula', *Revista Internacional de Estudos Africanos* 4, 5.

Gentili A 2005. 'Party, Party Systems and Democratisation in Sub-Saharan Africa'. Paper presented at the Sixth Global Forum on Reinventing Government, Seoul, Republic of Korea.

Harrison, G 1996. 'Democracy in Mozambique: The significance of multi-party elections'. *Review of African Political Economy*, 67.

___. 1999. 'Mozambique between two elections: a political economic of transition'. *Democratization*, 6. London: Frank Cass.

___. G 2000. *The politics of democratization in rural Mozambique: grassroots governance in Mecufi*. New York: The Edwin Mellen Press.

Ihonvbere, JO 1998. 'Where is the third wave? A critical evaluation of Africa's non-transition to democracy', in Mkabu John Mukum and Ihonvbere Julius O (eds.) *Multiparty Democracy and Political Change: Constraints to Democratization in Africa*. Aldershot: Ashgate.

Kadima D and Matsimbe Z 2006. 'RENAMO-Electoral Union: Understanding the longevity and challenges of an opposition party coalition in Mozambique', in Kadima D (ed), *The Politics of Party Coalitions in Africa*. Johannesburg: EISA/KAS.

Lipset MS and Rokkan S 1967. 'Cleavage structures, party system and voter alignment: An introduction', in Lipset MS and Rokkan S (eds). *Party Systems and Voter Alignments: Cross-National Perspectives*. New York: Free Press.

Lundin L 1996. 'Political parties: A reading of the ethnic and regional factor in the democratisation processes', in Mazula B (ed), *Mozambique: Elections, Democracy, and Development*. Maputo: Elo Grafico.

Nuvunga A 2005. 'Multiparty Democracy in Mozambique: Strengths, Weakness and Challenges'. EISA Research Report no 14. Johannesburg: EISA.

Ottaway, M 1998. *Ethnic politics in Africa: State, conflict and democracy in Africa*. Boulder, Col: Lynne Rienner.

Patel N 2005. 'Political Parties as an Institutional Building Block of Democracy in Africa: Consolidation or Fragmentation?' Paper presented at the regional conference on political parties and democratisation in East Africa. Arusha, Tanzania.

Pereira J 1997. 'As primeira eleições multipartidárias e o comportamento eleitoral no distrito de Marromeu'. *Boletim do Arquivo Histórico de Moçambique*, 21.

Maputo: AHM.

___. 1999. 'The Politics of Survival: Peasants, Chiefs and RENAMO in Maringue district, Mozambique, 1982-1992'. MA dissertation. Johannesburg: University of the Witwatersrand.

Pottie, D 2003. 'Party finance and politics of money in Southern Africa.' *Journal of Contemporary African Studies*, 21(1).

Roesch O 1992. 'RENAMO and peasantry in Southern Mozambique: A view from Gaza province'. *Canadian Journal of African Studies*, 26.

___. 1993. 'Peasants, War and Tradition in Central Mozambique'. Paper prepared for the symposium 'Symbols of change: Transregional culture and local practice in Southern Africa'. Germany: Free University of Berlin.

Rokkan S 1970. *Citizens, Elections, Parties.* Oslo: Universitetsforlaget.

Simutanyi N 2005. 'Funding Political Parties in Zambia: Challenges and Opportunities'. Paper presented to the Netherlands Institute for Multiparty Democracy regional conference on rules of engagement between ruling and opposition parties and funding for political parties. Livingstone Zambia: NIMD.

Sitoe E et al 2005. *Parties and Political Development in Mozambique.* EISA Research Report No 22. Johannesburg: EISA.

Van de Walle N 2002. 'Presidentialism and clientelism in Africa's emerging party systems'. *The Journal of Modern African Studies*, 41.

Vines A 1991. RENAMO: *Terrorism in Mozambique.* York: Centre for African Studies, University of York.

___. 1996. RENAMO: *From terrorism to democracy in Mozambique.* York: Centre for African Studies, University of York.

Wole O 2003. 'Political parties and multi-party elections in Southern Africa'. *SADC Insight*, IV.

Election Observation Report
EU 2009. 'European Union Observation Report: Presidential, Legislative and Provincial Assembly Elections'. Maputo: EU.

Chapter 6
NAMBIA: STUCK IN THE SAND
André du Pisani and Bill Lindeke

Afrobarometer. 2003, 2004-5, 2006, 200. Survey summaries. At www.afrobarometer.org

and www.ippr.org.na.

Bratton M and Cho W (compilers) 2006. 'Where is Africa going? Views from below. A compendium of trends in public opinion in 12 African countries, 1999-2006', Working Paper No 60. Cape Town: IDASA.

Bukurura SH 2002. *Essays on Constitutionalism and the Administration of Justice in Namibia 1990-2002*. Windhoek: Out of Africa Publishers.

Chirawu TO 2003. 'Political parties and democracy in independent Namibia', in Salih MMA (ed.), *African Political Parties Evolution, Institutionalisation and Governance*. London: Pluto Press.

Diescho J 1996. 'Government and opposition in post-independence Namibia: Perceptions and performance'. *Building Democracy*. Windhoek: NID.

Du Pisani A 1986. *SWA/Namibia: The Politics of Continuity and Change*. Johannesburg: Jonathan Ball Publishers.

Groth S 1995. *Namibia: The Wall of Silence –The Dark Days of the Liberation Struggle*. Wupperthal: Peter Hammer Verlag.

Gyimah-Boadi E (ed.) 2004. *Democratic Reform in Africa: The Quality of Progress*. Boulder: Lynne Rienner Publishers.

Hopwood G 2006. *Guide to Namibian Politics*, second edition. Windhoek: Namibia Institute for Democracy.

___. 2005. 'Trapped in the past: The state of the opposition', in Hunter J (ed.), Spot the Difference. Namibia's Political Parties Compared. Windhoek: Namibia Institute for Democracy (NID) and Konrad-Adenauer-Stiftung.

Kandetu VB 1999. 'Democracy in Namibia: Wind of change or withering breeze?', in O'Malley P (ed.), *Southern Africa: The People's Voices: Perspectives on Democracy*. Cape Town: NDI.

Keulder C 2006. Afrobarometer *Survey Findings: Summary of Results, Survey in Namibia*. Cape Town: IDASA.

Leys C and Saul JS (eds.) 1995. *Namibia's Liberation Struggle: The Two-Edged Sword*. London: James Currey

Lindberg S 2006. 'The Surprising Significance of African Elections'. *Journal of Democracy*, 17 (1), January.

Little Eric and Logan Carolyn. 'The Quality of Democracy and Governance in Africa: New Results from the Afrobarometer Round 4'. Working Paper No108. At http://www.afrobarometer.org/abseries.html

Melber H (ed) 2003. *Re-examining Liberation in Namibia: Political Culture Since*

Independence. Uppsala: Nordic Africa Institute.

Office of the Prime Minister 2000. *Namibia: A Decade of Peace, Democracy and Prosperity 1990-2000.* Windhoek: OPM.

Republic of Namibia 1995. *Agenda for Change: Consolidating Parliamentary Democracy in Namibia.* Windhoek: Office of the Speaker.

Sheefni P, Humavinda J and Sherbourne R 2003. 'Less than 30,000 jobs in ten years? Employment trends in Namibia since 1991'. Institute for Public Policy Research Briefing Paper No 24. Windhoek: IPPR.

Thornberry C 2005. *A Nation is Born: The Inside Story of Namibia's Independence.* Windhoek: Gamsberg Macmillan.

World Bank 2003. *African Development Indicators 2003.* Washington, DC: The World Bank

___. 2006. *World Development Report 2006.* Washington, DC: The World Bank.

DOCUMENTS
Congress of Democrats (CoD) 1999. 'Programme for a Better Namibia'.¬¬¬

___. 2000. Political Declaration and Principles of the Congress of Democrats.

___. 2001. Congress of Democrats Constitution.

Democratic Turnhalle Alliance of Namibia (DTA) 1999. Manifesto,
___. 2004. Election Manifesto.

www.ecn.na. Accessed on various dates from 2009-2010.
National Unity Democratic Organisation (NUDO) 2004. Election Manifesto of the National Unity Democratic Organisation (NUDO). Windhoek: NUDO.

United Democratic Front of Namibia (UDF) 2000. Manifesto. Windhoek.

NEWSPAPER ARTICLES
Namibia Today

'Pohamba fires Ben Ulenga', 15- 21 November 1999

'What Uulenga told the enemy', 22-28 November 1999

'Ulenga's folly to be exposed', 1-7 November 1999

Chapter 7
SOUTH AFRICA: OPPOSITION POLITICS POST APARTHEID
Dirk Kotzé

Bobbio Norberto 1996. *Left and Right: The significance of a political distinction.*

Cambridge: Polity Press.

Dandala Mvume 2009. 'Mr Mvume Dandala – Congress of the People (COPE)'. *The Thinker*, April 2009.

De Lille Patricia 2010. Speech for the Democratic Alliance Federal Congress, 25 July 2010, ID homepage (www.id.org.za/newsroom/speeches/, accessed 2010/07/27)

Greben Jan and Ittmann Hans 2010. 'Election night forecasting'. Electronic presentation at the ORSSA Pretoria Chapter, CSIR, 3 August 2010.

Holomisa Bantu 2008. 'South African democracy at a crossroad: Turning a new page'. UDM input at the National Convention: 1 November 2008, Sandton Convention Centre. Mimeo.

Independent Electoral Commission. 2009a. 'Elections 2009: to the future'. Information brochure. Pretoria: Electoral Commission.

___. 2009b. 'Represented Political Parties' Fund: Annual report 2008/2009'. RP 248/2009. Pretoria: Electoral Commission.

Kemmerzell Jörg 2010. 'Why there is no party ban in the South African Constitution'. *Democratization* 17(4).

Kleynhans WA 1987. *South African general election manifestos 191 –1981*. Pretoria: University of South Africa

Kotzé Dirk 2004. 'Public funding regulatory mechanisms to prevent the abuse of state resources' in Matlosa Khabele (ed.). *The politics of state resources: Party funding in South Africa*. Johannesburg: Konrad-Adenauer-Stiftung.

Kotzé Hennie and Greyling Anneke 1991. *Political organizations in South Africa A–Z*. Cape Town: Tafelberg.

Krüger DW (ed). 1960. *South African parties and policies 1910–1960: A select source book*. Cape Town: Human & Rousseau.

Leon Tony 2008. *On the contrary: Leading the opposition in a democratic South Africa*. Johannesburg and Cape Town: Jonathan Ball

Lodge Tom 2006. 'The future of South Africa's party system'. *Journal of Democracy* 17(3).

Ndletyana Mcebisi 2009. 'COPE – The beginning of the resolution of ideological contestation within the African National Congress'. Seminar paper presented at UNISA, 29 July 2009. Mimeo.

Przeworksi, Adam et al. 2000. *Democracy and development: Political institutions and well-being in the world, 1950–1990*. Cambridge: Cambridge University Press.

Southall Roger 2001. 'Opposition in South Africa: Issues and problems' in *Special issue:*

Opposition and democracy, Southall Roger (ed.). Democratization 8(1).

___. 2009. 'The Congress of the People: Challenges for South African democracy'. *Representation* 45(2).

___. and Daniel John (eds.) 2009. *Zunami!: The South African elections of 2009*. Auckland Park: Jacana and Konrad-Adenauer-Stiftung.

Tabane Rapule and Ludman Barbara (eds.). 2009. *The Mail & Guardian A–Z of South African politics: The essential handbook 2009*. Auckland Park: Jacana.

Zille Helen 2008. Speech by Helen Zille, Leader of the Democratic Alliance. Constitution Hill. Johannesburg, 15 November 2008. Mimeo.

___. 2009. 'The power of (more than) one'. Focus 54(2).

Documents
Coetzee, Ryan. 2006. "Becoming a party for all the people: A new approach for the DA". (Internal document distributed by email and leaked to the media via ryancoetzeedocument@webmail.co.za, 28 November 2006).

COPE 2009. Constitution. COPE homepage: www.congressofthepeople.orgza. COPE_Consti_2009.doc, accessed 2010/10/24.

COPE, 20 May 2010. The full letter of the General Secretary, document distributed by e-mail

(COPE 2010. COPE branches reject leaders' deal, press statement distributed by e-mail info@congressofthepeople.org.za, 29 May 2010)

Zille, Helen 2008. 10 November 2008. Press statement: 'The re-launch of the Democratic Alliance'. Democratic Alliance homepage: www.da.org.za, accessed 2008/11/13.

Newspaper Articles
Business Day, 24 July 2010 (DA not for minorities: Zille), www.businessday.co.za/articles/, accessed on 2010/07/27

Chapter 8
SWAZILAND : OPPOSITION POLITICS WITHIN A FEUDAL SYSTEM
Petros Magagula and Zwelibanzi Masilela

Aphane, Doo former National Coordinator of Women and Law in Southern Africa (WLSA) Swaziland, http://www.genderlinks.org.za/gencomm/genncommall

Establishment of the Parliament of Swaziland Order,1978.

Matlosa, K. (2003) Constitutional Development. Swaziland Elections Dossier 2003,

Matlosa, K. (2003) Review of Previous Elections in Swaziland. Swaziland Elections Dossier 2003, No.1.

Olaleye, W. (2004) Chiefdom Politics vs Electoral Processes in Swaziland, Electoral Institute of Southern Africa Election Update 2003 Swaziland Number 2, 20 April 2004.

Statement of the National Democratic Institute for International Affairs, August 24-29, 1998 Assessment Mission to Swaziland.

Booth, A.R. (1983) Swaziland: Tradition and Change in a Southern African Kingdom Colorado: Westview Press.

Kuper, H. (1978) Sobhuza II: Ngwenyama and King of Swaziland London: Duckworth.

Parliamentary Debates (1967-1968) Vol. 759 London.

Command Paper No.3568, March 1968

Swaziland House of Assembly Official Report (Hansard) 7th to 21st April 1967.

Swaziland House of Assembly Official Report (Hansard), Vol. II 12th April 1973.

Stevens, R.P. (1967) Lesotho, Botswana and Swaziland: The High Commission Territories in Southern Africa. London: Pall Mall Press.

Mzizi J.B. (2005) Political Movements and the Challenges for Democracy in Swaziland, Johannesburg: EISA.

Daniel J. (1986), The Domestic and International Dimension of the Crisis of Political Legitimacy in Swaziland. Paper presented at the Research Seminar on Swaziland, Free University of Amsterdam.

Magagula P.Q. (1999) Constitutions and Constitutionalism. Paper presented at the NNLC Seminar held on 8 May 1999 at the Caritas Centre, Manzini.

Magagula P.Q. (1998) Beyond the 1973 Decree. Paper presented at the NNLC National Delegates Conference at Waterford on November 28, 1998.

Magagula P.Q. (1997) The Current Political System in Swaziland and the Way Forward: Paper presented at the NNLC Strategic Planning Workshop on October 10, 1997, at Ngenule Motel.

Magagula P.Q. (1994) Creating a Democratic Political Dispensation based on a National Constitution: Realities, Challenges and Prospects for Swaziland. Paper presented at a Seminar organised by the Institute for Democracy and Leadership in Swaziland, on October 15, 1994.

Constitution of the African United Democratic Party

Constitution of the People's United Democratic Movement

The SNAT Constitution and By-Laws

Constitution of the Swaziland Federation of Labour

Constitution of the Kingdom of Swaziland, September 1968

King's Proclamation, No.1 of 1981

Establishment of Parliament of Swaziland Order, 1992

The Voters Registration Order, 1992

Elections Order, 1992

The Constitution of the Kingdom of Swaziland Act, 2005

A Report by the International Bar Association (2003) Striving for Democratic Governance: An Analysis of the Draft Swaziland Constitution.

Chapter 9
ZAMBIA: BETWEEN THE POLITICS OF OPPOSITION AND INCUMBENCY
Jotham C. Momba

Bureau of Labour 2001. *Country Report on Human Rights*, February 2001.

Chanda AW. 'Public Order Act'. ZAMLII lecture series, available at http://zamlii.ac.zm/lecture-series.html.

___. 2002. 'Interim Statement on 27 December 2001 tripartite elections'. FODEP press briefing, 3 January.

Momba JC 2002. 'Political transition and the crises of an African nationalist party: The case of UNIP', in Salih M (ed), *African Political Parties: Evolution, Institutionalisation and Governance*. London: Pluto Press.

___. 2004. 'Civil Society and the Struggle for Human Rights and Democracy in Zambia', in Zeleza, Paul Tiyambe and McConnaughay, Philip J (eds), *Human Rights, the Rule of Law, and Development in Africa*. Philadelphia: University of Pennsylvania Press.

National Democratic Institute for International Affairs. *The 31 October 1991 National Elections in Zambia*. Available at http://www.ndi.org/ndi/library/192_zm_oct31_91_nat.txt.

ELECTION OBSERVATION REPORTS

Carter Center. 'Carter Center Observation Assessment of the 2001 Zambian Pre-election Period, 13 December 2001'. Available at http://www.cartercenter.org/documents/298.dpf.

Coalition 2001. 'Monitoring Report on the Mwandi Parliamentary By-election', 14 November 2000.

___. 'Monitoring Report on the Isoka East Parliamentary By-election', 7 September 2001.

Commonwealth Secretariat 2006. *Zambia Presidential, National Assembly and Local Government Elections 18 September 2006 – Report of the Commonwealth Observer Group.* At http://aceproject.org./ero en/regions/africa/ZM/zambia-final-report-general-elections-commonwealth.

Electoral Institute for Sustainability of Democracy in Africa 2006. Interim Statement EISA Regional Observation Mission to the Zambian 2006 Tripartite Elections, 28 September 2006: p6. At http://www.eisa.org.za/WEP/zam2006is6.htm

European Union Election Observation Mission Zambia 2006. Final Report, Lusaka, Novembeer, 2008: pp22-23. At http://www.delzmb.ec.europa.eu/en/EU%20EOM%20-%20Final%20Report.pdf

FODEP 1999. *Zambia's 1998 Local Government Elections Report.* Lusaka: Multimedia.

DOCUMENTS
Electoral Commission of Zambia, 'Election Results Index'. At http://www.elections.org.zm/indexGovernment of the Republic of Zambia 1995. The Societies Act CAP. 119 of the Laws of Zambia, Article 8.

___. Electoral (Conduct) Regulations (Statutory Instrument No.179 of 1996).

National Constitutional Conference Secretariat 2010. 'Initial Report of the National Constitutional Conference' at http://www.znbc.co.zm/documents/The_Initial_Report_of_the_National_Constitutional_Conference_June_2010.pdf http://www.parliament.gov.zm/index

NEWSPAPER ARTICLES
Le Monde, 2 December 1962
Times of Zambia, 8 October 1991
___. 11 July 1991
___. 11 January 1996

The Post, 7 February 2002
___. 2 June 2003
___. 3 June 2003
___. 8 August 2003

The Saturday Post, 22 July 2006.
Zambia Daily Mail, 18 December 1990.
___. 20 July 2006.
___. 28 July 2006
___. 29 July 2006.

Chapter 10
ZIMBABWE: OPPOSING AN AUTHORITARIAN SYSTEM - THE CASE OF THE MDC
John Makumbe

Makumbe J 2002.'Zimbabwe's hijacked election'. Journal of Democracy 13(4), October.

_____ 2003. 'The stolen presidential election', in Lee MC and Collard K (eds), *Unfinished Business: The Land Crisis in Southern Africa*. Pretoria: Africa Institute of South Africa.

_____and Compagnon D 2000. *Behind the Smokescreen: The Politics of Zimbabwe's 1995 General Elections*. Harare: University of Zimbabwe Publications.

Sachikonye L 2003. 'Between authoritarianism and democracy: Politis in Zimbabwe since 1990', in Lee MC and Collard K (eds). *Unfinished Business: The Land Crisis in Southern Africa*. Pretoria: Africa Institute of South Africa.

Sithole M 2003. 'In Search of a Viable Democratic Alternative in Zimbabwe: A Study of Opposition Political Parties Since Independence". Unpublished departmental monograph.

Documents
Government of Zimbabwe. Constitution of Zimbabwe

MDC 2006. National Council Report to the National Congress. 18-19 March.

_____2006. Constitution, as amended at the Second Congress. 19 March.